Willem Spanjers (Ed.)

Monetary Policy, Trade and Convergence

New Developments in Economic Research

edited by

Christian Richter, Edward Shinnick
and Jan Van Hove

Volume 2

The *International Network for Economic Research (INFER)* was established in 1998 as an independent, non-profit research network. It supports high quality research in all fields of economics and related areas through seminars, workshops and publications. The main objective of *INFER* is to foster interactions among academics, business practitioners and policy makers with a view to finding solutions to economic problems. Further details are available from the *INFER* website at: www.infer-research.net

The *INFER New Developments in Economic Research* series publishes leading-edge research findings across all aspects of economics. A multi-stage referee process and a Scientific Advisory Board of distinguished academics, business practitioners and policy makers ensures the quality of the publications.

LIT

Monetary Policy, Trade and Convergence

The Case of Transition Economies

edited by

Willem Spanjers

LIT

Bibliographic information published by the Deutsche Nationalbibliothek
The Deutsche Nationalbibliothek lists this publication in the Deutsche Nationalbibliografie; detailed bibliographic data are available in the Internet at http://dnb.d-nb.de.

ISBN 978-3-643-10021-4

A catalogue record for this book is available from the British Library

Fresnostr. 2 D-48159 Münster
Tel. +49 (0) 2 51-620 32 22 Fax +49 (0) 2 51-922 60 99
e-Mail: lit@lit-verlag.de http://www.lit-verlag.de

Distribution:

In Germany: LIT Verlag Fresnostr. 2, D-48159 Münster
Tel. +49 (0) 2 51-620 32 22, Fax +49 (0) 2 51-922 60 99, e-Mail: vertrieb@lit-verlag.de

In Austria: Medienlogistik Pichler-ÖBZ GmbH & Co KG
IZ-NÖ, Süd, Straße 1, Objekt 34, A-2355 Wiener Neudorf
Tel. +43 (0) 22 36-63 53 52 90, Fax +43 (0) 22 36-63 53 52 43, e-Mail: mlo@medien-logistik.at

In Switzerland: B + M Buch- und Medienvertriebs AG
Hochstr. 357, CH-8200 Schaffhausen
Tel. +41 (0) 52-643 54 85, Fax +41 (0) 52-643 54 35, e-Mail: order@buch-medien.ch

Distributed in the UK by: Global Book Marketing, 99B Wallis Rd, London, E9 5LN
Phone: +44 (0) 20 8533 5800 – Fax: +44 (0) 1600 775 663
http://www.centralbooks.co.uk/html

Distributed in North America by:

Transaction Publishers
New Brunswick (U.S.A.) and London (U.K.)

Transaction Publishers
Rutgers University
35 Berrue Circle
Piscataway, NJ 08854

Phone: +1 (732) 445 - 2280
Fax: + 1 (732) 445 - 3138
for orders (U. S. only):
toll free (888) 999 - 6778
e-mail: orders@transactionpub.com

Acknowledgements

This volume contains papers that were presented at the combined 5th INFER Workshop on Monetary Economics "Monetary Policy in Emerging Markets" and 5th INFER Workshop on International Economics "Trade, Convergence and Factor Mobility", which took place from 14th to 16th July 2006 at Kingston University, London, United Kingdom.

The papers greatly benefited from the contributions of the participants in the workshop, in particular from the useful comments and constructive discussions by the keynote speakers: Professor Jayasri Dutta (University of Birmingham), Professor Subrata Ghatak (Kingston University), Professor Charles van Marrewijk (Erasmus University Rotterdam), Professor Chris Milner (University of Nottingham) and Professor Helmut Wagner (University of Hagen).

The workshops, and therefore this volume, would not have been possible without the support of Kingston University, which provided facilities and access to dorminories for interested participants, the administrative support of its Faculty of Arts and Social Sciences, and the generous financial support of the School of Economics.

Particular thanks, however, go to Michael Pickhardt for his encouragement, to INFER for providing the framework which made organising the workshops seem the most natural thing in the world, and, last but not least, to the participants of the workshops for creating and sustaining a pleasant, friendly and productive atmosphere during these unusually warm summer's days.

The kind permission of Serials Publications to re-print the paper "Loss of Confidence and Currency Crises" by Willem Spanjers, originally published in 2008 in the International Journal of Economic Research, Volume 5, Issue 2, pp. 219-237, is greatfully acknowledged.

Willem Spanjers
Kingston-upon-Thames
January 2009

Contents

Introduction 1

Willem Spanjers
Loss of Confidence and Currency Crises 7

Anıl Akçağlayan and Ayşe Ertuğrul
The Effect of Monetary Policy on an Emerging Market Economy: Evidence from Turkey 29

Victoria Dobrynskaya
The Optimal Monetary Policy under Incomplete Pass-through and Asymmetric Price Rigidity: The Empirical Evidence from Russia 47

Elif Bascavusoglu-Moreau
Does International Trade Transfer Technology to Emerging Countries? A Patent Citation Analysis 79

Laura Ruud
Changes in Estonian Export Product Variety 125

Alan Mulhern
Small Firms and Diverging Regions: The Case of Poland 145

Václav Žďárek and Jaromír Šindel
Selected Issues Relating to Real and Nominal Convergence of New EU Member States 163

List of Contributors 194

Introduction

Willem Spanjers, Kingston University, United Kingdom[*]

1 Overview

During the past decade or so, transition economies have been a focus of economic policy making and advising. Following the changes in the political systems in Central and Eastern Europe, policy makers and economists alike were presented with the new and interesting task of identifying suitable paths for the transition of centrally planned economies to market based economies. The lack of experience with transitions of this kind added to the challenge, as it required dealing with the incalculable risks of implementing untested policies in complicated situations.

Although some of the papers of this volume do not address the first few years after this momentous change and/or may discuss countries that are not located in Central and Eastern Europe, in each of them the excitement of addressing important issues in only partially charted waters and be sensed. By focusing on monetary policy, trade, and convergence, this volume addresses the most urgent issues relating to economic policy making in Central and Eastern Europe and beyond.

The first three contributions to the volume focus on different aspects of monetary policy[1] and exchange rates: *Spanjers* on the effects of a loss of confidence in the context of exchange rate targets, *Akçağlayan* and *Ertuğrul* on the dynamic relationship between monetary policy and exchange rates, and *Dobrynskaya* on the optimal monetary policy in the context of asymmetric price rigidities when the pass-through of exchange rate movements is incomplete.

The second group of contributions considers the connections between technology and trade flows. *Bascavusoglu-Moreau* considers the empirical impact of trade flows on technology transfer, whereas *Ruud* analyzes the difference in changes in export variety between low-technology and high-technology sectors.

The final two contributions consider the issue of convergence between regions and countries and how this may affect local firms. *Mulhern* addresses

* Address for correspondence: Willem Spanjers, School of Economics, Kingston University, Kingston-upon-Thames, Surrey KT1 2EE UK. Email: w.spanjers@kingston.ac.uk

[1] For more a more general discussion of monetary policy in the presence of the incalculable risks that can be expected in transition economies see e.g. Ghatak / Spanjers (2007) and Spanjers (2008).

the lack of convergence in the performance of small firms in different regions in Poland. *Žďárek* and *Šindel* combine aspects of economic growth and monetary policy in their discussion of real convergence and price convergence for the Central and Eastern European accession countries (EU-10).

2 Monetary Policy and Exchange Rates

The point of departure for *Spanjers* is a group of transition economies with exchange rate targets. In this context he analyses the potential impact of a loss of confidence by international investors. A model with fragile financial systems is considered, which includes liquid low yield bonds and an illiquid potentially high yielding asset. Unsurprisingly, an *exogenous* interim loss of confidence may trigger a crisis, even when the economic fundamentals remain unchanged. The failure of monetary authorities to recognize the presence of incalculable risk (i.e. ambiguity) has a similar effect. Bad news may cause an unexpected *endogenous* loss of confidence, with investors seeming to overreact.

Although the model is based on the experience of the South-East-Asian crisis, it represents the basic structure of the EU-accession countries in the run-up to their adoption of the Euro. It is argued that transparency, competence, and political stability offer some protection against currency crises by increasing confidence. The best protection, however, is a stable financial system, which enables share prices to absorb the impact of a loss of confidence.

Akçağlayan and *Ertuğrul* examine the relationship between monetary policy and the exchange rate for Turkey. They use a Vector-Auto-Regressive model for monthly data from 1990 to 2004, applying the Toda and Yamamoto methodology. Regardless of the order of integration of the series and of the co-integration properties of the system, this enables them to test for Granger-causality.

A fundamental change in the monetary policy objectives of the Central Bank of the Republic of Turkey in 2000 makes it appropriate to divide the data into two distinct periods. The first period, from June 1990 to December 1999, is characterized by an emphasis on stabilizing financial markets. During the second period, from January 2000 to November 2004, the focus of monetary policy shifted to fighting high inflation rates. In the first period the interbank over-night nominal interest rate – the monetary policy instrument – Granger-causes foreign exchange reserves and the real exchange rate. In the second period it not only Granger-causes the real exchange rate, but also the inflation rate, output and the amount of reserve money.

A more general question concerns the optimal monetary policy for typical transition economies, and if central banks seem to be following such policy. In this context, *Dobrynskaya* discusses the monetary policy of the Central Bank of Russia. Dobrynskaya (2008) derives the optimal monetary policy under the assumptions of an incomplete pass-through of exchange rate movements in an economy that faces asymmetric price rigidities.

The theoretical results are obtained in a general equilibrium of a small open economy with sticky prices. An optimal interest rate rule is derived, which responds to real exchange rate changes. This responsiveness reduces the pass-through of movements in the exchange. Moreover, the optimal intervention is stronger when the level of pass-through is higher, but it is weaker when prices are more rigid. As a consequence, monetary policy should be more responsive in case of depreciation of the domestic currency than in case of its appreciation. On the basis of this result, the monetary policy of the Central Bank of Russia from January 1998 to May 2005 is subjected to an empirical evaluation. It is found that during this period monetary policy was overly inflationary and it is suggested that less effort should be made to prevent a nominal appreciation of the rouble.

3 Trade and Technology

Exchange rates also have effects on trade, on investment, and on technology transfer, and – therefore – on economic growth. *Bascavusoglu-Moreau* investigates whether trade flows represent a disembodied transfer of technology to transition economies. Combining an endogenous growth framework with a patent citation analysis, the question is addressed whether emerging countries that trade more tend to cite more foreign patents. A more frequent citation of patents is considered to indicate a stronger absorption of foreign knowledge and technology.

The empirical analysis takes place at a sector level, relating relative numbers of citations to bilateral trade flows. For the period from 1980 to 1998 18 emerging countries and 10 technological source countries are considered. It is found that trade does transfer technology across countries and sectors. But the extent of the diffusion is mainly determined by the technical capacity of host countries and by cultural and historical proximities. An increase in a country's product variety is identified as an important factor both for increasing its exports and for enhancing its economic growth in general.

The issue of the product variety of exports in transition economies is analysed in more detail by *Ruud*. In particular, the question is addressed if changes in the export variety of low-technology industries differ from those of high-technology ones. For this purpose, an empirical analysis of the changes in export product variety of Estonian manufacturing industries is conducted. It uses the econometric analogue of a shift-share approach to analyse Estonian exports of 27 industries to 213 countries in the period from 1994 to 2004.

Ruud's results distinguish between industry effects and destination country effects. Comparing industries in Estonia, it is found that the export product variety tends to increase in low-technology industries, rather than in high-technology ones. This result may find its cause in a redirection in Estonia exports from its traditional trade partners to the EU-15. With respect to its traditional partners, Estonia has a comparative advantage in high-technology industries, but with respect to the EU-15 its comparative advantage is in low-technology industries. This explanation is in line with the destination country effects, where Estonia's product variety in exports increases for the EU-15, but not for its more traditional trade partners.

4 Convergence

Although trade and technology transfer improve the growth prospects of transition economies, there are concerns over their effects both on different regions within countries and on firms in these regions. Does an increase in exports and export variety favour rural areas or does it tend to benefit urban areas?

If it is correct to associate high-technology industries with urbanized regions and low-technology industries with rural regions, the results of *Ruud* may suggest that in transition economies it is the rural areas, rather than the urban areas, that tend to benefit from increased exports. This would contribute to a convergence between the rural and urban areas.

Mulhern considers small firms in a rural region in the East of Poland and an urban region in the West of the country. In contradiction to the above hypothesis, empirical evidence indicates a divergence between these two typical regions, with the rural region losing ground. Against this background he compares the typical characteristic of small firms in the two regions.

Based on a survey from 1999, it is found that the firms in the developed region show more favourable characteristics on a number of variables, indicating a considerable range of organisational, behavioural and performance advantages. As a consequence, the small firms in the developed region are better positioned to benefit from new opportunities as they occur. Efforts to contain the divergence between the two regions may require targeted support for the small firms in the rural area.

The final contribution in this volume is by *Žďárek* and *Šindel*, who consider the convergence of the new EU member states in Central and Eastern Europe with the more established EU members, i.e. the EU-15. They discuss both real and monetary aspects of the convergence processes by also analysing price convergence, comparing the situation in 2000 with that in 2005.

During this period, the new member states experienced a robust economic growth, which contributed to real convergence with the EU-15. This convergence in standards of living is accompanied by a convergence in price levels, which is referred to as "nominal convergence". The latter process not only involves changes in relative prices but also shows an inflation rate above that in the EU-15. The process of price convergence has the potential to erode the competitiveness of the firms in the new EU member states. To prevent this from happening, the speed of the price convergence should not exceed the (relative) productivity growth.

5 Concluding Remarks

This volume addresses a broad range of issues relating to economic transition processes and the intended convergence of living standards to those of developed economies.

The individual contributions examine specific issues in considerable depth, at times by focussing on specific countries or regions, in other instances by analysing specific periods in time. Combined they sketch a distinctive picture of the mechanisms, interactions and complications that play a leading role in the transition processes in Central and Eastern Europe and elsewhere.

Still, the contributions leave many opportunities for creative thinking about and further research in this fascinating and highly relevant area of Economics.

References

Dobrynskaya, V. (2008): Asymmetric price rigidity and the optimal interest rate defense of the exchange rate: some evidence for the US, in: Journal of Policy Modelling, Volume 30, pp. 713-724.

Ghatak, S. / Spanjers, W. (2007): Monetary policy rules in transition economies: the impact of ambiguity, in: International Journal of Development Issues, Volume 6, pp. 26 – 37.

Spanjers, W. (2008): Central banks and ambiguity, in: International Review of Economics and Finance, Volume 17, pp. 85 – 102.

Reprinted with permission from the International Journal of Economic Research, 2007, Volume 5, Issue 2, pp. 219-237. [1]

Loss of Confidence and Currency Crises[2]

Willem Spanjers, Kingston University, United Kingdom[*]

1 Introduction

What causes currency crises? Clearly, there are some intrinsic problems in the economies affected, but it is striking that their outbreak often fails to be related to newly emergent information on fundamentals. Starting with the seminal paper by Krugman (1979), the literature on currency crises set out to address this problem. In the paper at hand, we argue that loss of confidence plays a role.[3]

Traditional microeconomics is not well equipped to model such loss of confidence. It only allows for changes in probability assessments based on new information. But this is not what has been suggested as the cause of some currency crises as, e.g., the South-East Asian crisis. A "loss of confidence" is due to a growing feeling of unease with the probability assessment, rather than to a change in this assessment itself. It relates to a change in investors' *perceptions*, not to a change in underlying parameters that reflect a shift in *economic fundamentals*. Including the concept of incalculable risk (i.e. ambiguity) may help where conventional approaches fail to provide a satisfactory explanation.

The conceptual difference between risk and ambiguity was already recognized by Keynes (1921, 1937) and Knight (1921), who distinguish between "calculable" and "incalculable" risk. Modern terminology refers to the latter as

---

[1] With minor changes and corrections.

[2] Suggestions and comments from Paul Auerbach, Jürgen Eichberger and David Kelsey led to significant improvements. Helpful comments of the participants of the 1999 Annual Conference of the Verein für Socialpolitik, the 2000 Royal Economic Society Annual Meeting, the 2002 Workshop on Ambiguity at The University of Birmingham, the 6th Pacific Rim Conference 2005 in Hong Kong, the 4th EEFS Conference 2005 in Coimbra, the 5th INFER Workshop on Monetary Economics in Kingston-upon-Thames and the 6th INFER Annual Meeting in Cork are gratefully acknowledged. The usual disclaimer applies.

[*] Address for correspondence: Willem Spanjers, School of Economics, Kingston University, Kingston-upon-Thames, Surrey KT1 2EE, UK. Email: w.spanjers@kingston.ac.uk

[3] See also Spanjers (2008).

ambiguity.[4] Risk may fail to be calculable for two basic reasons. Firstly, it may not be possible to assign a unique (subjective) probability distribution to different scenarios for the future. Secondly, it may be difficult to associate a unique outcome to each scenario. In either case there is ambiguity. Furthermore, decision makers may display different attitudes towards ambiguity: they may be ambiguity averse (*pessimistic*) or they may be ambiguity loving (*optimistic*).

Let us consider three specific examples of ambiguity. First, consider the BSE-crisis. Here the direct consequences of attaining the disease were relatively clear from the outset, the probability of becoming infected by consuming beef from infected cattle, however, was unknown. A second example is the concern about terrorist attacks after 11th September 2001. Although there were some rough indications about the likelihood of further attacks based on historic evidence, it remained highly unclear what damage and casualties future attacks might have caused. In both cases, the public reacted pessimistically. In our final example, that of New Economy technologies, the public reacted toward the ambiguity of these technologies in an optimistic way, by hoping for the best, rather than fearing the worst. When the bounds of possibility became tighter, the scope for optimism subsided and the dot.com bubble burst.

With his famous thought experiment, Ellsberg (1961) showed that the subjective expected utility approach of Savage (1954) does not capture the distinction between risk and ambiguity adequately. Two decades ago, Schmeidler (1989) provided a decision-theoretic foundation for modelling ambiguity. Within this framework, Eichberger and Kelsey (1998) focus on a special class of beliefs, called E(llsberg)-capacities. These beliefs are represented by a combination of an additive probability assessment and a level of confidence in this probability assessment. Not only are E-capacities suitable for analysing the effects of a loss of confidence, they also are relatively easy to work with.

In Obstfeld (1986) and more recently in Obstfeld (1996), currency crises are considered to be examples of coordination games that may have multiple equilibria. We deviate from this approach by focusing on specific equilibria, but extend it by including the stability of the banking sector in the model. By allowing for fragile financial systems in the countries under consideration, a micro-based model of twin crises is obtained.

The model of Morris / Shin (1998), which elaborates on the topic of multiple equilibria, can be interpreted as implicitly modelling ambiguity as a lack of common knowledge. In an economy that is ripe for a crisis, a speculative attack may be triggered when the fundamentals cease to be common knowledge to the investors. Thus, even if the fundamentals have not changed and each investor is aware of this fact, his "no longer knowing that the others know that

[4] Incalculable risk is sometimes referred to as *Knightian uncertainty*.

he knows that..." is sufficient to make a speculative attack the unique equilibrium. The focus on institutions and confidence firmly places our model in the category of *fourth generation models of currency crises* in the terminology of the survey article of Breuer (2005).

In contrast to this literature, the driving force behind the result in the current paper is a form of dynamic inconsistency. It occurs as a natural consequence of updating beliefs under ambiguity, which leads to an increase in the level of ambiguity and therefore to a decrease in the level of confidence. Investors tend to act more cautiously after receiving bad news, then they initially intended to. Eichberger / Kelsey (2004) argue that dynamic inconsistency in updating ambiguous beliefs is inevitable.

The current paper also relates to the intuition expressed by Keynes (1937). He considers ambiguity to be one of the most characteristic features of decision making under uncertainty (Keynes, 1937, pp.113 – 114):

> "By 'uncertain' knowledge, let me explain, I do not mean merely to distinguish what is known for certain from what is only probable. The game of roulette is not subject, in this sense, to uncertainty [...]. The sense in which I am using the term is that [...] there is no scientific basis on which to form any calculable probability whatever. We simply do not know."

In particular, Keynes (1937, pp. 114 – 115) highlights that decisions which are made in the presence of ambiguity are vulnerable to sudden violent changes:

> "Now a practical theory of the future [...] has certain marked characteristics. In particular, being based on so flimsy a foundation, it is subject to sudden and violent changes. The practice of calmness and immobility, of certainty and security, suddenly breaks down. New fears and hopes will, without warning, take charge of human conduct. The forces of disillusion may suddenly impose a new conventional basis of valuation. All these pretty, polite techniques, made for a well-panelled board room and a nicely regulated market, are liable to collapse. At all times vague panic fears and equally vague and unreasoned hopes are not really lulled, and lie but a little way below the surface."

In our opinion, both ambiguity and sudden violent changes in investor behaviour are leading characteristics in many currency crises and in the South-East-Asian crisis in particular.

The paper is organized as follows. In Section 2 the basic model is introduced. The equilibrium reserve policies are outlined in Section 3. In Section 4 the consequences of not recognizing ambiguity are analysed. Some stylized facts of the South-East Asian crisis are provided in Section 5: they accord with the logic of the model. The policy prescriptions in Section 6 support the policy followed by the IMF, except for its demands for fiscal and monetary austerity. Section 7 contains concluding remarks.

2 The Model

2.1 The Economy

Consider a three period world economy containing a region of identical countries, each of which is represented by its own monetary authority. As the expectation of stable exchange rates tends to promote trade and thus welfare, the monetary authority of each country commits itself to exchange rate targets. Apart from the effects on trade, this policy has consequences for foreign portfolio investment. The latter is at the focus of the analysis.

Suppose there are many identical investors from the rest of the world, represented by the interval [0,1]. Each investor owns one unit of Euros, (part of) which can be invested in the local asset of one of the countries in Period 0. Alternatively, (part of) it can be invested in a unit bond denominated in local currency. For simplicity, we assume the bond has a zero rate of return. The local asset pays out in local currency and either has a high or a low return in Period 2, provided it is not liquidated prematurely. The payouts of the bond and the asset, which apply for each country in the region, are summarized in Table 1, where $0 \leq \alpha_\ell < \alpha_l < 1 < \alpha_h$. Ad interim, in Period 1, investments in the asset can be traded as shares on the local stock market.

Table 1: Asset Payouts

Payout in local currency	Period 0	Period 1	Period 2
Bond	–1	1	0
Asset liquidated	–1	α_l	0
Asset successful	–1	0	α_h
Asset failure	–1	0	α_ℓ

Investment in the local asset generates output that may be sold on the world market. It generates an inflow of Euros for the local monetary authority. We assume this inflow equals the payoff in local currency at the initial exchange rate, independent of the actual exchange rate in Period 1 and Period 2.[5] Local bonds pay out in local currency in Period 1. As the proceeds cannot be reinvested in the local economy, they generate an interim outflow of foreign currency. The effective payout to foreign investors, denominated in Euros, depends both on the value of the claims in local currency and on the exchange rate. At exchange rate r, claims y in local currency yield $x = r \cdot y$ units of Euros. We assume that the initial exchange rate is 1.

Each monetary authority decides on the exchange rate targets r_1 for Period 1 and r_2 for Period 2. Furthermore, it determines what fraction of its initial capital inflow is to be held as currency reserves. For each unit of Euros held as reserve, it issues a bond that pays out one unit of local currency in Period 1. The remainder flows into the stock market and is invested in the local asset. Under such circumstances, the flexibility of share prices is a substitute for a flexible exchange rate.[6] The fragility of the local banking sector, however, complicates the matter.

The banking sector in each country is endowed with a portfolio of collateralised loans denominated in local currency with a total nominal value of v, whereas the ex-ante value of the collateral depends on the share price and equals c. A fall in the interim share price may reduce the value of the collateral below that of the outstanding debt. This leads to the technical bankruptcy of the banking sector and threatens the stability of the local financial system. The local monetary authority can not allow such a fall in share prices without risking the breakdown of the financial system. Bearing this in mind, in each period the monetary authority determines the actual exchange. We use $(c-v)/c$, the fraction of collateral c at ex-ante prices in excess of the amount necessary to secure the debts v, to indicated the *soundness* of the local banking sector.

Through its choice of the actual exchange rate, the monetary authority has the possibility to make "hold up profits" on foreign investors: after foreign capital is invested in Period 0 at an exchange rate of one, the monetary authority may be tempted to devalue in Periods 1 and 2. Thus, it repays investors fewer Euros than it otherwise would have, which increases its profit. Foreign investors would be less willing to invest in a country that is suspected of applying such practices. Therefore, monetary authorities may want to establish a reputation for abiding by the exchange rate targets they announce.

---

[5] This may occur when the local asset produces output for an international market where prices are quoted in Euros.

[6] The interim decisions of the international investors are driven by the payouts *in Euros* of the expiring bonds Period 1 compared to the expected payout (in Period 1) of investing these proceeds in local shares in Period 1. For a given exchange rate in Period 2, this trade-off depends both on the share price in Period 1 and on the exchange rate in Period 1.

Each monetary authority is assumed to have established its credibility in the past and to be committed to retaining it in the future. This credibility can be secured in two ways, first, by realizing the announced exchange rate, or, second, when the target proves impossible to reach, by implementing the toughest monetary policy available before allowing a devaluation to occur. Faced with the choice between preventing a currency crisis and securing the survival of its financial system, however, the monetary authority will choose the latter.

A tough ad interim monetary policy forces some assets into premature liquidation. Therefore, we may identify the toughness of the monetary policy with the fraction of assets liquidated: the toughest monetary policy leads to the liquidation of all assets. Per Euro of initial investment it leaves foreign investors with claims of α_l units of local currency and the monetary authority with α_l Euros.

Ad interim, in Period 1, the economy receives a public signal $\sigma \in \{b,g\}$ about the economy's prospects, which applies for the region as a whole. When the bad signal b is received, the probability of a high asset return in Period 2 is low. When the signal is good, g, this probability equals one. The joint probability distribution of signals and asset payouts is summarized in Table 2 where $\rho \in \{h,\ell\}$ and π_{bh}, $\pi_{b\ell}$, $\pi_{gh} > 0$.

Table 2: Probability Distribution of Signals and Returns

Asset state (σ,ρ)	Signal	Return	Probability
(b,h)	b	α_h	π_{bh}
(b,ℓ)	b	α_ℓ	$\pi_{b\ell}$
(g,h)	g	α_h	π_{gh}
(g,ℓ)	g	α_ℓ	0

For analytical convenience, we assume all investments in the local asset have the same return. Either all investments are successful, or they all fail.[7] The probability of success equals $\pi_h := \pi_{bh} + \pi_{gh}$, whereas the probability of failure is $\pi_\ell := \pi_{b\ell}$. With a conditional probability of $\pi_h^b := \pi_{bh} / \pi_b$ the assets are successful after the bad signal is received. Similarly, we have $\pi_h^g := 1$.

In Period 1, each investor learns his preference for liquidity. This liquidity preference is private information and is described by his type $t \in \{H,L\}$. Type H investors obtain a relatively high utility from Euros in Period 1. The corresponding utility of L-type investors is relatively low. The fractions of H-types and L-types are denoted by π_H and π_L respectively, with $0 < \pi_H < 1$. These fractions equal the ex-ante probability that an investor will have a high or a low

[7] Thus, we effectively focus on "systemic" or "undiversifiable" risk.

liquidity preference. The probabilities are independent of the asset state (σ,ρ). For the probability distribution π over $\{H,L\}\times\{b,g\}\times\{h,\ell\}$ we have $Pr\{(t,\sigma,\rho)\} = \pi_t \cdot \pi_{\sigma\rho}$. We denote by $S := \{H,L\}\times\{b,g\}\times\{h,\ell\}$ the relevant state-space for each individual investor.

2.2 Beliefs

The investors face ambiguity with respect to the joint distribution of signals and investment returns. This ambiguity is modelled by E-capacities as axiomatised in Eichberger / Kelsey (1998), who also provide an extensive motivation for using E-capacities.

The *E-capacity* $(\pi,\{E_H,E_L\},\gamma)$, which describes the ex-ante beliefs of the investors, is characterized by three components:

- the probability assessment π,
- the (finest) partition E of the state-space S in unambiguous events, $\{E_H,E_L\}$, with:
  $E_H := \{(H,b,h), (H,b,\ell), (H,g,h), (H,g,\ell)\}$
  $E_L := \{(L,b,h), (L,b,\ell), (L,g,h), (L,g,\ell)\}$ and
- a level of confidence in the probability assessment, $\gamma \in [0,1]$.

The probabilities of the unambiguous events E_H and E_L are unambiguously known. So each investor has full confidence in the probabilities that concern his type. Effectively, there is restricted confidence only in (appropriate combinations of) strict sub events of E_H and E_L.

The risk attitude of an investor of type $t \in \{H,L\}$ is described by his von Neumann-Morgenstern utility index u: $\mathbb{R}_+^2 \times \{H,L\} \rightarrow \mathbb{R}$. We assume

$$(1) \quad u(x_1,x_2;t) := \beta_t \cdot x_1 + x_2,$$

with $\beta_H > \beta_L > 1$. Thus, the investors are risk-neutral. The utility a type t investor derives from the state contingent consumption $(x_1(s),x_s(s))_{s\in S}$ is defined below as his Choquet expected utility with respect to u and the relevant beliefs.

For consumption $(x_1(s),x_2(s))_{s\in S}$ and beliefs (π,E,γ) with $E:=\{E_H,E_L\}$, we denote the minimal expected utility on an unambiguous event $E_t \subseteq S$ by

$$(2) \quad M_t(x) := \min_{s\in E_t} u(x(s)).$$

The *Choquet expected utility* of $(x_1(s),x_2(s))_{s\in S}$ for the E-capacity (π,E,γ) equals

(3) $\mathsf{CE}_s\{u(x(s))\} := \gamma \cdot \mathsf{E}_s\{u(x(s))\} + (1-\gamma)\cdot \mathsf{E}_t\{M_t(x)\}$,

where $\mathsf{E}_s\{u(x(s))\} := \sum_{s\in S}\pi_s \cdot u(x(s))$ and $\mathsf{E}_t\{M_t(x)\} := \sum_{t\in\{H,L\}}\pi_t \cdot M_t(x)$.

As stated above, in Period 1 each investor learns his liquidity preference as represented by his type and observes the signal about the prospective asset returns. As in the additive case, he adjusts his beliefs about returns to incorporate this information. For updating additive beliefs Bayes' rule is used.

When beliefs are represented by capacities, Gilboa / Schmeidler (1993) show that Bayes' rule can be generalized in a number of ways. Of those rules, we focus on the Dempster-Shafer rule, which is most widely used.[8]

The Dempster-Shafer update of an E-capacity is once again an E-capacity, the updated probability assessment of which is the Bayesian update of the original one. A formula for updating E-capacities by the Dempster-Shafer rule is provided in Eichberger / Kelsey (1998).

Suppose the beliefs of the investors are represented by (π,E,γ) as above and the signal σ is received. The Dempster-Shafer rule now yields the updated beliefs $(\pi^\sigma,E^\sigma,\gamma^\sigma)$ with:

	$\sigma = b$	$\sigma = g$
π_h^σ	π_{bh}/π_b	1
γ^σ	$\gamma\cdot[\pi_b/(1-\gamma\cdot\pi_g)] \le \gamma$	$\gamma\cdot[\pi_g/(1-\gamma\cdot\pi_b)] \le \gamma$
E_t^σ	$\{(t,b,h),(t,b,\ell)\}$	$\{(t,g,h),(t,g,\ell)\}$

where the inequalities are strict for $0 < \gamma < 1$.

Given $\sigma = g$ and in spite of $\pi_h^g = 1$, investors are not certain that the asset pays out α_h in Period 2. This is due to the remaining ambiguity within the unambiguous component E_t^σ. No sub event of E_t^σ is unambiguously ruled out from occurring.

When an investor learns $\sigma = b$, the assessed probability of an unfavourable result increases from $\pi_\ell := \pi_{b\ell}$ to $\pi_\ell^b := \pi_{b\ell}/\pi_b$. The bad signal also decreases his confidence in his updated assessment π^b, as does a good signal with respect to the confidence in π^g. In the remainder of the paper we make the following assumptions:

- $\alpha_\ell = 0$: when assets fail, their payout is zero.
- $\beta_H > \alpha_h > \beta_L$: when the assets are successful, their payout is sufficiently high to be of interest to the L-types, but sufficiently low not to be desirable for H-types when compared to holding Euros in Period 0.

[8] As is shown in Spanjers (1999, Sect. 8.6) for the above beliefs (π,E,γ), the Dempster-Shafer rule and its closest competitor, Full Bayesian Updating, result in the same updated E-capacity.

3 Reserve Policies

In this section we determine the equilibrium reserve policies of the monetary authorities. At the outset, there are no foreign investments in the local economy. The monetary authority neither has nor needs any currency reserves. The role of currency reserves in our model follows solely from the interplay of foreign investment in Period 0 and the exchange rate targets. A *reserve policy* is represented by the associated exchange rate targets r_1 and r_2 for the Periods 1 and 2, and a fractional currency reserve ratio μ.

3.1 The Representative Monetary Authority

Monetary authorities choose reserve policies that maximize their profits from the inflow of foreign investment, while avoiding to lose their reputation for not making "hold up profits".[9] Ex-ante the countries' economies are identical, as are the foreign investors. The reserve policies that result from competition between these identical monetary authorities can be obtained as the result of a single decision problem.[10] In this decision problem a representative monetary authority maximizes the ex-ante Choquet expected utility of a representative investor under suitable constraints. These constraints are:

- feasibility constraints, which are identical to those of the local monetary authority due to the linearity of the investment technologies,
- a stability constraint that ensures the local financial system does not break down and
- a condition of "withdrawal equilibrium" regarding the outflow of foreign currency.

In the model under consideration, the stock market essentially transfers local bonds from type *L* investors to *H*-types in Period 1, in exchange for shares in the illiquid asset. A higher transfer results from lower ad interim share prices.[11]

[9] Alternatively, one could assume that monetary authorities try to maximize the inflow of foreign investment, while avoiding losses on their foreign exchange reserves. In the context of our analysis both assumptions lead to the same equilibrium behaviour.

[10] The approach has been used in the context of a competitive banking sector in Allen / Gale (1998). See also Spanjers (1999).

[11] Suppose that at the beginning of Period 1 each investor holds the same amounts of shares and bonds. Consider the share price for which *H*-types sell all their shares in exchange for all bond held by *L*-types. When the share price declines by a small amount, *H*-types may still sell their shares, but *L*-types pay less for them. They therefore end up holding some bonds in addition to the shares. Similarly, when the initial share price increases by a small amount, *H*-types will still buy all bonds, but will continue to hold some shares as well.

Let $\xi \geq 0$ denote the maximal fraction of local bonds that can be held by L-types at the end of Period 1 without threatening financial stability. As share prices at which L-types have an incentive to buy bonds will not occur, this maximal amount cannot exceed $\pi_L \cdot \mu$. We assume ξ is related to the soundness of the local banking sector as

(4) $\xi = \pi_L \cdot \frac{c-v}{c}$, with $c \geq v$.

For high values of $\xi \in [0, \pi_L]$ the financial system is *stable*, for low values it is *fragile*. At the exchange rate target r_1, the local currency paid out by $\xi \cdot \mu$ bonds buys $r_1 \cdot \xi \cdot \mu$ Euros.

The equilibrium share price in Period 1 may fail to be unique. This is due to the linearity of the preferences of investors for immediate consumption and for shares.[12] It is assumed that the monetary authority acts in the ex-ante interest of the investors and targets the highest equilibrium price.[13]

Investors correctly anticipate the effective payouts in Euros from withdrawing their investments in Period 1, x_1, and for withdrawing them in Period 2, x_2, as functions of the signal σ, the exchange rate targets r_1 and r_2, the fractional withdrawal ϖ in Period 1, and the success or failure of the assets. Each individual investor is negligible, so he takes the withdrawal behaviour of the others as given.

Since $\beta_H > \beta_L > 1$, it is optimal to have the currency reserves depleted in Period 1 rather than transferring some reserves to Period 2. Taking this into account, the optimization problem of the representative monetary authority, given the beliefs (π, E, γ) of the investors, is:

$$\max_{(x_1(\cdot), x_2^h(\cdot), x_2^\ell(\cdot), r_1, r_2, \mu, \varpi, \lambda)} \mathsf{CE}\{u(x)\}$$

such that for each $\sigma \in \{b, g\}$:

$$
\begin{array}{llcll}
 & \varpi := \varpi(\sigma;\mu,r_1,r_2) & \in & \varpi^*(\sigma;\mu,r_1,r_2) & \text{(E)} \\
\text{(5)} & \varpi \cdot x_1(\varpi;\cdot) & = & \mu + \alpha_1 \cdot \lambda \cdot (1-\mu) & (\text{F}_1) \\
 & (1-\varpi) \cdot x_2^h(\varpi;\cdot) & = & \alpha_h \cdot (1-\lambda) \cdot (1-\mu) & (\text{F}_{2h}) \\
 & (1-\varpi) \cdot x_2^\ell(\varpi;\cdot) & = & 0 & (\text{F}_{2\ell}) \\
\text{and for } \lambda < 1 & (\varpi - \pi_H) \cdot x_1(\varpi;\cdot) & \leq & r_1 \cdot \xi \cdot \mu + \alpha_1 \cdot (1-\mu) & \text{(S)}
\end{array}
$$

[12] The possible non-uniqueness follows directly by consultation of the appropriate Edgeworth-Box.

[13] Thus, for given reserves μ, the representative monetary authority minimizes the actual redistribution of bonds from H-types to L-types in the withdrawal equilibrium in Period 1. This keeps the ex-ante utility loss from transferring reserves away from investors with the high marginal utility of immediate consumption as small as possible.

where $\varpi^*(\sigma;\mu,r_1,r_2)$ is the set of withdrawal equilibria for signal σ, given the reserve policy μ and the exchange rate targets r_1 and r_2, and λ denotes the fraction of assets liquidated.[14]

Condition (E) states that the withdrawals in Period 1 are compatible with a withdrawal equilibrium. (F_1) is the feasibility constraint for Period 1. The feasibility constraints for Period 2 when assets are successful and when assets fail, are denoted by (F_{2h}) and ($F_{2\ell}$) respectively. Finally, (S) is the condition of financial stability in the absence of a currency crisis. It states that the amount withdrawn in Period 1 in excess of the reserves paid out to the *H*-types, does not exceed the maximal transfer to *L*-types plus the revenues from the liquidation of assets.

In general, the currency reserves of the monetary authority depend on which of the withdrawal equilibria in Period 1 is anticipated to occur. In the above formulation of the optimization problem, it is assumed that after a signal is received, the "best" withdrawal equilibrium is obtained. This implies that we rule out currency crises that are the consequence of coordination problems only. Thus, we focus on *fundamental currency crises.* Following the terminology of Freixas / Rochet (1997) for bank runs, a crisis is "fundamental" when it is caused by beliefs concerning the asset returns, as opposed to beliefs about the withdrawal behaviour of the other investors.

3.2 Equilibrium

In analysing the equilibrium, we start by looking at the effect that competition between local monetary authorities has on the exchange rate targets they set. After finding that the result greatly simplifies our further analysis, we turn to the withdrawal equilibrium and the equilibrium fractional reserve holdings.

Earlier, we assumed that in each period the inflow of Euros generated by the local asset equals its payouts in local currency valued at the ex-ante exchange rate. A local monetary authority with an exchange rate target r_1 less than one does not return the entire inflow of Euros in Period 1 to foreign investors. Rather, it keeps some of the Euros obtained in Period 1 as reserves to carry over to Period 2. This "undervaluation" of the exchange rate target can be helpful, as it generates a surplus of Euros that protects the local currency against unexpectedly high capital outflows in Period 1.

The surplus, however, reduces the ex-ante utility of the foreign investors. It could either have been paid out in Period 1 to a utility of at least β_L or be

[14] *Withdrawal equilibrium* in this setting is defined similar to that in the context of bank runs. See also Spanjers (1999, Chapter 5). The withdrawal equilibrium is analysed below.

invested in local assets, with an ex-ante Choquet expected payout which exceeds that of Euros carried over to Period 2.

Foreign investors in a country that offers an exchange rate target $r_1 < 1$ will find another country that is prepared to offer a preferred exchange rate policy with an exchange rate target $\tilde{r}_1$ between r_1 and 1. The investors will reconsider and invest in the latter country, making it better off as well, as it increases its profits from foreign investment. As a result, in equilibrium no country offers an exchange rate target $r_1 < 1$. An exchange rate target $r_1 > 1$ will not occur in equilibrium either. For $r_1 = 1$, the target $r_2 > 1$ is not feasible. For $r_1 = 1$ and $r_2 < 1$, some of the Euros remain with the local monetary authority and are not returned to investors. Now another country can improve its position by offering $\tilde{r}_2$ between r_2 and 1.

This is summarized in the following Property.

Property 1. *We may assume without loss of generality that in equilibrium* $r_1 = r_2 = 1$.

The nature of competition between monetary authorities leads to reserve policies μ that maximize the ex-ante utility of the representative investor. The ex-ante utility of *H*-types from the payouts in Period 2 of wealth invested in successful assets equals that of *L*-types. But their utility from consuming the same initial wealth as Euros in Period 1 is even higher. So maximizing ex-ante utility amounts to transferring wealth from *L*-types to *H*-types.

Due to the linear structure of preferences, this problem has corner solutions. In particular, the limits of the transfers are determined by the incentive compatibility constraints of *L*-types. We proceed by looking at these incentive constraints in more detail. In doing so, we denote the ad interim Choquet expected payout of assets when signal σ has occurred as

(6) $$\tilde{\alpha}^{\sigma} := \mathrm{CE}\,\{\alpha_p|\sigma\} = \gamma^{\sigma} \cdot \pi_h{}^{\sigma} \cdot \alpha_h.$$

Consider the situation after signal σ occurs, given fractional withdrawals $\varpi = \pi_H$. The incentive constraint assuming that at the end of Period 1 all reserves are held by *H*-types, is denoted by (IC_L^{σ}). For a given reserve policy μ the constraint reads

(7) $$\tilde{\alpha}^{\sigma} \cdot \frac{1-\mu}{\pi_L} \geq \beta_L \cdot \frac{\mu}{\pi_H}.$$

It holds with equality for

(8) $$\mu_\sigma(\gamma) := \frac{\pi_H \cdot \tilde{\alpha}^\sigma}{\pi_L \cdot \beta_L + \pi_H \cdot \tilde{\alpha}^\sigma}.$$

If constraint (7) is violated, this does not necessarily mean that a currency crisis is inevitable after obtaining signal σ. Rather, a fall in share prices may restore equilibrium, leading to an inefficient allocation in which L-types end up obtaining some of the currency reserves in Period 1. However, due to the fragility of the financial system, the monetary authority can only allow for a limited fall in share prices. The incentive compatibility constraint ($IC_L^{\sigma\xi}$) considers the effective payouts after the maximal decline in share prices the monetary authority can allow. When this constraint is violated the monetary authority will abandon its exchange rate target and a currency crisis occurs.

Consider the reserve policy μ and the stability parameter ξ. The incentive constraint of L-types after signal σ and redistribution $\xi \cdot \mu$ through share prices reads:

(9) $$\beta_L \cdot \frac{\xi \cdot \mu}{\pi_L} + \tilde{\alpha}^\sigma \cdot \frac{1-\mu}{\pi_L} \geq \beta_L \cdot \frac{(1-\xi) \cdot \mu}{\pi_H}.$$

It is referred to as ($IC_L^{\sigma\xi}$) and holds with equality for

(10) $$\mu_{\sigma\xi}(\gamma) = \frac{\pi_H \cdot \tilde{\alpha}^\sigma}{(\pi_L - \xi) \cdot \beta_L + \pi_H \cdot \tilde{\alpha}^\sigma}.$$

Clearly, if both $\tilde{\alpha}^\sigma > 0$ and $\xi > 0$, it follows for each level of confidence $\gamma > 0$ and each signal σ that

(11) $$\mu_{\sigma\xi}(\gamma) > \mu_{\sigma 0}(\gamma) = \mu_\sigma(\gamma),$$

which indicates that a more stable financial system leads to higher equilibrium currency reserves.

It should be noted that out of equilibrium and for given exchange rate targets, *higher* currency reserves make a currency crises *more* likely. The reason for this is that it is not *fractional reserve holdings* that offer protection against currency crises, but the *inflow in Euros that is not returned to the foreign investors* in Period 1. As follows from Property 1, in equilibrium – due to competition between the local monetary authorities – the entire inflow of Euros in Period 1 is instantly returned to the foreign investors.

For the equilibrium exchange rate policy the representative monetary authority either chooses one of the above mentioned currency reserves or $\mu^*(\gamma) = 1$, which implements a currency board.

Theorem 2. [15] *In equilibrium we have currency reserves:*

$$(12)\quad \mu^*(\gamma) \in \{\mu_b(\gamma), \mu_{b\xi}(\gamma), \mu_g(\gamma), \mu_{g\xi}(\gamma), 1\}.$$

The intuition behind Theorem 2 is as follows.

When the probability of a good signal is sufficiently low, the monetary authority focuses on the situation after a bad signal, and chooses the liquidity reserves $\mu_b(\gamma)$. Reserve holdings $\mu_{b\xi}(\gamma)$ will occur when both a good signal and a bad signal are sufficiently likely, and the cost of liquidation is high. The monetary authority now prefers high reserves – which are benefical when a good signal occurs – but without risking a currency crisis after a bad signal. By choosing reserves $\mu_{b\xi}(\gamma)$ it sails as close to the wind as possible.

When the probability of a bad signal is sufficiently low, the monetary authority focuses on the situation after a good signal. When the costs of liquidation are sufficiently low, the reserve holdings will be $\mu_g(\gamma)$. If however, both the costs of liquidation and the probability of a bad signal are sufficiently high, it chooses reserve holdings $\mu_{g\xi}(\gamma)$. These reserve holdings exceed their optimal level for a good signal, but reduce the liquidation loss after a bad one. In the extreme case, the monetary authority implements a currency board.

4 Failing to Recognize Ambiguity

What happens when the monetary authorities fail to recognize the presence of ambiguity? This question is answered for two guises in which this failure may occur. Firstly, they may (falsely) believe that investors are fully confident about their probability assessments. The consequences of this belief resemble those of an exogenous loss of confidence. Secondly, monetary authorities may interpret the weights the investors ex-ante assign to the different states of nature as a subjective probability estimate. It should be noted that these weights change when alternatives are considered that obtain their lowest payouts in different states of nature.

To focus on the consequences of the failure to recognize ambiguity, the behaviour of the investors, which is based on their actual beliefs, must be constrained from "correcting" the mistaken beliefs of the monetary authorities in

[15] The proof of Theorem 2 involves a significant amount of rather tedious, though not overly complicated, calculations. It closely follows the proof in Spanjers (1999, Proposition 5.12) in the context of bank runs. An outline of the proof is available on request.

the perfect foresight equilibrium.[16] Therefore, we make the ad hoc assumption that the information policy of the monetary authority ex-ante convinces each individual investor that all other investors share the monetary authority's beliefs about asset states. Since each individual investor is negligible, only the ad interim behaviour, and therefore the beliefs, of the *other* investors matter as to whether or not the incentive constraint is violated and a currency crisis occurs.

Suppose the monetary authority considers the uncertain probability assessment to be certain, i.e., it falsely believes $\gamma = 1$. It therefore chooses reserves $\mu^*(1)$. The actual interim incentive constraint of L-types, however, is the one implied by γ. Therefore, L-types demand a higher ambiguity premium than the monetary authority implicitly offers in its exchange rate policy. If the currency reserves equal $\mu_{b\xi}(1)$, the signal b causes a currency crisis. For reserves $\mu_b(1)$ a currency crisis may or may not occur after a bad signal, depending on the fragility of the financial system. After the signal g a currency crises may or may not arise. For reserves $\mu_g(1)$ a currency crisis is imminent after either signal if the financial system is sufficiently fragile.

A second way in which the monetary authority may fail to recognize ambiguity is by interpreting the specific ex-ante weights the investors assign to the different states of nature as their subjective probability distribution $\hat{\pi} := (\hat{\pi}^H, \hat{\pi}^L)$ which is described as in Table 3.[17]

Table 3: Ex-ante Assigned Weights

	(t,b,h)	**(t,b,ℓ)**	**(t,g,h)**	**(t,g,ℓ)**
$t = H$	$\pi_H \cdot (1-\gamma \cdot \pi_g)$		$\pi_H \cdot \gamma \cdot \pi_g$	0
$t = L$	$\pi_L \cdot \gamma \cdot \pi_{bh}$	$\pi_L \cdot \gamma \cdot \pi_{b\ell}$	$\pi_L \cdot \gamma \cdot \pi_{gh}$	$\pi_L \cdot (1-\gamma)$

The E-capacity (π, E, γ), representing the actual beliefs, is updated using the Dempster-Shafer rule, whereas $\hat{\pi}$ is updated by the conventional Bayes' rule. We obtain the following weights for the asset states when considering the equilibrium withdrawal behaviour of L-types. As the difference in weights shows, the dynamics of the actual beliefs after a bad signal fail to be reproduced by additive probabilities and Bayesian updating.

16 As is indicated in McAfee (2004), many large firms fail to recognize the importance of confidence, which he refers to as "trust". In this light, the possibility that monetary authorities may fail to recognize the full impact of the absence of full confidence seems more than plausible.

17 The existence of such a unique distribution of additive weights depends crucially on the co-monotonicity of the state-contingent payouts that the relevant investment strategies generate for the representative investor. Its derivation is available on request.

Table 4: Ex-ante Assigned Weights for Asset States for L-types

	(*b*,*h*)	**(*b*,*ℓ*)**	**(*g*,*h*)**	**(*g*,*ℓ*)**
Dempster-Shafer weight	$\gamma \cdot \pi_{bh}$	$1-\gamma \cdot \pi_{bh}$	$\frac{\gamma \cdot \pi_g}{1-\gamma \cdot \pi_b}$	$\frac{1-\gamma}{1-\gamma \cdot \pi_b}$
Bayes' weight	$\frac{\pi_{bh}}{\pi_b}$	$\frac{\pi_{b\ell}}{\pi_b}$	$\frac{\gamma \cdot \pi_g}{1-\gamma \cdot \pi_b}$	$\frac{1-\gamma}{1-\gamma \cdot \pi_b}$

The fractional currency reserve ratio for which (IC_L^g) binds for the subjective probability distribution $\hat{\pi}$ is denoted by $\mu_g(\hat{\pi},1)$. When the representative monetary authority chooses this reserve policy, the failure to recognize the presence of ambiguity does not influence the withdrawal equilibrium, since $\mu_g(\hat{\pi},1) = \mu_g(\gamma)$ and $\mu_{g\xi}(\hat{\pi},1) = \mu_{g\xi}(\gamma)$. After a good signal, the updated probabilities equal the weights assigned by the updated E-capacity. The incentive compatibility constraint of type-*L* investors holds. Any fundamental crisis that the monetary authority may anticipate after the bad signal also occurs when the Dempster-Shafer rule is applied. For similar reasons as outlined below, however, there may be a currency crisis after a bad signal is received when no crisis is expected.

For currency reserves $\mu_{b\xi}(\hat{\pi},1)$ the misjudgment of the monetary authorities has serious consequences. The same holds for reserves $\mu_b(\hat{\pi},1)$. When a bad signal is received and currency reserves are $\mu_{b\xi}(\hat{\pi},1)$, the incentive constraint for *L*-types just holds for the updated probability $\hat{\pi}_L^b$ after the maximal fall in share prices that the monetary authority can allow. But the investors assign weights according to Dempster-Shafer updated E-capacity. They put a weight on (*b*,*ℓ*) which exceeds the probability assigned by the monetary authority. Therefore, the incentive constraint of *L*-types is violated and a currency crisis becomes inevitable.

The monetary authority may interpret such unexpected crises as caused by an "irrational overreaction" of the *L*-type investors who "lose their nerves". After a bad signal is received, the falsely perceived "*panic reaction*" of the investors in fact is a *fundamental currency crisis*.

5 The South-East Asian Crisis

Having analysed our model of currency crises in the presence of ambiguity, we now confront it with the stylised facts of the South-East Asian Crisis.[18] This

[18] For an excellent paper on the South-East Asian Crisis in a broader perspective (disguised as a book review) see Williamson (2004).

crisis affected a number of more or less similar economies in the same geographical region. It provides an example where monetary authorities of similar countries used exchange rate policies to compete for foreign investments.

In the light of our model, two distinct phases of the South-East Asian crisis can be recognized. The first phase was characterized by an *exogenous* loss of confidence. It has its roots in the clumsy and at times incompetent reactions to the crisis of the Thai Baht. The second phase was characterized by an *endogenous* loss of confidence. The latter was caused by bad news concerning the fundamentals of the economies in the region.

The initial "speculative attack" on the Baht may well have been caused by a worsening of the prospects for Thai assets. In terms of the model, the incentive constraint of some patient investors was violated. Either a more rapid decline in stock prices or giving in to the international pressure to devalue might have solved the problem at an early stage.

The Thai government, however, failed to link the attack to fundamental problems. Its stubborn reaction led to a loss of confidence in its economic competence, inducing a further outflow of capital. After depleting its currency reserves in trying to defend its exchange rate peg, it was forced to let the Baht float. As the mutual stand-by treaties with its neighbours failed to stop the fall, confidence in its neighbours also declined, as did their stock markets and currencies.

The reaction of the region's governments to the devaluations merely increased doubts about their economic competence. The economic policy of the governments in the region and the Malayan prime minister in particular during the following two months or so, can best be described as follows[19]

> "So illiterate is some of the bluster coming from top policy makers, and so discomforting some of their actions, that investors' confidence has been badly battered..."

As the investors lost confidence in the policy makers, shares and currencies lost value. After the crisis had calmed down by October, bad signals about the economic prospects of South Korea (and to a lesser extent Japan) hit the market. Updating beliefs based on this adverse information led to a further loss of confidence. The increase in ambiguity induced a stronger reaction than the change in the probability assessment about fundamentals seemed to justify. The internal political situation in Korea prevented a swift and prudent reaction and

[19] *The Economist*, September 6th, 1997, "Too late for a gentle landing".

added to the sense of incompetence.[20] It led to a further loss of confidence and a corresponding outflow of capital.

Thus, in our opinion, the story of the South-East Asian crisis fits our model. In particular, the perceived "overreactions", often interpreted as "speculative attacks", seem to be adequately modelled by incorporating ambiguity.

6 Policy Prescriptions

The logic of the model suggests the following policy prescriptions. When a crisis is imminent – as possibly indicated by the combination of a sharp fall in share prices in a country with a fragile financial system and an increased outflow of capital – it is likely to be prevented by an independently approved devaluation: if the monetary authority is pressured to devalue by, say, the IMF, it may retain its credibility. At the same time, one should be careful not to harm the long term prospects of the local economy.

The anticipation of such policy does not reduce its effectiveness. On the contrary, a credible commitment to it leads to second best efficiency, provided there are no unexpected changes in the level of confidence. The reason is similar to that in the corresponding model of bank runs.[21]

At times, the policy may lead to an increase in the number of potential currency crises. But this is not the unfortunate consequence of an avoidable moral hazard problem. Rather, the policy removes the need for excessive caution by the monetary authorities, which is due to the fragility of their financial systems. A commitment to it may increase the number of currency crises to its second-best efficient level.[22]

Furthermore, measures should be taken to enhance the confidence in the economies involved. An increased transparency regarding the financial position of companies and banks might do a lot of good. It could be obtained, for instance, by disentangling industrial conglomerates, liberalizing financial markets and increasing foreign (confidence enhancing!) takeovers. By contrast,

[20] With a presidential election coming up in a few weeks' time, the temptation in South Korea to take firm action and restore confidence was at a minimum. In the beginning of December, it negotiated the, up until then, largest bail out ever with the IMF. Even this rescue failed to restore confidence, mainly because of a failing resolve by the Korean government to deal with the crisis and presidential candidates who seemingly had no clue what to do. The incumbent president was severely damaged and the country was in effect leaderless.

[21] See Spanjers (1999, Section 5.6.3).

[22] In the context of bank runs, this argument builds on Allen / Gale (1998) and more recently, Allen / Gale (2004). It more closely follows Spanjers (1999, Chapter 5).
This argument was made in technical detail in a previous version of the paper, but is left out here to improve the focus of the present version. It will form the basis of a separate paper.

a restrictive monetary policy only damages the prospects of the investments even further.

To prevent currency crises from becoming imminent, measures to strengthen the local financial sectors should have the highest priority. A stable financial system enables share prices to perform their task of absorbing the shocks caused by changes in the fortunes of investments and in the preferences of their owners.

Accordingly, as far as the logic of the model is concerned, the IMF handled the crisis quite well. By providing bailout packages, it prevented large scale bankruptcies of companies and banks under distress. Furthermore, its support may have stopped the fundamental crisis from turning into a panic after the inevitable devaluation of the currencies involved. The demands for liberalization of financial markets and the lifting of restrictions on foreign ownership increased transparency and may, after a period of transition, have helped to increase confidence. The "all purpose" recipe of a restrictive monetary and fiscal policy was, however, counter-productive. But perhaps these requirements, which are the most painful for the governments involved, serve as a warning to others that the political price of a bailout is high. It may convince them to implement confidence enhancing measures and stabilize their financial systems before the next round of bad news hits.

7 Conclusions

The (qualitative) results derived for an *exogenous* loss of confidence may also be obtained for risk averse agents in the absence of ambiguity. As Spanjers (1999, Conjecture 8.1) suggests, qualitative results that depend on a risk premium can be replicated (after suitable adaptations of the model) by using an ambiguity premium, and vice versa. This by no means disqualifies the results. On the contrary, it raises the question whether, at times, premia for ambiguity are mistakenly interpreted as risk premia.

Such misinterpretations are far from harmless, since they may suggest that policy measures are useless, which are, in fact, effective. Policy makers can do little to reduce risk or to change risk attitudes, so they may not be able to effectively change risk premia. But they may well be able to reduce the premia for ambiguity by increasing transparency and predictability. Confusing the premia for ambiguity with risk premia may grossly underestimate the gains of such "prudent" policy making.[23] The "terror premium" on oil prices illustrates this point.

The dynamic inconsistency that leads to an *endogenous* loss of confidence cannot be replicated by assuming risk aversion. Decision makers with

[23] See also Spanjers (1999 and 2008).

ambiguous beliefs who ex-ante plan a course of action contingent on interim information, may deviate from these contingent plans once the information is actually obtained. This drives the main results of Section 4, where the monetary authorities fail to recognize the presence of ambiguity.

In the context of our model, ambiguity can easily be detected once it is known what to look for. It should not be accepted at face value that, ex-ante, investors superstitiously perceive a correlation between their liquidity preference and asset returns. Rather, one should compare the weights assigned to the asset states by the same type of investor, for actions that obtain their worst utility level in different states. When these weights change with the action of the investor, there is a strong indication that he faces ambiguity about asset returns.[24]

The stylized facts of the currency crisis which best fits the assumptions of the model, the South-East Asian crisis, are in line with the conclusions. For the countries in Central and Eastern Europe that intend to adopt the Euro, the model indicates that a stable financial sector may be the best guarantee for achieving this goal.

References

Allen, F. / Gale, D. (1998): Optimal Financial Crises, Journal of Finance, Volume 53, pp. 1245–1284.

Breuer, J. (2005): An Exegesis on Currency and Banking Crises: in Issues in Monetary, Financial and Macroeconomic Adjustment Policies, edited by S. Sayer, pp. 69–96, Blackwell Publishing, Malden MA.

Eichberger, J. / Kelsey, D. (1998): E-Capacities and the Ellsberg Paradox, Theory and Decision, Volume 46, pp. 107–138.

Eichberger, J. / Kelsey, D. (2004): CEU Preferences and Dynamic Consistency, Department of Economics Discussion Paper 04–02, The University of Birmingham.

Ellsberg, D (1961): Risk, Ambiguity and the Savage Axioms, Quarterly Journal of Economics, Volume 75, pp. 643–669.

Freixas, X. / Rochet, J. (1997): Microeconomics of Banking, MIT Press, Cambridge: Mass.

Gilboa, I. / Schmeidler, D. (1993): Updating Ambiguous Beliefs, Journal of Economic Theory, Volume 59, pp. 33–49.

Keynes, J. (1921): A Treatise on Probability, Macmillan, London.

[24] That is, one should compare the weights of the asset states for actions that fail to be comonotonic. See, e.g. Schmeidler (1982/89).

Keynes, J. (1937): The General Theory of Employment, from: Quarterly Journal of Economics, in: Collected Writings, Volume 14, pp. 109–123, MacMillan, London.

Knight, F. (1921): Risk, Uncertainty and Profit, Houghton Mifflin, London.

Krugman, P. (1979): A Model of Balance-of-Payment Crises, Journal of Money, Credit and Banking, Volume 11, pp. 311–325.

McAfee, R. (2004): Real Lessons of Enron's Implosion: Market Makers are in the Trust Business, The Economists' Voice, Volume 1, Issue 2, Article 4.

Morris, S. / Shin, H. (1998): Unique Equilibrium in a Model of Self-Fullfilling Currency Attacks, American Economic Review, Volume 88, pp. 587–597.

Obstfeld, M. (1986): Rational and Self-Fulfilling Balance-of-Payments Crises, American Economic Review, Volume 76, pp. 72–81.

Obstfeld, M. (1996): Models of Currency Crises with Self-Fulfilling Features, European Economic Review, Volume 40, pp. 1037–1047.

Savage, L. (1954): The Foundations of Statistics, Wiley, New York.

Schmeidler, D. (1982/89): Subjective Probability and Expected Utility without Additivity, Econometrica, Volume 57, pp. 571–587.

Spanjers, W. (1999): Liquiditätsversorgung bei Knight'scher Unsicherheit: Ein theoretischer Vergleich von Banken und Märkten, Habilitation Thesis, University of Saarland, Saarbrücken, Engelsdorfer Verlag, Leipzig, 2008.

Spanjers, W. (2008): Central Banks and Ambiguity, International Review of Economics and Finance, Volume 17, pp. 85–102.

Williamson, J. (2004): The Years of Emerging Market Crises: A Review of Feldstein, Journal of Economic Literature, Volume 42, pp. 822–837.

The Effect of Monetary Policy on an Emerging Market Economy: Evidence from Turkey[1]

Anıl Akçağlayan,[2] Ankara University, Turkey
Ayşe Ertuğrul,[3] Université Paris 1 Panthéon Sorbonne, France

1 Introduction

The first empirical analyses of monetary policy within the vector autoregressive (VAR) framework were conducted by Sims (1972) for the US economy. Since then numerous studies have used the VAR or structural VAR framework to analyze the effects of monetary policy in developed economies. In recent studies, however, it has been argued that the monetary policy for developing countries faces additional challenges. In this regard, Turkey is an interesting case because of its structural changes.

The Turkish monetary policy is investigated in various studies. The recent literature has focused greatly on the response of the Central Bank of the Republic of Turkey (CBRT) to exogenous monetary shocks and on the estimation of its reaction function. Turkish monetary policy is analyzed using the VAR approach.

Berument (2001), by conducting vector autoregression, impulse response function, and variance composition analysis, identifies monetary policy shocks. The empirical evidence in his paper is in line with what the theory suggests and does not produce well-known puzzles, e.g. the price-puzzle, in Turkey. Introducing a new monetary policy tool – the spread between the CBRT's *interbank* interest rate and the depreciation of the domestic currency – Berument shows for the period 1986:05-2001:10 that a tight monetary policy was associated both with a decrease in income and prices and with the appreciation

---

[1] We would like to thank Phillippe de Peretti for his valuable comments as well as the participants of the AEA Colloquium on "Exchange Rate Econometrics" April, 8, 2005, Luxembourg, the "Journées of the French Economics Association", May, 11, 2006, Strasbourg, the 5th INFER Workshop on Monetary Economics and Financial Markets, July 14-16, 2006, London, U.K., and the "International Conference of the Turkish Economics Association", September, 11-13, 2006, Istanbul. The usual disclaimer applies.
[2] Ankara University, Department of Economics, 06590 Cebeci, Ankara, Turkey Phone: + 90 312 3197720 Fax: + 90 312 3197736 e-mail: gokkus@politics.ankara.edu.tr
[3] Centre d'Economie de la Sorbonne (UMR 8174), Université Paris 1 Panthéon Sorbonne, CNRS, Maison des Sciences Economiques 106-112, Bd. de l'Hôpital, 75647 Paris Cedex 13, e-mail: Ayse.Ertugrul@malix.univ-paris1.fr

of the currency in the short run. The findings also indicate that the effect was permanent for prices and the exchange rate but was transitory for income.

Berument / Dogan (2003) assess how openness influenced the effectiveness of monetary policy on output and prices. Using quarterly data for the 1987:01-2001:01 period on Turkey, they empirically show that a reduction in the money supply led to a smaller output. They also find that an expansionary monetary policy had an upward impact on inflation. Us (2004), by conducting a VAR analysis, showes that between 1990 and 2002 high inflation has not been a result of an expansionary monetary policy. In Gumus (2002), the relationship between the exchange rate and interest rate is analyzed during the 1994 currency crisis in Turkey using a vector error-correction model (VECM). Estimation results show that higher interest rates were associated with exchange rate depreciation in the long run.

Still one another paper which aims at explaining Turkish monetary policy focused the reaction function of the CBRT. Berument / Malatyali (2000) estimate the implicit reaction function of the CBRT. Their empirical results indicate that CBRT responded to the lagged inflation rate, M2 growth was targeted on annual basis, and a serious output targeting policy was implemented during the period 1989:07-1997:03. Berument / Tasçi (2004) estimate a forward-looking monetary policy reaction function of the CBRT for the period 1990-2000. Their results indicate that the CBRT responds to its foreign exchange reserves, output, and M2 growth, but not the forward, current or lagged inflation. Finally, Emir et al. (2000) measure the degree of sterilization, the offset coefficient, and the degree of the relation between the central bank's reactions and macroeconomic variables. They find that the link between the high sterilization and low inflation, which is generally accepted in the literature, was not observed in Turkey since 1994.

The purpose of this paper is to evaluate the long run effect of Turkish monetary policy on a number of variables. To the best of our knowledge, this is the first paper applying the Toda-Yamamoto methodology to study monetary policy in Turkey for the period 1990-2004. This period includes the 1994 and 2000/2001 financial crises. To account for changes in monetary policy, we divide the sample into two sub-periods corresponding to 1990:06-1999:12 and 2000:01-2004:11. The contributions of our study are twofold. First, we examine variables upon which the CBRT policy has an effect using the Toda-Yamamoto method. Second, by dividing the period in two sub-periods, we explore whether there is a difference in the affected variables in each sub-period. In particular, we estimate a VAR model applying the Toda / Yamamoto (1995) methodology, which allows testing Granger causality regardless of the order of integration of the series of monthly data. In this paper, we use the interest rate as an indicator of monetary policy. The paper is organized as follows. In Section 2 the monetary policy implemented in Turkey under the constraints of fiscal dominance is provided. Section 3 describes the data and methodology. We present and interpret the estimation results in this section. Concluding remarks are given in the last section, Section 4.

2 Monetary Policy in the Turkish Economy from a Historical Viewpoint

In this section, we provide a brief account of the monetary policy followed by the CBRT during the last fifteen years.

In the 1980's a structural change takes place as a reform program is implemented.[4] One of the aims of the structural adjustment program was the liberalization of the repressed financial system. The foreign exchange regime was liberalized, banks were allowed to accept foreign deposits, and convertibility of the Turkish Lira was realized. At the same time restrictions on interest rates were removed, a money market for short-term transactions was established, and the CBRT started to engage in open market operations.[5] The liberalization of the capital account in 1989 ensured a short-term capital inflow into the domestic economy.

After the stabilization and structural adjustment program of 1980's, monetary developments in 1990's were dominated by the public sector borrowing requirement (PSBR) and its financing. In the early 1990's the rapid expansion of credits to the public sector made it impossible for the CBRT to achieve its monetary targets and to take the measures necessary to reduce the inflation rate. Instead, the main policy objective was maintaining stability in the money and foreign exchange markets.

In 1990's the CBRT followed monetary programs and targeted different items of its balance sheet and/or monetary aggregates with or without declaring this to the public. In 1990 the first monetary program was announced, which targeted the size of balance sheet of the CBRT, its total domestic assets, its total domestic liabilities, and its reserve money. As determined within its first monetary program targets, the CBRT succeeded in controlling the balances sheet aggregates and the growth of domestic credit. In this period, the Turkish lira is appreciated and no remarkable fluctuations were observed in the interest rate level. Because of the first Gulf War and the emerging political instability caused by the decision of the government to call an early election, the CBRT didn't announce a monetary program in 1991. In addition, huge increases in the

[4] See Ertugrul / Selcuk (2001), for detailed account of the Turkish macroeconomic experience during 1980-2001.

[5] See Nas / Odekon (1988), Aricanli / Rodrik (1990), Rodrik (1991) and Yeldan (1997) for many aspects of Turkish structural adjustment.

PSBR put a pressure upon the exchange rate. Thus, the interest rate increased and the currency depreciated due to the loss of foreign reserves. The CBRT aimed to ensure the stability in the foreign exchange market and to control the growth rate of the reserve money without incurring large losses in foreign reserves. As a result of increases in the credit extended to public and banking sectors, its level of domestic assets could not be controlled.

In 1992, the CBRT announced a monetary program alike that in the 1980's aiming to control the growth of its balance sheet aggregates. However, the expansion of credit extended to the public sector forced it to abandon its targets and to try to decrease the extreme fluctuations in the exchange rate without allowing foreign reserve losses instead. The following year the CBRT did not announce a monetary program because of the financing needs of the public sector. The main objective of the central bank was once again to ensure the stability of the financial markets without losses in its foreign reserves.

In the last month of 1993, the government changed its financing methods of the fiscal deficit in order to decrease the cost of domestic borrowing. The government did not borrow in some of its loan auctions, despite the increasing public sector deficits. Instead, the Treasury heavily used the CBRT's resources. The resulting excess liquidity put pressure on foreign exchange rate. In the last quarter of 1993, some rating agencies downgraded Turkish government bonds. These developments, combined with unresolved structural problems, triggered the financial crisis in the first quarter of 1994. The currency devaluated, the tight monetary and fiscal policies as well as structural reforms were implemented on the 5th of April 1994. As can be seen in Table 1, the results of the crisis were destructive. The average growth rate, which was as 6 % in 1990-1993 period, declined to -6.1% in 1994 as a result of the crises. The inflation rate increased to three digits.

The 1994 financial crisis influenced the monetary policy of the CBRT. Before 5 April 1994, the designated monetary policy was almost the same as the policies applied between 1990 and 1993. In the post crisis period, in accordance with the standby agreement signed with IMF, the CBRT tried to control the high inflation by using an unannounced predetermined exchange rate path as a peg on one hand and stressed the increase of the foreign assets on the other. In line with IMF's conditions, the monetary authority put a ceiling on the level of its domestic assets and a floor under its net foreign reserves, and tried to control the growth of the monetary base by sterilizing the foreign exchange reserves. However, the destructive results of the crisis left their mark on the Turkish economy during the second half of 1994 and the first half of 1995.

Table 1: Selected Macroeconomic Indicators: 1990-2004

	1990	1991	1992	1993	1994	1995	1996	1997	1998	1999	2000	2001	2002	2003	2004
PSBR/GDP	7.4	10.2	10.6	12.0	7.9	5.0	8.6	7.7	9.4	15.5	11.8	16.4	12.7	9.4	5.0
PSPS/GDP(1)	0.2	-1.4	-0.6	-0.9	3.8	3.3	1.7	0.1	4.6	2.1	6.0	5.8	4.6	6.6	6.5
TPDS/GNP(2)	na	na	na	na	na	na	48.7	47.5	47.2	58.3	57.7	101	89.4	84.0	79.0
Growth (3)	9.4	0.3	6.4	8.1	-6.1	8.0	7.1	8.3	3.9	-6.1	6.3	-9.5	7.9	5.9	10.0
Inflation (4)	60.0	66.0	70.0	66.0	106	94.0	80.0	86.0	85.0	65.0	55.0	54.0	45.0	25.0	10.6
CA/GDP(5)	-1.7	0.2	-0.6	-3.6	2.0	-1.4	-1.4	-1.4	1.0	-0.7	-4.9	2.3	-0.8	-3.3	-5.2
Reserves(6)	5.9	4.9	6.1	6.2	7.1	12.9	16.2	20.8	19.7	23.5	22.1	18.7	26.8	33.6	na

1. Primary Surplus of Public Sector/GNP
2. Total Public Sector Debt Stock /GNP
3. Real Gross National Product (% Change)
4. Consumer Price Index With Different Base Years
5. Current Account /Gross Domestic Product
6. International Reserves ($, Billion)

Source: Central Bank, Treasury

Due to the expiring of the stand-by agreement with the IMF, Turkey's engagement in the Customs Union of the European Communities, and the early general elections held at the end of 1995, the instability in the financial markets increased considerably. Concerned about the instability in the markets, the CBRT centered its monetary policy on achieving stability in financial markets rather than decreasing the inflation rate. The CBRT continued its surveillance of the exchange rate and also tried to control its balance sheet aggregates. The new monetary program became effective in the middle of the second quarter of 1996. It was similar to the programs of the previous two years and depended on controlling both the CBRT's domestic assets growth and the increases in its domestic liabilities, in order to increase its foreign assets. Since the short-term advances to the Treasury were limited by the law and as no credit was extended to other public sector institutions, domestic assets showed a controlled and slow growth. Exchange rate policy was conducted in line with forecasted inflation rates.

In 1997 monetary policy was not so different from the previous years. The details of the monetary program, as in 1996, were not made public. Exchange rates were conducted in line with the expected inflation. This policy ensured not only real effective exchange rate stability but competitiveness in the export sector and a sustainable current account deficit as well. At the same time, official reserves of CBRT reached 27 billion US dollars, which reduced the CBRT's vulnerability to speculative attacks.

Figure 1: Effective Exchange Rate Index

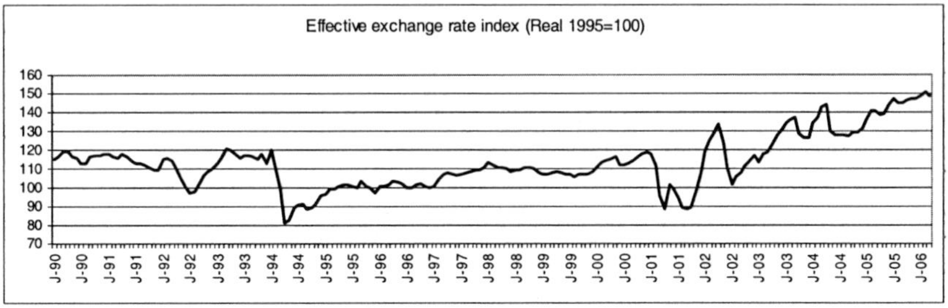

Source: CBRT

Figure 2: Interbank Interest Rate

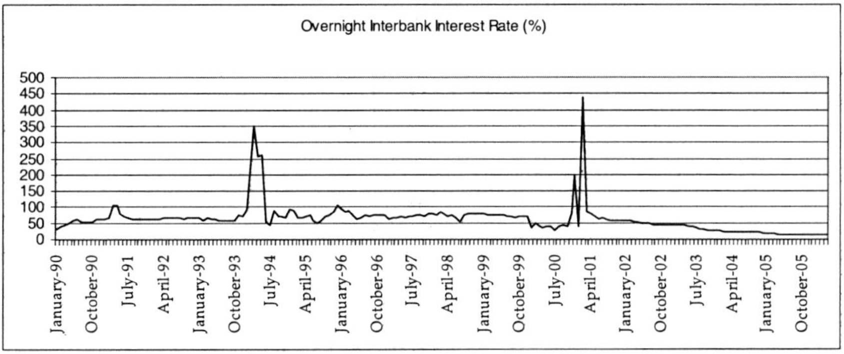

Source: CBRT

In 1998, a new monetary program was announced, which aimed not only at ensuring stability in financial markets but also at fighting inflation. According to the Annual Report of the CBRT, the monetary policy in 1998 was formulated to support the fiscal policy, which was set mainly to reduce the rate of inflation. In the first half of the year reserve money target bands were announced. The bands were determined by money demand projections. However, the Russian crisis, the uncertainty about civil servants' salary increases, an early election, and developments in the international financial markets led to a change in the targets and the priorities in the second half of the year. While fighting inflation was the main aim in the first half of the year, the stability policy gained importance in the second half of the year. In June, Turkey signed a Staff Monitoring Program (SMP) with IMF. According to this program net domestic assets were redefined and targeted. Throughout the year, the targeted aggregates were below the targeted limits. But foreign capital outflows occured, as a result of the developments in the second half of year. The lack of borrowing in international markets forced the Treasury to domestic borrowing which exacerbated the upward pressure on interest rates. Thus, at the beginning of 1999, the Turkish economy entered into a recession whilst facing worsening debt dynamics.

The monetary policy implementation under the SMP agreement continued in the next year. As in 1998, the monetary policy in 1999 was based on the targets of controlling inflation and stabilizing financial markets. In order to remove uncertainties in the economy, priority was given to controlling the inflation rate in 1999 and the exchange rate policy was used to contribute to this aim. The SMP program achieved some improvements in the inflation rate and fiscal imbalances but it could not relieve the pressure on interest rates. The capital inflows were more than expected, which led to CBRT to achieve the program targets regarding reserve money bands and primary budget surplus. The Russian crisis in August 1998, the general election in April 1999 and two devastating earthquakes in August and October 1999 led to a deterioration of the fiscal balance of public sector. At the same time, the overall public sector deterioration and rapid increase in interest payments caused the inflation rate to get out of control. The economy contracted by 5 percent in this year.

The SMP was designed as a bridge to a future comprehensive disinflation program. In December, the government signed a stand-by agreement with IMF to implement the disinflation program. The aim of the program was to reduce inflation from 60-70 % per year to single digits by the end of the year 2002. The monetary policy in 2000 was determined in line with the Disinflation Program.

The main tool of the stabilization program – a crawling peg, i.e. the percent change in the Turkish lira against the exchange rate basket of 1 US dollar and 0.77 euro – was announced daily during the year 2000. A band for domestic assets held by the CBRT was the other important feature of the monetary policy implemented in 2000. In addition, it was presumed that increases in base money demand would be met by increases in the net foreign items of the CBRT's balance sheet.

In the beginning of the year, the disinflation program brought about a sharp reduction in interest rates. Even though the performance criteria of the program were realized, the interest rate on government securities increased in the second half of the year because of accumulated problems like the increase of the current account deficit, the delay in structural reforms and persistence in the inflation rate. While there was turmoil in financial markets in November,[6] the program

[6] Increased interest rates caused problems for the banks that held a high volume of government securities in their portfolios in November. The liquidity needs were met by the CBRT's funding through open market operation and the interbank money market. This, in turn, caused

seemed on track until February of 2001. However, the liquidity crisis of November 2000 increased the interest rates to sky-high levels. The exchange rate based disinflation program came to a halt due to developments in the financial markets that occurred in February. At this date, the exchange rate collapsed and depreciated more than 40%.[7]

During the remainder of 2001, the monetary program was focused on reducing the destructive effects of the crisis. According to Annual Report, the CBRT set its short-term priorities so as to provide stability in the financial system.[8] The new program[9] which followed after May 2001 was designed to control the base money by implementation of monetary targeting. The values of the net domestic assets (NDA) and periodical changes in the net international reserves (NIR) of the CBRT became the performance criteria. Within the framework of new monetary program, short-term interest rates became the most important monetary policy tool for controlling liquidity and inflation pressures.

Following the February 2001 financial crisis, the exchange rate was determined to a large extend by market conditions and this remained so in the following years. In the beginning of the floating exchange rate system, the CBRT announced that the exchange rates would be determined by market forces. It would intervene in the foreign exchange market in a limited fashion to prevent excessive volatility without targeting a certain trend level. Moreover, the CBRT announced that it would hold foreign exchange auctions in order to strengthen the exchange rate.

In the beginning of the year 2002, the monetary policy was designed in line with the stabilization program called Transition Program to a Strong Economy covering the period 2002-2004. According to Annual Reports of the CBRT, an implicit inflation targeting policy which focused only on future inflation was implemented.[10] In the new monetary framework, short-term interest rates are used as the main policy instrument to fight inflation. The CBRT also monitored the monetary performance criteria and indicative targets.

---

its net domestic assets to exceed their limit and the demand of foreign exchange increased. The CBRT sold a substantial amount of foreign exchange. Thereafter the CBRT returned to the domestic assets targets.

[7] The effect of crisis on economy was devastating. GDP shrunk 7.5 percent. PSBR/GDP ratio increased from 12 % in 2000 to 16% in 2001.

[8] The new program aimed mainly at arranging the role of the state banks and reducing their extensive short term liabilities.

[9] Transition Program to a Strong Economy as implemented by K. Dervis.

[10] In preparation for inflation targeting, important changes were made in the structure of monetary policy in 2002. On August, the Turkish Banks' Association launched the Turkish Lira Interbank Offer Rate (TRLIBOR). Furthermore, a Primary Dealership System was initiated by Treasury and the Central Bank.

At the end of 2002, the CPI inflation rate was at 30 percent, which was the lowest level in 20 years. The growth rate of GDP was 8 per cent in 2002.

In 2003 and 2004, there has been no substantial change in the monetary policy, which had been followed since 2001. The Central Bank intervened in the exchange market to balance foreign exchange purchases in cases where rates displayed signals for excessive fluctuations in either direction. During this period, the short-term interest rate was used as the main policy instrument as it was before.

Thus, in this context, it is possible to devide 1990-2004 in two sub-periods as pre-2000 and post-2000. In summary, the CBRT focused its monetary policy on achieving stability in financial markets rather than decreasing the inflation rate in the pre-2000 period, because of the difficulty in controlling its balance sheet items and monetary aggregates due to the financial needs of the public sector. However, in the 2000-2004 periods the monetary policy formulation of the CBRT was based on the challenge to decrease the high inflation rates. The fight against inflation became the priority at the beginning of 2000.

The ongoing monetary and fiscal discipline together with the progress in structural reforms allowed the CBRT to determine the disinflation target as the first priority of the monetary policy. Certain conditions beyond its control also contributed to achieving the disinflation target. First of all, the maintenance of budgetary discipline changed the macroeconomic conditions in recent years. Second, just after the 2001 financial crises, the CBRT gained legally sound institutional independence and regulations. Third, the problems in banking sector were resolved in 2000's. Fourth, thanks to the favorable conditions, economic uncertainty declined and market confidence increased. Finally, inflationary expectations decreased in the last three years.

3 Empirical Analysis and Results

3.1 Specification

In this study we use the methodology to test for Granger causality in the VAR framework developed by Toda / Yamamoto (1995). The advantages of this test stem from the ability to overcome many shortcomings of alternative econometric methods. There are some problems regarding Granger causality testing in time series analysis. In the empirical literature sometimes the Wald test is use for unrestricted vector autoregressive models. Toda / Phillips (1993) show that the asymptotic distribution of the test in the unrestricted models in levels involves nuisance parameters and non-standard distributions. They concluded that, in general, there is no sound basis for undertaking non-causality tests in levels vector autoregressive models with non-stationary variables. The Wald test, which determines whether some parameters of a stable VAR model are jointly zero, is not valid for non-stationary processes, as the test statistics do not follow a standard distribution.

The cointegration techniques proposed by Engle / Granger (1987), Johansen (1988) and Johansen / Juselius (1990) have been used in some studies for testing causality. But they are cumbersome and involve pre-testing for integration and cointegration. The Johansen cointegration method is based on the error-correction representation of the VAR(k) model. As Giles / Mirza (1999) show, it is necessary to pre-test the rank conditions. If either of the rank conditions is not satisfied then the problems of nuisance parameters and non-standard distributions show up. The Monte Carlo experiment of Giles / Mirza shows also that applied unit root and cointegration tests suffer from size distortion and often have low power. As Engle / Granger (1987) demonstrate, if the original series are non-stationary, valid results in Granger causality are obtained simply by first differentiating the VAR model. Nevertheless, this transformation may lead to loss of information about long run relations between the trend components of the original time series.

To deal with these problems Toda / Yamamoto (1995) develop a technique that can be applied irrespective of the integration and cointegration properties of the system. This method uses a modified Wald statistic (MWALD) for testing significance of the parameters of a VAR(k), where k is the lag length in the system. The MWALD statistics has an asymptotic chi-square distribution when a VAR($k+d_{max}$) is estimated, where d_{max} is the maximal order of integration suspected to occur in the system. Monte Carlo experiments presented by Zapata / Rambaldi (1996) provide evidence that the MWALD test performs well in terms of size and power in large samples. Overfitting and underfitting does not affect the size and power of the test.

According to Toda / Yamamoto (1995), one of the advantages of this procedure is that it does not require precise knowledge of the integration properties of the system. It can be applied even when there is no integration and/or stability and rank conditions are not satisfied insofar as the order of integration does not exceed the true lag length of the model. The better size and power of Wald test over other tests have been supported by Giles / Mirza (1999)'s Monte Carlo study. The authors showed that the performance of Granger non-causality testing depends on the accuracy of the prior cointegration test for the pre-test methods, not only in terms of detecting whether or not there is cointegration but also in terms of accurate assessment of the cointegrating rank. The results of their experiments showed that the consistent performance of the MWALD method over the pre-testing approaches helps detecting the unidirectional causality and non-causality. On the other hand, they concluded that the MWALD test is expected to have lower power than WALD and LR tests based on VECM. However, as the simulation study covers cases where there is cointegration and rank conditions are satisfied, the results of this study must be explained carefully.

Before applying the Toda-Yamamoto technique, it is necessary to determine the order of integration. In the Section 3.2, the information about data and integration properties are given. Results of Granger causality test are presented and interpreted in Section 3.3.

3.2 Data and Integration Properties

The data used in this study are real GDP, real effective exchange rate, foreign reserves, inflation rate, real reserve money, interest rate, oil prices and foreign interest rate. They are labeled as in Table 2. Data are monthly and cover the period 1990-2004. All data series except interest rates are in natural logarithms and obtained from the CBRT and the Board of Governors of the Federal Reserve System.[11] The real effective exchange rate index is calculated by the Central Bank of Turkey, a rise in this index indicates real appreciation. The inflation rate is calculated as monthly change in the log of consumer price index that is used to deflate the monetary aggregate. Since GDP is not available on a monthly basis, the monthly GDP is calculated by using monthly industrial production index and is deflated by using the wholesale price index. The real GDP series are seasonally adjusted by running the X-11 multiplicative filter.

Table 2: Data

p:	log of monthly inflation rate[(a)]
m:	log of real reserve money[(b)]
y:	log of real GDP
i:	interest rate
e:	log of reel effective exchange rate index[(c)]
r:	log of central bank's reserves
ia:	effective federal funds rate
o:	log of oil price

(a) $p = log(CPI_t) - log(CPI_{t-1})$ CPI (1987=100)
(b) $m = log$(reserve money/CPI) CPI (1987=100)
(c) The index is calculated by Central Bank Of Turkey. CPI based real effective exchange index calculated using the IMF weights for 19 countries including Germany, USA; Italy; France; United Kingdom, Japan; Netherlands, Belgium, Switzerland, Austria, Spain, Canada, Korea, Sweden, Taiwan, Iran, Brazil, China and Greece (1995=100) . An increase in the index denotes an appreciation.

---

[11] Federal funds rate and monthly oil prices are collected from Board of Governors of the Federal Reserve System.

Prior to applying the Toda-Yamamoto technique for Granger non-causality, it is necessary to establish the optimal lag length of the system and the maximum order of integration of variables. The order of integration of the series is tested by means of the Augmented Dickey-Fuller (ADF) and Kwiatkowski, Phillips, Schmidt and Shin (KPSS) tests.[12] The results of both tests are reported in Table 3.

As shown in Table 3, the hypothesis a unit root is not rejected for *p*, *m*, *y*, *e*, *i*, *r*, *ia*, and *o*. However, results for first difference clearly show that the null hypothesis of *I(2)* can be easily rejected. The results indicate that all series are stationary in first difference. In other words, all series are *I(1)*.

Table 3: Results of Stationary of Series

Variables	Level				First-difference			
	t_u	t_t	LM_u	LM_t	t_u	t_t	LM_u	LM_t
p	-0.85 (12)	-2.13 (12)	1.226	0.634	-6.13 (11)	-6.22 (11)	0.088	0.068
m	-0.14 (12)	-3.14 (12)	1.356	0.251	-3.46 (11)	-3.75 (11)	0.307	0.070
y	-1.90 (11)	-2.55 (11)	1.429	0.222	-4.29 (10)	-4.35 (10)	0.378	0.415
i	-3.62 (4)	-3.69 (4)	0.321	0.306	-9.53 (3)	-9.54 (3)	0.281	0.179
e	-1.27 (12)	-2.34 (12)	0.808	0.182	-5.19 (11)	-5.27 (11)	0.033	0.023
r	-1.15 (12)	-2.46 (12)	1.545	0.208	-3.69 (11)	-3.68 (11)	0.043	0.043
ia	-2.34 (4)	-2.47 (4)	0.652	0.200	-3.65 (3)	-3.67 (3)	0.121	0.121
o	-1.25 (13)	-2.36 (13)	0.745	0.248	-3.15 (12)	-3.33 (12)	0.180	0.036
Critical Values								
1%	-3.471	-4.016	0.739	0.216	-3.471	-4.016	0.739	0.216
5%	-2.879	-3.437	0.463	0.146	-2.879	-3.437	0.463	0.146
10%	-2.576	-3.142	0.347	0.119	-2.576	-3.142	0.347	0.119

Notes: The *t* and LM statistics are for ADF and KPSS test respectively. t_u and LM_u are for the model with constant term. t_t and LM_t are for the model with a constant and a trend. The critical values are taken from MacKinnon (1991) and KPSS (1992).

[12] See Enders (1995, Chapter 4), Hamilton (1994, Chapter 17), Dickey / Fuller (1979) and Kwiatkowski *et al.* (1992)

3.3 Results of Granger Causality Test

To select the lag structure of the VAR model, Akaike Informative criterion (AIC) and Hannan-Quinn criterion (HOC) are used.[13] A series of diagnostic tests (i.e. autocorrelation, normality, heteroskedasticity) are conducted to ensure that the underlying statistical assumptions hold.[14] When they do not, we chose the minimal lag-length to ensure the whiteness of residuals. We separated our estimation into two subperiods. The first period runs from 1990:01 to 1999:12, the optimal lag order of VAR is six, hence the order of the VAR to apply the Wald test is seven. The second period covers 2000:01 to 2004:12, the optimal lag order of VAR is two, therefore the order of VAR to apply the Wald test is three.

In this paper we used the interest rate as the indicator of monetary policy applied in Turkey. To measure the monetary policy of the CBRT, alternativley some of its balance sheet items could be used. As explained above, the CBRT has announced its monetary policies at various times and targeted different monetary aggregates and items in its balance sheet, like NDA and NIR. However, the CBRT cared more about the interest rate than about the announced target variables. Therefore, here the interest rate is used as an indicator of monetary policy.[15] Likewise, in Berument / Malatyalı (2000), the overnight interbank interest rate is taken to be the instrument fort the CBRT's monetary policy. Bernanke / Blinder (1992) provide empirical evidence that the federal funds rate might be used to measure the Fed's monetary policy.

In Table 4, we report the chi-square test statistics obtained by Granger non-causality testing together with the estimated *p*-values.[16] In the first sub-period, there is strong evidence of causal relationship running from interest rate to exchange rate (Wald test=24.08, *p*-value=0.03), given the information set. The null hypothesis of Granger non-causality from interest rate to central bank's official reserves is also strongly rejected at 1 percent level (Wald test=13.86, *p*-value=0.031). Our findings indicate however that there is no causal relationship running from interest rate to inflation rate and income.

In the second period, the results of causality test are in accordance with what we expect. Economic theory suggest that a contractive monetary policy should reduce price levels and real output. According to chi-square test statistic the null hypothesis of Granger non-causality from interest rate to inflation rate is

[13] See Akaike (1973) and Hannan / Quinn (1979).

[14] The results of diagnostic tests are available upon request.

[15] As indicated in Section 1, Berument (2001) argues that spread between interbank interest rate and depreciation rate of the local currency can be used as an indicator or the stance of the CBRT's monetary policy.

[16] For Granger causality, sec Granger (1969) and Enders (1985, Chapter 5).

rejected. The result of this test also suggests a Granger causal relation going from interest rate to income in the second period.

The findings support the hypothesis that, in the 1990's, the Central Bank's priority was the stability of the financial markets. Fighting inflation became priority from the beginning of the year 2000.

Table 4: Granger Causality Test

H_o	Lag length /VAR order	Mwald	p-value
1990-1999			
$i \xrightarrow{/} m$	6/7	8.43 (6)	0.208
$i \xrightarrow{/} p$	6/7	7.47 (6)	0.279
$i \xrightarrow{/} y$	6/7	8.46 (6)	0.206
$i \xrightarrow{/} r$	6/7	24.08 (6)	0.000*
$i \xrightarrow{/} e$	6/7	13.86 (6)	0.031*
2000-2004			
$i \xrightarrow{/} m$	2/3	9.52 (2)	0.008*
$i \xrightarrow{/} p$	2/3	10.65 (2)	0.004*
$i \xrightarrow{/} y$	2/3	11.49 (2)	0.003*
$i \xrightarrow{/} r$	2/3	3.77 (2)	0.151
$i \xrightarrow{/} e$	2/3	5.99 (2)	0.049*

Notes: $\xrightarrow{/}$ denotes does not cause (significance at 5%). Figures in parentheses are degree of freedom.

4 Conclusion

In Turkey, bearing the characteristics of a developing country with high inflation, the main targets of the monetary policy are not evident. In some years, the CBRT explicitly declared that it has used its balance sheet items as the policy objective but it was also concerned about the stability of financial markets and inflation.

In the beginning of the 1990's, the CBRT targeted items on its balance sheet, such as net domestic assets or reserve money. Also, the CBRT used various tools between 1990 and 1999 in controlling inflation such as exchange rate and monetary aggregates. During this period the CBRT applied monetary policy under the constraints of the financing needs of the public sector. In this regard, the constraint of the CBRT was to stabilize the value of the Turkish Lira against other currency and to eliminate any potential attack on the exchange rate. However, despite the recurring disinflation programs, inflation rates had been high until 2002.

The positive effects of a sound fiscal discipline and the progress achieved in structural reforms combined with the favorable conditions in international markets allowed the fight against inflation to be set as a priority by the beginning of 2000. Following implicit inflation targeting, the Central Bank achieved to decrease inflation rate from 60-70 percent to one digit level in 2004.

The main motivation of this paper is to explain the relation between monetary policy and monthly macroeconomic variables between 1990 and 2004. In particular, we estimated a VAR model applying the Toda / Yamamoto (1995) methodology, which allows testing for Granger causality regardless of the order of integration of the series to monthly data. We used the interest rate as an indicator of monetary policy.

The causality results support our hypothesis that during 1990's the Central Bank centered its monetary policy on achieving stability in financial markets rather than decreasing the inflation rate. Our findings indicate that, between 1990 and 1999, there is strong evidence of causal relationship running from interest rate to exchange rate and official reserves.

The results also support the hypothesis that since the end of 1999 the first priority of the Bank is to reduce inflation rate. We find a causal relationship between interest rate and inflation for the 2000-04 period. According to our findings Granger non-causality from interest rate to income and to the exchange rate are rejected as well.

References

Akaike, H. (1973): Information theory and an extension of the maximum likelihood principle, in: 2nd International Symposium on Information Theory, edited by B. Petrov and F. Csaki, Budapest Akademiai Kiado, pp. 267-281.

Aricanli, T. / Rodrik, D. (Eds.) (1990): The Political Economy of Turkey Debt, Adjustment and Sustainability, Mac Millan, New York, USA.

Bernanke, B. / Blinder, A. (1992): The federal funds rate and the channels of monetary transmission, in: American Economic Review, Volume 82, pp. 901-921.

Berument, H. / Dogan, B. (2003): Openness and the effectiveness of monetary policy: empirical evidence from Turkey, in: Applied Economic Letters, Volume 10, pp. 217-221.

Berument, H. (2001): Measuring monetary policy for a small open economy: Turkey, unpublished manuscript, Bilkent University, Ankara, Turkey.

Berument, H. / Malatyalı, K. (2000): The implicit reaction function of the central bank of the republic of Turkey, in: Applied Economic Letters, Volume 7, pp. 425-430.

Berument, H. / Tasçi, H. (2004): Monetary policy rules in practice: evidence from Turkey, in: International Journal of Finance and Economics, Volume 9, pp. 33-38.

The Central Bank of the Republic of Turkey (1996, 1997, 1998, 1999, 2000, 2001, 2002, 2003, 2004): Annual Report, Ankara, Turkey. [http://www.tcmb.gov.tr].

Dickey, D. / W. Fuller (1979): Distribution of the estimators for autoregressive time series with a unit root, in: Journal of the American Statistical Association, Volume 74, pp. 727-431.

Emir, O. / Karasoy, A. / Kunter, K. (2000): Monetary policy reaction function in Turkey, Working Paper, Research Department of the Central Bank of the Republic of Turkey, Ankara, Turkey.

Enders, W. (1995): Applied Econometric Time Series, John Wiley and Sons, New York, USA.

Engle, R. / Granger, C. (1987): Cointegration and Error Correction: Representation, Estimation and Testing, in: Econometrica, Volume 55, pp. 251-276.

Ertugrul A. / Selcuk, F. (2001): Turkish economy: 1980-2001, in: Inflation and Disinflation in Turkey, edited by A. Kibritcioglu, L. Rittenberg and F. Selcuk, Ashgate Publishing, Hampshire, United Kingdom, pp. 13-40.

Giles, J. / Mirza, S. (1999): Some pretesting issue on testing for Granger non-causality, Econometrics Working Paper from Department of Economics, No 9914, University of Victoria, Victoria BC, Canada.

Granger, C. (1969): Investigating causal relations by econometric models and cross spectral methods, in: Econometrica, Volume 37, pp. 48-58.

Grasa, A. (1989): Econometric Model Selection: A New Approach, Kluwer Academic Publishers, Dordrecht, Netherlands.

Gumus, I. (2002): Effects of the interest rates on exchange rates during the 1994 crisis in Turkey, Working Paper No 14, Research Department of the Central Bank of the Republic of Turkey, Ankara, Turkey.

Hamilton, J. (1994): Time Series Analysis, Princeton University Press, Princeton, NJ, USA.

Hannan, E. / Quinn, B. (1979): The determination of the order of an autoregression, in: Journal of the Royal Statistical Society, Series B, Volume 41, pp 190–195.

Johansen, S. (1988): Statical analysis of cointegrated vectors, in: Journal of Economic Dynamics and Control, Volume 12, pp. 231-54.

Johansen S. / Juselius, K. (1990): Maximum likelihood estimation and inference on cointegration-with applications to the demand for money, in: Oxford Bulletin of Economics and Statistics, Volume 52, pp. 169-210.

Kesriyeli, M. (1997): 1980'li Yıllardan Günümüze Para Politikası, Working Paper, No 4, The Central Bank of the Republic of Turkey, Ankara, Turkey. In Turkish: Monetary policy from 1980s to today.

Kwiatkowski, D. / Phillips, P. / Schmidt, P. / Shin, Y. (1992): Testing the null hypothesis of stationary against the alternative of a unit root, in: Journal of Econometrics, Volume 54, pp. 154-178.

MacKinnon, J. (1991): Critical values for cointegration tests, in: Long-run Economic Relations: Reading in Cointegration, edited by R. Engle and C. Granger, Oxford University Press, Oxford, United Kingdom, pp. 267-276.

Nas, T. / Odekon, M. (Eds.) (1988): Liberalization and the Turkish Economy, Contributions in Economics and Economic History, No 86, Greenwood Press, New York, USA.

Rodrik, D. (1991): Premature liberalization, incomplete stabilization: the Ozal decade in Turkey, in: Lessons of Economic Stabilization and Its Aftermath, edited by M. Bruno, S. Fisher, E. Helpman, N. Liviatan, and L. Meridor, MIT Press, Cambridge, MA, USA, pp 323-353.

Sims, C. (1972): Money, income and causality, in: American Economic Review, Volume 66, pp. 213-216.

Toda, H. / Phillips, P. (1993): Vector autoregression and causality, in: Econometrica, Volume 6, pp. 1367-1393.

Toda H. / Yamamoto, P. (1995): Statistical inferences in vector autoregression with possibly integrated processes, in: Journal of Econometrics, Volume 66, pp. 225-250.

Us, V. (2004): Inflation dynamics and monetary policy strategy: some prospects for the Turkish economy, in: Journal of Policy Modeling, Volume 26, pp. 1003-1013.

Yeldan, E. (1997): Financial liberalization and fiscal repression in Turkey: policy analysis in a CGE model with financial markets, in: Journal of Policy Modeling, Volume 19, pp. 79-117.

Zapata, H. / Rambaldi, A. (1996): Monte Carlo evidence on cointegration and causation, in: Oxford Bulletin of Economics and Statistics, Volume 59, pp. 285-298.

Optimal Monetary Policy under Incomplete Pass-through and Asymmetric Price Rigidity: The Empirical Evidence from Russia.

Victoria Dobrynskaya,[1]
State University - Higher School of Economics, Russia

1 Introduction

The welfare analysis of the monetary policy has been in the centre of macroeconomics since the Great Depression. Empirical observations of the Phillips curve suggest that prices are sticky in the short run and, therefore, the monetary policy may be used to smooth the business cycle and increase social welfare.

In an open economy where foreign shocks may be passed into the domestic economy the task of the monetary policy becomes even more complicated. Under high pass-through of the exchange rate onto the domestic prices, monetary policy stops to be independent and should adjust to exchange rate shocks. Such a policy of smoothing exchange rate fluctuations is common in western economies (see e.g. Parsley / Popper 1998).

The problem of optimal monetary policy is extremely relevant for Russia. Although the monetary authority claims that inflation targeting is the main goal of the monetary policy, empirical finding suggest that the real exchange rate targeting is of major importance (see Vdovichenko / Voronina 2004). Due to the rising flow of petrodollars, the rouble is currently experiencing a significant real appreciation. The fear to harm exports causes the monetary authority to respond by accumulating dollar reserves and increasing the money supply, thus preventing a nominal appreciation. Such policy leads to high inflation which benefits of some groups at the expense of others. That is why the optimal degree of intervention is in the centre of the current political and economic debate.

A number of theoretical papers suggest that the optimal degree of intervention depends on the effect of exchange rate changes on domestic price level (see e.g. Devereux / Engel 2000). If this pass-through is high, in the absence of a monetary policy reaction an exchange rate shock will have clear impact on do-

[1] Email: v.v.dobrynskaya@lse.ac.uk Tel: +7 916 6864264, fax: +7 495 6257933. Personal website http://new.hse.ru/sites/dobrynskaya. The author is grateful to all participants of the Macroeconomic Workshop at State University – Higher School of Economics and a research seminar at the Central Bank of Russia for their valuable comments and suggestions. This research was supported by individual research grant of State University – Higher School of Economics # 05-01-0008

mestic prices. Therefore, some degree of policy intervention is desirable in order to reduce the pass-through effect and, thus, domestic price volatility. But the pass-through effect, in turn, appears to be endogenous to the local monetary policy (see Devereux / Yetman 2003). It tends to be higher in countries with higher average inflation rates and a lower degree of monetary policy intervention.

Most theoretical models developed in this field are welfare-based optimizing general equilibrium models which try to capture real life peculiarities and, hence, are too complicated to be solved analytically. The authors obtain their results from calibrations, but they typically fail to apply a comparative static analysis. In an attempt to fill this gap, we propose a simple general equilibrium sticky price model of a small open economy with incomplete pass-through. Our model is similar to the New Keynesian model of a closed economy, described in Clarida et al. (1999). By minimizing a social loss function, we obtain an optimal monetary policy rule and analyse the parameters that determine the optimal degree of monetary intervention. In particular, we find that the higher the pass-through and the more flexible prices in an economy are, the stronger should the monetary policy intervention be in the case of an exchange rate shock.

Recent empirical literature finds that prices are more sticky downwards than upwards. This effect it called "asymmetric price rigidity" and may result from money illusion of workers, collusive behaviour of firms or search behaviour of consumers. Therefore, in our model we assume downward price rigidity and determine the optimal monetary policy in case of positive and negative exchange rate shocks. We find that while a depreciation of the domestic currency should lead to a significant rise in the interest rate, an appreciation of the same size requires a much smaller reduction in the interest rate.

The empirical part of the paper deals with analysing the monetary policy of the Central Bank of Russia. Since the pass-through effect is important for determination of the appropriate monetary policy, we estimate its size for different types of consumer goods using a Vector Error Correction Model and constructing impulse-response functions. We analyse the period from the crisis of 1998 to 2005 and trace changes in the pass-through effect over this time span. Then we estimate the impact of the monetary policy on the pass-through in general and in cases of appreciation and depreciation of rouble. Finally, we compare the estimation results with the predictions of the theoretical model and make policy recommendations.

The remainder of the paper is organised as follows. In Section 2 we review the most relevant literature on the pass-through effect, on optimal monetary policy and on asymmetric price rigidity. In Section 3 we lay out the theoretical model and determine the optimal monetary policy within this setting. Empirical estimations of the pass-through effect and the monetary policy in Russia are presented in Section 4. Section 5 draws conclusions, makes recommendations, and provides suggestions for further research.

2 Literature Review

2.1 Pass-Through Effect and Monetary Policy

In the early days of open economy macroeconomics it was common to think that purchasing power parity (PPP) is the reason why domestic prices react to exchange rate movements. According to PPP, an exchange rate shock should be passed onto the domestic price level in its full extent, implying a complete pass-through and the absence of arbitrage opportunities of trade between countries.

But an extensive literature on the pass-through effect (PTE) in different countries find empirical evidence that it is far from complete, although significant, and varies greatly across countries, industries and other parameters under consideration. For example, the pass-through in developing countries appears to be much higher than in developed ones (see, for example, Dubravco / Marc 2002). Korhonen / Wachtel (2005) find that the pass-through effect in CIS countries during 1999-2004 is quite high, although once again far from complete. They report that the extent of pass-through is clearly higher in the CIS countries than in their comparison group of other emerging market economies. A couple of studies estimate the PTE in Russia. For example, Dobrynskaya / Levando (2005) study the period 1995-2002 and estimate an average pass-through elasticity of 40% on the consumer price index and of 23% on the producer price index within 6 months. Shmykova / Sosunov (2005) study the period after the crisis of 1998 and estimate a pass-through of 6% on CPI within 6 months during 1999-2001 and of 26% during 2002-2004.

A number of theories have been proposed to explain why the pass-through tends to be incomplete. Some authors argue that the ultimate explanation comes from microeconomics. The Obstfeld / Rogoff (2000) model assumes transportation costs, which increase the prices of imported goods and preclude their perfect substitutability for the competing domestic goods. Also the presence of non-traded goods in consumption may explain a low degree of pass-through (Betts / Kehoe 2001). Another argument is that the costs of imported inputs constitute only a small part of the costs of a final good, a large share of the costs being attributable to local inputs and non-traded services, such as marketing and distribution (see Corsetti / Dedola 2002 and Burstein et al. 2003).

Several authors (see e.g. Bergin / Feenstra 2001, Bergin 2001, Corsetti / Dedola 2002 and Bachetta / Wincoop 2002) argue that the pass-through may be below 100% due to imperfect competition, which may create incentives for optimal price discrimination or strategic pricing. A theoretical basis for most of these studies is the work of Dornbusch (1987), which appeals to arguments from theories of industrial organization. Specifically, it explains the differences in the pass-through by looking at market concentration, the degree of import penetration and the substitutability of imported and local goods. For instance, if profit-maximizing firms have significant market power in a given industry, the pass-through is expected to be high in spite of other factors (see Phillips 1988). On the other hand, if firms aim to maximise their market share instead of profits, pass-through will be lower (see Hooper / Mann 1989 and Ohno 1990). Moreover, if opportunities to discriminate between markets exist, then a policy of pricing to market may occur, which will lead to different degrees of pass-through in differently segmented markets (see Krugman 1987 and Gagnon / Knetter 1992).

Finally, if the imported good is an intermediate good which has locally produced substitutes priced in the domestic currency, local producers may replace the imported input by the domestic one in response to exchange rate changes (see Obstfeld 2001). This "expenditure-switching effect" may also exist in the market for final goods, reducing the degree of pass-through (see Burstein et al. 2001).

Other authors claim that incomplete pass-through is more a macroeconomic phenomenon, which results from price stickiness. For example, Chaudry / Hakura (2001) present cross-country evidence that pass-through varies systematically with the average inflation rate. They claim that high inflation countries exhibit a higher degree of pass-through. Table 1 presents pass-through elasticities for three groups of countries, different by their inflation rates.

Table 1: Average Pass-Through Elasticity of Consumer Prices

	1 quarter	**4 quarters**
Countries with inflation lower than 10% pa	0.04	0.14
Countries with inflation between 10% and 30% pa	0.09	0.33
Countries with inflation higher than 30% pa	0.22	0.50

Source: Chaudry / Hakura (2001)

But if pass-through is systematically related to the level of inflation, which, in turn, is determined by monetary policy, this would have important implications for appropriate monetary policy in an open economy. Thus, endogeneighty of the degree of pass-through is studied both theoretically and empirically in Devereux / Yetman (2003). They develop an open economy sticky price model where the degree of pass-through is determined by the frequency of price adjustments by importing firms. Since higher inflation implies a higher frequency of price changes for given menu costs, they claim that pass-through will be endogenous to the monetary policy regime. Their empirical test for 118 countries confirms that countries with higher inflation tend to have higher pass-through, but this relationship is non-linear.

The degree of intervention in foreign exchange markets also seems to affect the extent of pass-through. For example, Coricelli et al. (2004) find in a cross-country study that the pass-through is larger when there is less exchange rate management.

So, what should be the optimal monetary policy in an open economy with sticky prices and incomplete pass-through? In a closed economy the main problem of monetary policy is to overcome the trade-off between inflation and unemployment, which has been extensively studied in the New Keynesian Theory (e.g. Clarid et al. 1999). In open economies there is an additional trade-off between inflation and exchange rate targeting. An economy may leave the exchange rate freely floating and use its monetary policy to target domestic inflation. But then the economy will be more vulnerable to external shocks. Alternatively, the economy can be made less dependent on external shocks by targeting the exchange rate by means of interventions in the foreign exchange market. But then the monetary policy will be endogenous to exchange rate changes and inflation targeting will be impossible. The problem of finding the optimal degree of intervention has been extremely relevant for Russia in recent years since the economy faces a clear trade-off between an appreciating exchange rate and high inflation.

A highly relevant study of optimal exchange rate intervention is performed in Devereux / Engel (2000). This seminal paper attempts to analyze exchange rate regimes within an expected-utility-maximizing framework in the presence of nominal rigidities and incomplete pass-through. Specifically, it distinguishes between two types of pricing strategies in an economy: producer currency pricing (which implies full pass-through) and local currency pricing. In a welfare-based two-country general equilibrium model they analyze to what extent monetary policy should be employed to maintain the exchange rate target. They find that under local currency pricing, a fixed exchange rate regime is optimal in presence of country specific real shocks, while freely floating exchange rate is desirable when real shocks are insignificant and country's monetary sector is stable. On the other hand, under producer currency pricing, a country would never choose a clean float, even if it had a completely stable monetary sector, because exchange rate volatility would have a direct impact on expected consumption and would lead to welfare losses.

Another theoretical paper on optimal monetary policy under incomplete pass-through is Devereux / Lane (2001). They build a general equilibrium sticky price model for an emerging market economy, which is assumed to be small and subject to external shocks to its real interest rate and its terms of trade. The key features of their model are a) the presence of nominal rigidities; b) lending constraints on investment financing; and c) incomplete exchange rate pass-through onto import prices. In this setting, they evaluate three types of monetary rules: a fixed exchange rate rule, a CPI inflation targeting rule and non-tradable goods inflation targeting rule – using the second order approximation of utility function as the social welfare criterion. In their calibration of the model they find that the degree of pass-through in import prices is central in determining the appropriate monetary policy rule. Under high a pass-through it is advisable to stabilize the prices of non-tradable goods, since both the fixed exchange rate rule and the CPI targeting rule stabilize inflation at the expense of real output stability. With delayed pass-through, the trade-off between real stability and nominal stability disappears and the best rule is to stabilize CPI inflation. Thus, they claim, a low degree of short-term exchange rate pass-through may be an important prerequisite for the success of inflation targeting in emerging markets.

But since a lower pass-through is both theoretically and empirically associated with lower inflation, it becomes even more important to stabilize domestic inflation. This mutual endogeneighty of the pass-through effect and inflation should be taken into account in designing appropriate monetary policy.

Another welfare analysis of different monetary policy rules is presented in Gali / Monacelli (2005). They lay out a New Keynesian small open economy general equilibrium model with an endogenous monetary policy. In contrast to the above study, they assume that the law of one price holds for the individual goods all the time. Three types of rules are analyzed: CPI inflation targeting, domestic inflation targeting and a nominal exchange rate peg. As in Devereux / Lane (2001), they use second order approximation of utility function as the social welfare criterion. Again, they calibrate the model in order to rank the rules according to the welfare losses they generate. They find that the domestic inflation-based Taylor rule dominates the CPI-based Taylor rule, which, in turn, dominates the exchange rate peg.

Sosunov / Zamulin (2005) analyze several types of monetary policy rules in a simulated model of the Russian economy which faces external oil price shocks. Their results suggest that "the rule of responding to consumer inflation and the real exchange rate, allegedly followed by the Russian monetary authorities, gives better results in terms of output-inflation volatility than other conventional rules".

2.2 Asymmetric Nominal Rigidity

The studies quoted above assume symmetrically rigid prices. They usually analyse the effects of currency depreciation on inflation. But what would happen if the domestic currency appreciates, which is what Russia has been experiencing recently? According to the above studies, there should be a similar outburst of deflation due to pass-through effect. Following the optimal rules, monetary policy should adjust to the same extent, but in the opposite direction.

But in reality we rarely observe deflation resulting from domestic currency appreciation (see Dobrynskaya / Levando 2005). Similarly, we hardly observe deflation resulting from a negative money supply shock, while we do observe a more significant drop in output, than in case of a positive money supply shock (see Cover 1992). The recent literature proposes asymmetric nominal rigidities as an explanation for this phenomenon. In this context, asymmetric price rigidity means that prices are more sticky downwards than upwards.

Several theories are proposed to explain this phenomenon. The more traditional view is that the labour market is the primary source of asymmetry. Many papers show that a wage cut is a much rare phenomenon than a wage increase (see e.g. Altonji / Devereux 1999, Holden / Wulfsberg 2004 and Holzer / Montgomery 1993). In labour economics this is termed the "ratchet effect" and the first intuitive explanation for it was found in the possible money illusion of workers, as proposed by Keynes. Neo-Keynesian models (e.g. Ball et al. 1988) see wage rigidity arising endogenously in the bargaining process because of implicit contracts, imperfect information, efficiency wages and/or insider-outsider considerations. Most recent explanations of downward wage rigidity including fairness considerations, reference points and loss aversion of workers, come from behavioural economics.

Asymmetry is also widely observed in changes in prices of final goods. Peltzman (2000), for example, studies over 240 markets for consumer as well as producer goods and finds that asymmetries are persuasive, substantial and durable, and that they exist in periods of low inflation as well as in periods of high inflation. These asymmetries also apply to price indices (see Verbrugge 1998). Bakytzhanova (2005) finds an asymmetric response of retail gasoline prices in Moscow to positive and negative shocks in wholesale gasoline prices. Some theoretical explanations for asymmetric price rigidity are: consumer search with learning from prices (Benabou / Getner 1993), consumer search with reference prices (Lewis 2003), tacit collusion among firms with past price serving as a focal price (Borenstein et al. 1997), implicit coordination among firms in an industry to rise prices after a positive cost shock while not to reduce prices after a negative one (Bhaskar 2002), and the positive trend inflation in the economy (Ball / Mankiw 1994).

As claimed by DeLong / Summers (1988) and Ball et al. (1988), asymmetries in wages and prices may have important implications for the appropriate stabilization policy. Nevertheless, such asymmetries are rarely incorporated into theoretical models of optimal monetary policy.

For example, Holden (2002) builds a theoretical model of wage setting in which the institutional framework crucially affects the existence and importance of downward nominal wage rigidity. His model predicts that the downward nominal wage rigidity is likely to be stronger when the coverage of collective agreements is higher and employment protection legislation is stricter. Under such conditions, aiming for very low inflation may involve considerable costs in the form of higher unemployment and lower output. Hence, downward nominal rigidities may provide a rationale for a positive inflation target.

A similar conclusion is drawn in Itskhoki (2004). He adds exogenously asymmetric menu costs to Ball / Mankiw (1994) model of a closed economy in order to introduce asymmetric price rigidity even in case of zero trend inflation. In this setting, he finds that a positive long run inflation rate minimizes social losses.

So, the literature on the optimal monetary policy under asymmetric price rigidity is not overly rich in its recommendations. The main prescription is drawn for a closed economy and argues for a positive long-run trend inflation, as this alleviates price stickiness and smoothens the business cycle.

3 The Model of the Optimal Monetary Policy

3.1 Set-up of the Model

In this section we lay out a simple stochastic sticky price model for a small open economy. The set-up of the model is similar to Dobrynskaya (2008), but a more detailed analysis is presented here.

The *demand side* of the economy is represented by a forward-looking IS-type equation of the following form:

$$(1) \quad y_t = a + E_t[y_{t+1}] - b(i_t - E_t[\pi_{t+1}]) + cE_t[\Delta q_{t+1}] + \varepsilon_{1t},$$

where y_t is the output gap, i_t is the nominal interest rate, q_t is the real exchange rate, an increase in which indicates a real depreciation of the domestic currency, ε_{1t} is a demand shock (e.g. a government expenditure shock), which is assumed to be normally distributed with a mean of zero, and a, b and c are positive coefficients.

The IS curve has survived the New Keynesian revolution and is nowadays derived from maximization of expected discounted utility function of a representative consumer. For a micro-founded derivation of an IS curve similar to (1) see Gali / Monacelli (2005), where the parameters *a*, *b* and *c* are functions of the primitive parameters of their model. If the parameter *c* equals zero, equation (1) corresponds to the closed economy version of the IS curve used in Clarida et al. (1999). Its step-by-step derivations are available in, for example, Woodford (1996) and Bernanke et al. (1998). Such New Keynesian IS curve is different from a traditional one as current output depends positively on expected future output due to consumption smoothing and negatively on real interest rate due to the intertemporal substitution of consumption. Since net export is another component of the aggregate demand in an open economy, the output gap also depends on expected changes in the real exchange rate.

The *supply side* of the economy is presented by a New Keynesian Phillips curve. In order to derive it, we distinguish between two types of firms in the economy.

Firms of the first type are importing firms and they set prices according to the Law of One Price:

(2) $$P_{it} = P_{it}^{*} S_t$$

where P_{it} and P_{it}^{*} are the domestic and foreign prices of the *i*-th import good respectively and S_t is the nominal exchange rate. Aggregating (2) over all such firms and log-linearizing, we obtain the following relationship for the inflation in this "full pass-through" (FPT) sector of the economy:

(3) $$\pi_t^{FPT} = \pi_t^{*} + \Delta s_t$$

Firms of the second type are either local firms or importing firms. They adopt a pricing-to-market strategy. This means that the pricing decisions of these firms are not affected by exchange rate considerations, implying a zero pass-through. Rather, pricing decisions are affected solely by local economic conditions. We assume that these firms set prices in a staggered fashion as in Calvo (1983). This time-dependent modelling has become very popular in deriving the New Keynesian Phillips curve, mainly because it allows for an explicit analytical solution to firms' profit maximization problem. The model assumes that in every period each firm receives with some probability θ a signal that it should keep its price fixed in this period. With probability $1-\theta$ receives a signal that its price should adjust. Hence, the average time over which a firm's price is fixed is $1/(1-\theta)$. The higher is θ, the higher is the degree of price stickiness in the economy. Aggregating the pricing decisions of the firms of the second type and log-linearizing around the steady state, we obtain the following relationship for inflation in this "pricing-to-market" (PTM) sector of the economy:

$$(4) \qquad \pi_t^{PTM} = E_t[\pi_{t+1}] + dy_t + \varepsilon_{2t},$$

where the parameter d depends negatively on θ and, hence, captures the degree of price stickiness. Equation (4) is usually called the New Keynesian Phillips curve and its step-by-step derivation can be found in, for example, Gali / Monacelli (2005). It is different from the traditional Phillips curve as inflation depends on the expected future inflation and not on the expected current inflation. In our case this relationship is valid for the second-type firms only and it shows that their inflation depends on the expected overall inflation, the current output gap, and a random supply shock with the mean of zero.

To derive a Phillips curve for our economy with two types of firms we assume that there is a share e of the firms of the first type and a share 1-e of the firms of the second type. Then the overall inflation is:

$$(5) \qquad \pi_t = e\pi_t^{FPT} + (1-e)\pi_t^{PTM}$$

Substituting (3) and (4) into (5) and using the following relationship for the real exchange rate:

$$(6) \qquad Q_t \equiv \frac{S_t P_t^*}{P_t} \quad \text{or} \quad \Delta q_t \equiv \Delta s_t + \pi_t^* - \pi_t$$

we obtain the following version of a New Keynesian Phillips curve for the economy:

$$(7) \qquad \pi_t = \frac{e}{1-e}\Delta q_t + E[\pi_{t+1}] + dy_t + \varepsilon_{2t}$$

This Phillips curve is different from the ones used in the literature since it explicitly shows the degree of the real exchange rate pass-through on overall consumer price inflation, measured by the coefficient $e/(1$-$e)$. The higher the share of first-type firms e is, the higher is the pass-through effect in the economy. Our model assumes e it to be exogenous, but in reality it may vary depending on economic conditions. For example, Devereux / Yetman (2003) model the pass-through effect to be endogenous to the local monetary policy. They claim: "'Looser' monetary policy, which implies a higher mean inflation and a higher volatility of the exchange rate, will lead to more frequent price changes and a higher rate of pass-through".

So, there are two reasons for price stickiness in our model: incomplete pass-through measured by parameter *e* (the higher is *e*, the further shifts the Phillips curve as a result of exchange rate changes) and staggered pricing measured by parameter *d*, which in turn depends on parameter θ (the higher is θ, the flatter is the Phillips curve).

The equilibrium in the economy is described by the system of the IS and the Phillips curves holding simultaneously.

To complete the model, we assume that the real exchange rate follows non-stationary AR(1) process (a random walk):

$$(8) \qquad q_t = q_{t-1} + \eta_t$$

where η_t is a normally distributed shock with a mean of zero. Such specification is close to reality, since real exchange rates are often observed to be non-stationary. For example, a unit root test for the real exchange rate of Russian rouble did not allow us reject the null hypothesis of a unit root even on a 1% confidence level.

3.2 Optimal Monetary Policy under Discretion

As has become common in the literature on optimal monetary policy, we assume that the monetary authority minimizes the following loss function:

$$(9) \qquad L_t = (\pi_t - \pi^T)^2 + \lambda y_t^2$$

Such a loss function is not *ad hoc* and can be derived by second order approximation of the utility losses by a representative consumer (see Rotemberg / Woodford 1999 and Woodford 2003).

Substituting the Phillips curve (7) into the loss function (9) and making use of (8) and minimizing with respect to π_t we obtain the following reaction function of optimal inflation to expected inflation:

$$(10) \qquad \pi_t = \frac{d^2}{d^2+\lambda}\pi^T + \frac{\lambda}{d^2+\lambda}E[\pi_{t+1}] + \frac{e\lambda}{(1-e)(d^2+\lambda)}\eta_t + \frac{\lambda}{d^2+\lambda}\varepsilon_{2t}$$

Taking expectations of both sides of (10), solving for expected inflation and substituting it back into the reaction function, we obtain the expression for the equilibrium inflation, which minimizes the losses of society:

(11) $$\pi_t = \pi^T + \frac{e\lambda}{(1-e)(d^2+\lambda)}\eta_t + \frac{\lambda}{d^2+\lambda}\varepsilon_{2t}$$

We see that in order to minimize the social loss, inflation should be adjusted to exchange rate and supply shocks. It should be noticed that there is no dynamic inconsistency here since the expected inflation equals the target inflation and there is no incentive to deviate from this target unless there are some unexpected shocks.

Substituting (11) into (7) we find the equilibrium output gap:

(12) $$y_t = -\frac{ed}{(1-e)(d^2+\lambda)}\eta_t - \frac{d}{d^2+\lambda}\varepsilon_{2t}$$

The final step is to derive the optimal policy instrument rule where the real interest rate serves as the instrument for monetary policy. To do this we substitute (12) into the IS curve (1) and solve for r:

(13) $$r_t^{opt} = \frac{a}{b} + \left[\frac{ed}{b(1-e)(d^2+\lambda)}\right]\eta_t + \frac{d}{b(d^2+\lambda)}\varepsilon_{2t} + \frac{1}{b}\varepsilon_{1t}$$

This rule states that in order to minimize the social losses the real interest rate should be adjusted to all types of shocks in the economy: exchange rate shock, supply shock and demand shock – with positive coefficients. This means, for example, that positive shocks, being inflationary, should be accompanied by a contractionary monetary policy, leading to negative output gap and lower equilibrium inflation, than what it would have been without intervention.

Figure 1 illustrates the optimal reaction of the real interest rate to a positive exchange rate shock η_t, assuming that demand and supply shocks equal zero. Assume that initially the economy is at point *A* with the target inflation and zero output gap. The corresponding interest rate is r_0. An unexpected positive exchange rate shock (i.e. a depreciation of the domestic currency) shifts the Phillips curve upwards due to pass-through effect and shifts the IS curve rightwards due to higher net export. If the interest rate is not adjusted, the economy will move to point *B* with positive output gap and very high inflation. The corresponding losses of society can be illustrated by the circle coming through point *B*. We can see that in order to minimize social losses the interest rate should be increased to r_1 so that the economy moves to point *C*. So, a contractionary monetary policy is desirable in case of depreciation of domestic currency. By the same logic, a negative exchange rate shock should be accompanied by a reduction in the interest rate meaning expansionary monetary policy.

Figure 1: Monetary Policy Reaction to a Positive Exchange Rate Shock

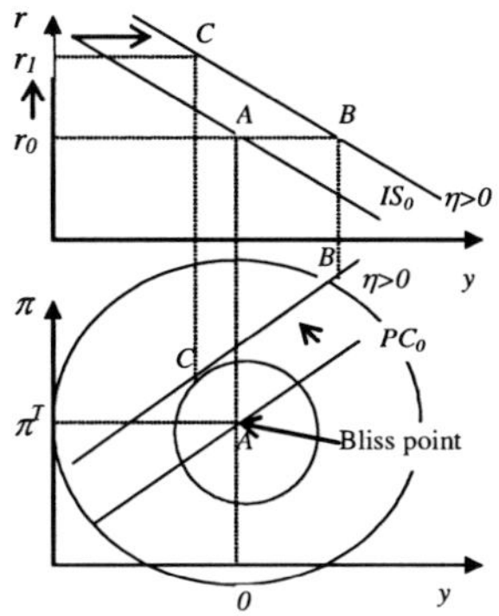

Proposition 1. The optimal monetary policy should react to exchange rate movements and should counteract the exchange rate changes by reducing pass-through onto domestic prices. The adjustment in the interest rate should be more significant if:

- pass-through effect is higher (i.e. the parameter e/(1-e) is higher)
- prices are less sticky (i.e. the parameter d is higher, provided that $d < \sqrt{\lambda}$)
- elasticity of consumption with respect to interest rate is lower (i.e. the parameter b is lower)
- the government cares less about output gap (i.e. the parameter λ is lower).

Proof. To prove this we differentiate the coefficient associated with the exchange rate shock in equation (13) with respect to each of the parameters and determine the signs of the corresponding derivatives.

This finding is in line with Devereux / Engel (2000) who claim that although under a low pass-through a freely floating exchange rate (i.e. a monetary policy in which exchange rates are not taken into consideration) may be optimal in some circumstances. This is, however, never true in case of producer currency pricing leading to a full pass-through.

The above analysis assumes that prices are symmetrically rigid upwards and downwards. But the empirical evidence described in Section 2.2 convincingly suggests that prices are more rigid downwards than upwards. Such asymmetric price rigidity can be captured by two parameters in our model: *d* and *e*. First, parameter *d* may be higher for upward changes in prices than for downward ones. This will result in a kink of the Philips curve at zero level of inflation. Secondly, the pass-through may be lower in cases of appreciation of domestic currency than in cases of depreciation (see Dobrynskaya / Levando 2005) as more firms may adopt a pricing-to-market strategy instead of reducing their prices. The model of Devereux / Yetman (2003) also suggests that a lower pass-through is associated with higher price stickiness and vice versa. Asymmetric pass-through will result in unequal shifts of the Phillips curve due to positive and negative exchange rate shocks of the same size.

Figure 2 analyses the optimal monetary policy in cases of a positive and a negative exchange rate shocks of the same size under asymmetric price rigidity.

Figure 2: Monetary Policy Reaction under Asymmetric Price Rigidity

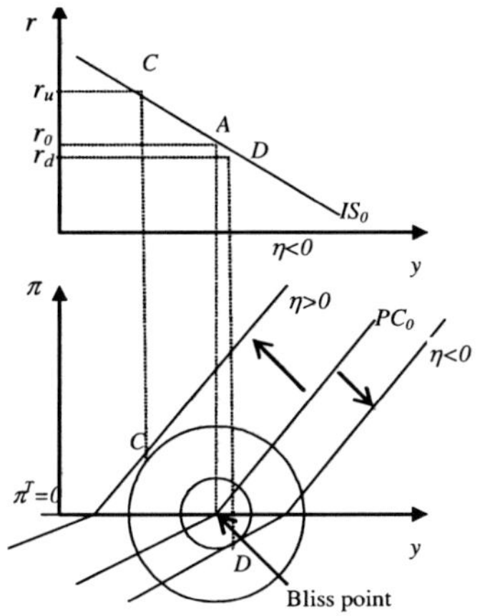

The shifts in the kinked Phillips curve are larger for a positive exchange rate shock than for a negative one, due to the asymmetric pass-through effect. In case of a positive shock the loss minimizing point is point *C*, which corresponds to an increased interest rate to r_u. In case of a negative shock the optimal point is point *D*. To reach this point interest rate should be reduced, but the magnitude of the change should be much less. The same conclusion will be true for positive target inflation, although the difference in required interest rate changes will be less significant.

Proposition 2. The optimal monetary policy is asymmetric depending on appreciation or depreciation of the domestic currency. The degree of monetary intervention should be higher in case of a positive exchange rate shock than in case of a negative one of the same size due to higher downward price rigidity and lower downward pass-through.

Proof. Recall from the proof of the Proposition 1 that the derivative of the coefficient associated with the exchange rate shock in equation (13) with respect to pass-through effect (*e/(1-e)*) is positive and the derivative of the same coefficient with respect to price flexibility (*d*) is also positive, provided that $d < \sqrt{\lambda}$. Since is it assumed that the pass-through effect and price flexibility are higher in case of an inflationary shock than in case of a deflationary one, the adjustment in the interest rate should also be higher.

This result is new to the Keynesian literature and has interesting practical implications for the conduct of the monetary policy. It predicts that in order to minimise the social losses, the monetary authority should not only determine the direction of the required policy instrument change, but also its magnitude depending on the sign of a shock. If the monetary policy rule is specified in a way that does not take such asymmetries into account, then following this rule may result an the equilibrium inflation and an output gap, that are far from optimal.

Our model predicts that in a country with a high pass-through, relatively flexible prices and a low sensitivity of consumption to the interest rate, the optimal monetary policy should adjust to exchange rate changes asymmetrically in order to minimize the losses to society. The next section of the paper is devoted to the empirical testing of the assumptions and prescriptions of the model for Russia.

4 Empirical Estimations

4.1 Data

We perform our analysis for Russia for the period from January 1998 to May 2005. The year 1998 is remarkable due to the default of the Russian government and the resulting balance of payments crisis when rouble lost more than half of its value within a month, causing a number of structural changes in the economy, such as import substitution. That is why we include this year in our sample, but we study it separately and compare it to the more recent period. The following monthly time series, all in natural logarithms, are used:

Endogenous variables:

- Consumer prices (*p*). We analyse consumer price index on the aggregate level and at 2 levels of disaggregation:

- foodstuffs: bread and bakery products, groats and beans, pasta products, meat and poultry, fish products, milk and diary products, butter, vegetable oil, fruit and vegetables, granulated sugar, alcoholic beverages;
- non-food goods: fabrics, clothing, knitwear, footwear, detergents, tobacco products, electric appliances, TV and radio sets, gasoline, medicine;
- services: housing and public utilities, public health, passenger transport, communications, cultural institutions, sanatoria, resorts and health care institutions, child care in pre-school institutions, education, everyday services.

All price indices are transformed into Laspeyres-type indices with the base period either January 1998 or the first month when a series began to be calculated and published.

The source of the data is monthly journal "Socio-economic performance of Russia" published by Rosstat (State Statistical Committee of Russian Federation).

- Money supply (*m*) is the monetary aggregate M2, provided by Rosstat.
- Nominal effective exchange rate (*neer*) is the trade-weighted exchange rate of the rouble, an increase in which reflects a depreciation of the rouble against a basket of currencies. The source is the IMF International Financial Statistics.

Exogenous variables:

- Real income (*ry*) is the seasonally adjusted real money income of the population, as published by Rosstat. The base period is December 1992.
- Price of oil (*oil*) is the price of crude oil in the USA, measured in cents per barrel. Source: Energy Information Administration Monthly Energy Review, July 2005.

All time series have been tested for stationarity. ADF test has not allowed us reject the hypothesis of a unit root. But the unit root hypothesis has been rejected for the first differences. Therefore, we treat the data as non-stationary I(1) processes.

4.2 The Pass-Through Effect

4.2.1 Methodology

Our theoretical model predicts that the degree of pass-through is crucial for determining the optimal monetary policy: under a high pass-through adjusting money supply to exchange rate shocks is more welfare enhancing than under a low degree of pass-through. That is why we start our empirical analysis by estimating the pass-through effect for different consumer goods.

As we deal with several endogenous variables, to take account of their mutual influence we estimate the following Vector Error Correction Model:

$$(14)\quad \Delta y_t = A + \sum_{i=1}^{3} B_i \Delta y_{t-i} + C\Delta x_t + D\nu_{t-1} + \psi_t$$

where y_t is a vector of endogenous variables (*p*, *m*, *neer*), x_t is a vector of exogenous variables (*ry*, *oil*), ν_{t-1} is a series of lagged residuals obtained from cointegration of the endogenous variables, ψ_t is an error term and *A, B, C* and *D* are coefficient matrices. We include three lags of endogenous variables because the major adjustments usually occur within a quarter. Inclusion of more lags would lead to too many coefficients to be estimated and less power of the test. If a cointegration between the endogenous variables exists, the model can be estimated by OLS method since all variables are stationary.

Such model allows us estimate the influence of lagged exchange rate changes on inflation separately from the influence of the other variables by constructing impulse-response function with the Cholesky ordering:

$m \rightarrow neer \rightarrow p$

We use E-Views 4.0 to estimate the VEC-model and the accumulated responses of prices to Cholesky degrees of freedom adjusted impulses to the exchange rate.

4.2.2 Results

First of all we concentrate our analysis on the *aggregate consumer price index*. We find that pass-through is 35% during 12 months. Since our sample includes the year of crisis, a number of changes might have occurred in Russian economy. Therefore, we are interested in changes in the pass-through over this time period. We estimate model (14) for a two-year rolling window starting from 1998 and ending 2005 because we are interested in changes in the pass-through from year to year, but 12 observations are not enough to estimate the model. Hence, we obtain pass-through elasticities for 7 two-year sub-periods. Twelfth-month elasticities are shown on Figure 3.

We see that the average pass-through of 35% is a biased estimate since pass-through effect was significantly different during the crisis, compared to the rest of the sample. During the crisis a shock to the exchange rate caused 40% change in CPI in 6 months and 63% change in 12 months. This confirms the result in Dobrynskaya / Levando (2005), where an Error Correction Model was used and the pass-through on CPI over 6 months during 1998-1999 was estimated to be 43%.

Figure 3: 12-Month PTE on CPI over Time

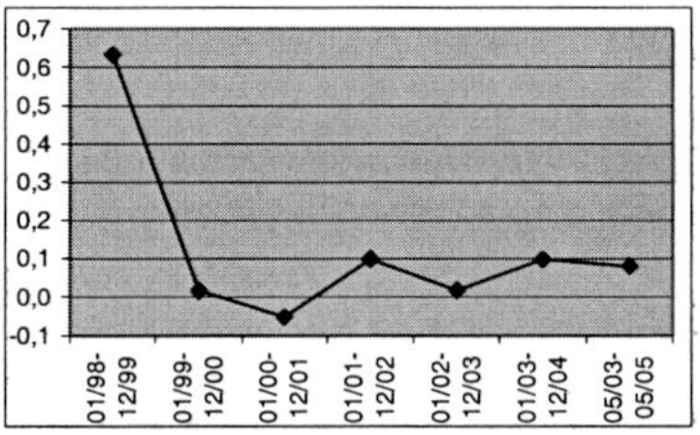

After the crisis we observe a significant drop in pass-through to almost zero probably due to a high degree of import substitution. Again, a similar result is obtained by Dobrynskaya / Levando (2005), who found a 6% pass-through over 6 months during 2000-2002. But as the Russian economy recovers, the yearly pass-through effect stabilises at about 8% after 2003. This looks similar to the findings for some European countries before introduction of Euro, as presented by Hufner / Schroder (2002). They estimate 7% pass-through after 12 months in France, 8% in Germany, 12% in Italy, 11% in the Netherlands and 8% in Spain. So, our further analysis will concentrate on analysing the period from 2003 to 2005.

To obtain further insight into changes in pass-through during this period, we estimate model (14) for three categories of consumer prices: *foodstuffs, non-food goods and services.* We estimate the pass-through elasticity for the whole period and separately for 2003-2005. The corresponding impulse responses are presented on Figure 4.

The figures show that all estimates of the pass-through effect are much higher for the whole sample than for the later period. The reason is the same as for the CPI: inclusion of the crisis period, characterized by a high pass-through, biases our estimates upwards. Nowadays the pass-through effect on all consumer prices is much lower than during the crisis but higher than in its immediate aftermath. The high pass-through during the crisis may be explained by foreign currency pricing, which prevailed during that period.

The sharp depreciation of the rouble made Russian citizens substitute purchases of import goods by domestic ones. Also some firms which previously exported goods to Russia, established their production locally using local inputs. All these facts can explain the almost zero pass-through at that period. Nowadays, real income of Russian citizens grows steadily and purchases of import goods increase, rising the degree of pass-through and making economy more vulnerable again to external shocks. Therefore, it becomes more important to follow a policy of exchange rate targeting by adjusting the money supply to exchange rate shocks.

Figure 4: Impulse-Responses of CPI, Foodstuffs, Non-Food Goods and Services

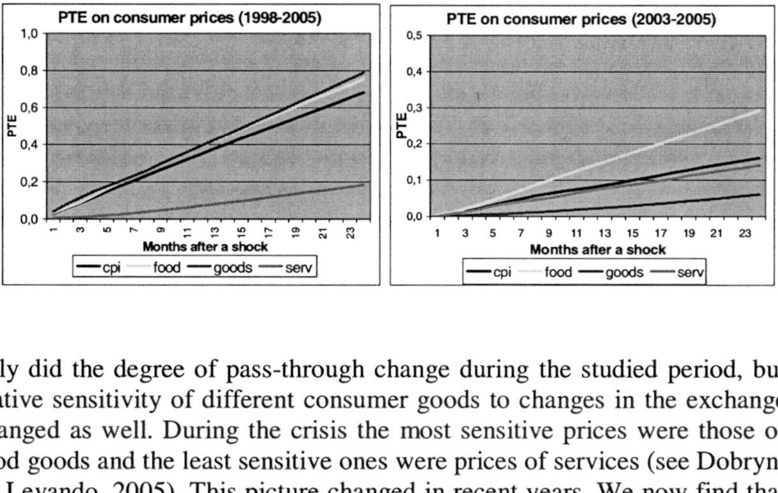

Not only did the degree of pass-through change during the studied period, but the relative sensitivity of different consumer goods to changes in the exchange rate changed as well. During the crisis the most sensitive prices were those of non-food goods and the least sensitive ones were prices of services (see Dobrynskaya / Levando, 2005). This picture changed in recent years. We now find that food prices are the most exchange rate elastic, the elasticity of service prices remained approximately the same as before, and prices of non-food goods have become almost insensitive to exchange rate changes. Since services are non-tradable goods, it does not come as a surprise that the pass-through on prices of services remains low. The most interesting is the behaviour of non-food goods prices. Their low pass-through may be explained by an expansion in the local production of non-food goods and the wide-spread adoption by exporting companies of the pricing-to-market strategy. Probably, in order to secure market shares, exporting companies choose to change their mark-ups in response to exchange rate changes rather than change prices.

To get better understanding of why food prices are now much more exchange rate elastic than the prices of non-food goods and why the prices of services still have some pass-through, we estimate the pass-through effect for *detailed categories of consumer goods*. In Table 2 we report 6, 12 and 24 month accumulated responses of prices to exchange rate impulses.

The prices of all goods have pass-through elasticities of less than 100% during 12 months. This finding supports our assumption that pass-through is incomplete and the parameter "*e*" in our model is less than 0.5. Among food prices the highest pass-through is observed for fruit and vegetables (112% during a year), bread and bakery products (22%) and groats and beans (14%). The least exchange rate elastic appeared to be prices of alcoholic beverages (1%) and vegetable oil (2%). Only the price of sugar appears to have negative pass-through. All non-food goods are insensitive to exchange rate changes with the highest pass-through of 4-5% during one year on prices of knitwear, clothing and tobacco products. In contrast, the prices for most services seem sensitive to exchange rate shocks. The prices of communications exhibit a high pass-through of 70% during one year, probably due to foreign currency pricing for internet and mobile services. We can also observe that education, services of cultural institutions, sanatoria, resorts, health care institutions and child care in pre-school institutions show a pass-through effect of about 10% during a year.

So, we can conclude that although at present the pass-through is much lower that is was during the crisis period – probably due to more stable exchange rates resulting from an exchange rate targeting policy of the central bank – the prices of some goods still show a significant sensitivity to exchange rate changes, which makes the Russian economy vulnerable to exchange rate shocks. Our optimal interest rate rule (13) is derived from minimization of the loss function (9). This loss function can be derived from maximizing the of expected discounted consumer's utility function of the form:

$$(15) \quad \max U_t = E_t \sum_{\tau=t}^{\infty} \beta^{\tau-t} u(\sum_i \alpha_i C_t; L_t)$$

where α_i denotes the share of good *i* in consumer's basket. This stresses the importance to adjust money supply to unexpected exchange rate shocks in order to minimize consumers' welfare losses, in particular when the goods with a high degree of pass-through are necessities and constitute largest the shares in consumer spending.

The structure of the consumption basket in Russia is presented in Appendix 1. It shows that among the three aggregate categories, foodstuffs constitute the largest share of consumption (about 43 %) and food prices have the largest pass-through among these categories. The share of food in low-income families is even higher, since food is the basic necessary good. Therefore, if the government cares about welfare of consumers, exchange rates should be targeted more carefully, since a shock is to a great extent reflected in food prices. When we look at particular goods, meat and poultry (10.71% of total consumption), alcoholic beverages (7.12%), fruit and vegetables (3.96%), clothing and underwear (5.19%), and housing and public utilities (8.9%) are the main components of consumption basket and all of them, with the exception of alcoholic beverages, have high degrees of pass-through of exchange rate shocks onto domestic prices.

Table 2: Estimates of Pass-Through on Detailed Categories of Consumer Goods

Prices \ Period after a shock	6 months	12 months	24 months
CPI	**0.04**	**0.08**	**0.16**
Foodstuffs	**0.06**	**0.14**	**0.29**
Bread and bakery products	0.08	0.22	0.50
Groats and beans	0.05	0.14	0.37
Pasta products	0.03	0.09	0.19
Meat and poultry	0.00	0.02	0.09
Fish products	0.02	0.07	0.05
Milk and diary products	0.05	0.11	0.21
Butter	0.02	0.06	0.12
Vegetable oil	0.00	0.02	0.05
Fruit and vegetables	0.47	1.12	2.33
Granulated sugar	-0.03	-0.12	-0.28
Alcoholic beverages	0.01	0.01	0.02
Non-food goods	**0.01**	**0.01**	**0.03**
Fabrics	0.00	0.01	0.02
Clothing	0.02	0.04	0.08
Knitwear	0.02	0.05	0.10
Footwear	0.01	0.02	0.04
Detergents	0.01	0.02	0.04
Tobacco products	0.01	0.04	0.09
Electric appliances	0.00	0.01	0.30
TV and radio sets	0.00	0.01	0.02
Gasoline	0.01	0.01	0.01
Medicine	0.00	0.00	0.03
Services rendered to population	**0.04**	**0.05**	**0.14**
Housing and public utilities	0.03	0.05	0.10
Public health	0.01	0.02	0.05
Passenger transport	0.02	0.05	0.09
Communications	0.20	0.70	2.17
Cultural institutions	0.06	0.12	0.25
Sanatoria, resorts and health care institutions	0.03	0.09	0.22
Child care in pre-school institutions	0.05	0.10	0.20
Education	0.04	0.09	0.17
Everyday services	0.01	0.02	0.03

Thus, we can conclude that following a monetary rule like (13) and adjusting money supply to unexpected exchange rate shocks is preferable to a freely floating exchange rate regime from social welfare point of view.

4.3 Monetary Policy Analysis

4.3.1 Symmetric Case

In order to analyze the impact of monetary policy on pass-through and prices we estimate a VEC model similar to (14) but we omit the money supply variable:

$$(16) \quad \Delta z_t = A + \sum_{i=1}^{3} B_i \Delta z_{t-i} + C\Delta x_t + D\upsilon_{t-1} + \psi_t$$

where z_t is a vector of endogenous variables (*p*, *neer*) and υ_{t-1} is a series of lagged residuals obtained from cointegration of these endogenous variables. Our theoretical model confirms the findings of Vdovichenko / Voronina (2004), indicating that a positive shock to the exchange rate should be accompanied by a rising interest rate and a falling money supply. This counteracts the inflationary effect of the currency depreciation by the contracting effect of monetary policy. The opposite should be true for a negative shock. Thus, by omitting money supply from the model we observe a lower pass-through, which is biased downwards by the money supply effect.

Such monetary policy is common in western economies. For example, the European Central Bank cited the possible inflationary effect of the weak euro as one factor behind the tightening of its monetary policy in 2000.[2] A similar conclusion was obtained empirically by Parsley / Popper (1998) for the USA. But Dobrynskaya / Levando (2005) come to the opposite conclusion for Russia: during 1995-2002 monetary policy did not eliminate pass-through, but, on the contrary, increased it.

In order to see whether Russian monetary policy has changed recently, we estimate model (16) for the aggregate consumer price index both for the whole period from 1998 to 2005 and separately for the recent period from 2003 to 2005. Then we construct impulse responses using Cholesky ordering *neer* $\rightarrow$ *cpi*. On Figure 5 shows impulse-responses we obtained for the model (14) (solid lines) and the model (13) (dashed lines).

As the dashed line lies above the solid line for the whole period, omission of money supply leads to higher estimates of pass-through. Since the whole period includes both the crisis period and the recent period, in which we observe the opposite behaviour of monetary policy, they seem to average out in our estimated. The difference between the dashed line and the solid line for the crisis period would be even more significant than what is presented in the figure. This

[2] European Central Bank Monthly Bulletin, May 2000.

indicates that the sharp depreciation of the rouble during the crisis was accompanied by an expansionary monetary policy which caused an additional inflationary effect on domestic prices. This finding is similar to what Dobrynskaya / Levando (2005) report. Such monetary policy led to greater social losses due to higher inflation than would have been incurred if the money supply did not change or decreased during that period.

Figure 5: Impulse Responses of CPI With and Without Money Supply

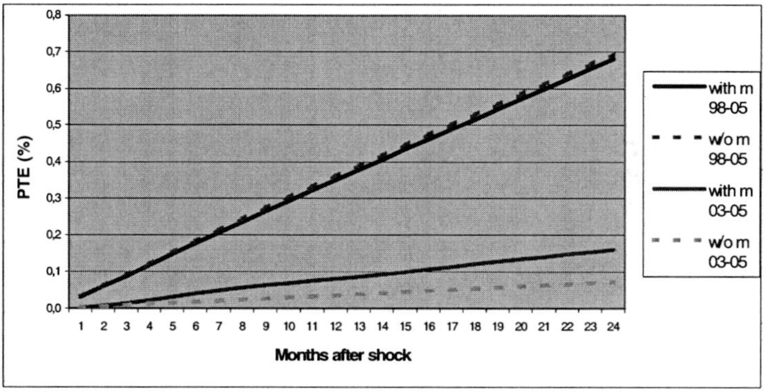

But the picture is remarkably different in the recent period. Here we see that monetary policy nowadays reduces pass-through. The combined effect of the money supply and exchange rate changes on CPI is 3.5% during one year, while it would have been 8% if money supply were not adjusted. Therefore, we can conclude that the monetary policy at present counteracts exchange rate changes, thus reducing the pass-through on consumer price index and, hence, its volatility. So, nowadays the monetary policy of the Central Bank of Russia seems to be closer to optimal, since it leads to lower social losses than otherwise would have been suffered.

To isolate the effect of the current monetary policy on the prices of food, goods, and services we estimate model (16) for each price index separately. We find that the pass-through is reduced for all service prices and for the prices of non-food goods. For some prices it even becomes negative. Since the real exchange rate mostly appreciated during this period and, hence, money supply increased, for the inflationary effect of money supply for these prices outweighed the deflationary effect of the exchange rate, making the biased pass-through negative.

But the behaviour of some food prices is surprising. For 4 food categories (bread and bakery products, pasta products, fish products and vegetable oil) the pass-through, as estimated in model (16) is higher than the true one. This means that prices of these goods rise in response to decreased money supply and visa versa. A possible explanation for this phenomenon is the negative income elasticity of demand for these goods.

4.3.2 Asymmetric Case

We find that during 2003-2005 the monetary policy in Russia was endogenous to exchange rate changes and real that the appreciation of the rouble was accompanied by an increase in money supply, thus reducing pass-through. Such a policy is highly desirable from theoretical point of view. If the monetary authority follows the optimal monetary policy rule, then depreciation of the rouble should be accompanied by a reduction in money supply. Moreover, our model predicts that the change in money supply should be stronger in case of a depreciation than in the case of an appreciation, due to the asymmetric price rigidity. Therefore, we would hope to observe in the data that a depreciation of the rouble leads to a reduction in the money supply, while only major appreciations are counteracted by increasing it. Unfortunately, we observe the opposite in our data: among 88 observations in our sample there are 45 observations of nominal depreciations and 38 observations of real depreciations of Rouble, but only 12 observations of a reduction in money supply. This means that the money supply tends to be increased no matter what happens to the exchange rate. Such policy may be optimal in the 50 observations of a real appreciation, but is overly inflationary in the other 38 cases of real depreciation.

As the monetary authority claims that its monetary policy is aimed at real exchange rate targeting, a real appreciation should be accompanied by an increase in money supply, making nominal appreciation less significant. A real depreciation should be accompanied by a reduction in money supply, making the nominal depreciation less significant as well. This relationship between changes in real and nominal exchange rates is illustrated by Figure 6A: under the optimal monetary policy rule changes in the nominal exchange rate should be smoothed, the blue line being less volatile than the red line. Moreover, positive changes should be smoothed more than negative ones. Figure 6B plots the actual changes in nominal and real exchange rates. We observe quite the opposite relationship: the blue line exhibits the same volatility as the red line and lies almost always above it. Again we see the most outspoken difference during the crisis when the real depreciation was accompanied by an increase in money supply, making the nominal depreciation even more pronounced. But in the later period the situation is similar. Real appreciations, indicated by negative changes in *neer*, are smoothed by increasing the money supply and hence result in lower nominal appreciations. Real depreciations, in contrast, are accompanied by increase in money supply as well, making nominal depreciations even more outspoken. Such monetary policy is asymmetric, but it differs from what our theoretical model proposes.

Figure 6: Changes in the Nominal and Real Exchange Rate of the Rouble

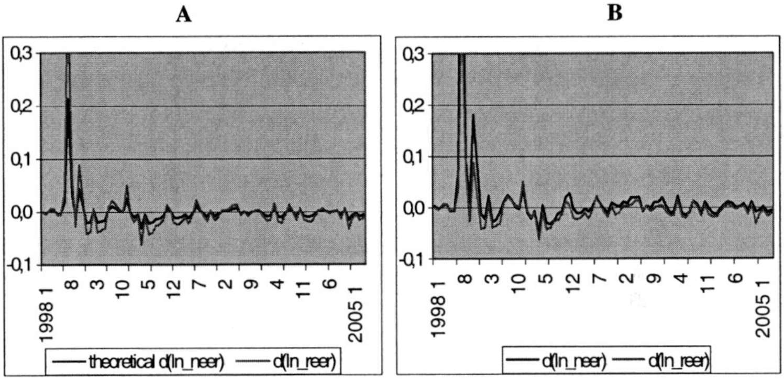

To perform a more formal test of the asymmetric monetary policy, we include a dummy variable $\hat{d}$, which equals 1 in case of a rising exchange rate, i.e. a depreciation, and 0 otherwise, into our VEC model:

$$(17)\quad \Delta y_t = A + \sum_{i=1}^{3} B_i \Delta y_{t-i} + E\hat{d}\Delta neer_{t-1} + C\Delta x_t + D v_{t-1} + \psi_t$$

We estimate the above model for the aggregate CPI for the period 2003-2005. We are interested in the sign and significance of the coefficient of $\hat{d}\,\Delta neer_{t-1}$ in the equation for the money supply. This coefficient was estimated to be positive with t-statistics of 1.78, which confirms that monetary policy is indeed asymmetric and inflationary.

The next step is to estimate responses of money supply to exchange rate impulses. We build impulse response functions separately for a positive shock, taking into account the dummy coefficient, and a negative shock. Each shock is normalised to 1 by absolute value. We find that money supply is increased by 3 after a negative shock. This confirms our hypothesis that an appreciation of the rouble is accompanied by an increase in money supply. But after a positive shock money supply also rises by 2.18 while in the symmetric case it should fall by 3.

The test formally shows that monetary policy of the Central Bank of Russia is asymmetric: money supply rises irrespectively of a change in the exchange rate. Such policy is too inflationary and leads to unnecessarily high social losses in case of a depreciation of the rouble. In order to fight inflation and to increase social welfare, the money supply should fall significantly when the rouble depreciates, but increase by less when the rouble appreciates. The extent of the optimal intervention depends on the degree of price stickiness in the economy. But as prices are more sticky downwards than upwards, it is not so important to intervene in the foreign exchange market in cases of an appreciation of the rouble. Since at present the rouble is experiencing a significant real appreciation, the Central Bank of Russia should not pay as much attention to its targeting as it currently does. If the Central Bank continues its present policy of preventing a nominal appreciation of the rouble by accumulation of foreign currency reserves, the rising money supply will only lead to a persistent inflation and higher social losses.

5 Conclusion

In the environment of rising oil prices and an appreciating rouble, Russian monetary policy faces a clear trade-off between loss of exports and inflation. Therefore, the debate on the extent to which monetary policy should be employed in managing nominal exchange rates has been in the centre of the political and economic debate in Russia.

In this paper we provide a general equilibrium model with sticky prices of a small open economy where the real exchange rate behaves like a random walk, as may, for example, be caused by exogenous oil price shocks. Using quadratic loss function as an approximation of social welfare losses, we find that the optimal monetary policy rule is to adjust interest rate to exchange rate shocks, thus reducing the pass-through of exchange rate shocks onto the domestic price level. The optimal degree of monetary policy intervention depends positively on the degree of pass-through and negatively on the stickiness of prices in the economy.

Since the pass-through is crucial for determining the appropriate monetary policy, we estimate the pass-through effect on prices of different types of consumer goods. We find that although the average pass-through elasticity has decreased remarkably since the crisis period, it is still significant for necessity goods such as foodstuffs. Since consumption of food constitutes the major share in total consumption, some degree of monetary intervention is desirable in order to reduce the impact of exchange rate shocks on consumption distortions.

But, according to our model, the optimal degree of intervention under asymmetric price rigidity should be different in cases of positive and of negative exchange rate shocks. We claim that more attentions should be paid to depreciations that to appreciations of the rouble, since prices are more sticky downwards.

We found evidence that, in line with the optimal monetary policy rule, the monetary policy in Russia responded to appreciations by increasing the money supply. Counter to the optimal policy rule, however, it responded to depreciations in the same way, leading to an overall monetary policy that was inflationary all the time.

So, based on our theoretical model and empirical estimation results, we have a number of propositions for Russian monetary policy. First, the degree of intervention during periods of appreciation of the rouble should be gradually reduced. This would help to reduce inflation and promote long run growth, even though in the short run the exporting sector may suffer. Furthermore, in case of a decline in oil prices or some other exogenous shocks which may affect exchange rate of the rouble adversely, a tight monetary policy should be followed in order to reduce the impact of exchange rate changes on domestic prices, acknowledging that the pass-through on prices of necessities is still significant.

A more general suggestion is that Russian Central Bank should start using interest rates as a policy instrument. Interest rates are easier to adjust, especially in cases of a contractionary policy as open market operations are ineffective in an economy with lost trust in its government. But in order for this transmission mechanism to work effectively, significant institutional developments, such as an increased transparency of Central Bank actions and of the banking system as a whole, are required, as are improvements in legal protection.

References

Altonji, J. / Devereux, P. (1999): The extent and consequences of downward nominal wage rigidity, NBER Working Paper #7236, National Bureau of Economic Research, Cambridge MA, USA.

Bacchetta, P. / Wincoop, E. (2002): Why do consumer prices react less than import prices to exchange rates? NBER Working Paper # 9352, National Bureau of Economic Research, Cambridge MA, USA.

Bakytzhanova Z. (2005): Asymmetric fuel pricing in transition economies: the case of Moscow, EERC Working Paper # 05/18, Economics Education and Research Consortium, Moscow, Russia.

Ball, L. / Mankiw, G. (1994): Asymmetric price adjustment and economic fluctuations, in: The Economic Journal, Volume 104, pp. 247-261.

Ball, L. / Mankiw, G. / Romer, D. (1988): The New Keynesian economics and the output inflation trade-off, in: Brookings Papers on Economic Activity, Volume 1, pp. 1-65.

Benabou, R. / Getner, R. (1993): Search with learning from prices: does increased inflationary uncertainty lead to higher mark-ups? in: Review of Economic Studies, Volume 60, pp. 69-94.

Bergin, P. (2001): One money one price: pricing to market in a monetary union, Mimeo, Department of Economics, University of California, Davis, USA.

Bergin, P. / Feenstra, R. (2001): Pricing-to-market, staggered contracts and real exchange rate persistence, in: Journal of International Economics, Volume 54, pp. 333-359.

Bernanke, B. / Gertler, M. / Gilchrist, S. (1998): The financial accelerator in a quantitative business cycle framework, NBER Working Paper #6455, National Bureau of Economic Research, Cambridge MA, USA.

Betts, C. / Kehoe, T. (2001): Real exchange rate movements and the relative price of non-traded goods, Research Department Staff Report, Federal Reserve Bank of Minneapolis, Minneapolis MN, USA. [http://www.econ.-umn.edu/~tkehoe/papers/nontraded.pdf]

Bhaskar, V. (2002): Asymmetric price adjustment: micro-foundations and macroeconomic implications, Economics Discussion Paper #547, University of Essex, Department of Economics, United Kingdom.

Borenstein S. / Cameron, C. / Gilbert, R. (1997): Do gasoline prices respond asymmetrically to crude oil price changes? in: Quarterly Journal of Economics, Volume 112, pp. 305-339.

Burstein, A. / Eichenbaum, M. / Rebelo, S. (2001): Why are rates of inflation so low after large devaluations? NBER Working Paper #8748, National Bureau of Economic Research, Cambridge MA, USA.

Burstein A. / Neves J. / Rebelo, S. (2003): Distribution costs and real exchange rate dynamics during exchange-rate-based stabilization, in: Journal of Monetary Economics, Volume 50, pp. 1189-1214.

Calvo, G. (1983): Staggered prices in a utility maximizing framework, in: Journal of Monetary Economics, Volume 12, pp. 129-152.

Chaudri, E. / Hakura, D. (2001): Exchange rate pass-through to domestic prices: does the inflationary environment matter? IMF Working Paper #01/194, International Monetary Fund, USA.

Clarida, R. / Gali, J. / Gertler, M. (1999): The science of monetary policy: a New Keynesian perspective, in: Journal of Economic Literature, Volume 37, pp. 1661-1707.

Corricelli, F. / Jazbec, B. / Masten, I. (2004): Exchange rate pass-through in acceding countries: the role of exchange rate regimes, in: Economics Working Paper #ECO2004/16, European University Institute, Italy.

Corsetti, G. / Dedola, L. (2002): Macroeconomics of international price discrimination, Mimeo, University of Rome III, Rome, Italy.

Cover, J. (1992): Asymmetric effects of positive and negative money supply shocks, in: Quarterly Journal of Economics, Volume 107, pp. 1261-1282.

DeLong, J. / Summers, L. (1988): How does macroeconomic policy affect output? in: Brookings Papers on Economic Activity, Volume 2, pp. 433-494.

Devereux, M. / Engel, C. (2000): Monetary policy in the open economy revisited: price setting and exchange rate flexibility, NBER Working Paper #7665, National Bureau of Economic Research, Cambridge MA, USA.

Devereux, M. / Lane, P. (2001): Exchange rates and monetary policy in emerging market economies, Trinity College Dublin CEG Working Paper #20017, Trinity College Dublin, Economics Department, Dublin, Ireland.

Devereux, M. / Yetman, J. (2003): Monetary policy and exchange rate pass-through: theory and empirics, Mimeo, Hong Kong Institute for Monetary Research, Hong Kong.

Dobrynskaya, V. / Levando, D. (2005): A study of the exchange rate pass-through effect in Russia, ICEF Working Paper 9/2005/02, State University – Higher School of Economics, Moscow, Russia.

Dobrynskaya, V. (2008): Asymmetric price rigidity and the optimal interest rate defense of the exchange rate: some evidence for the US, in Journal of Policy Modeling, Volume 30, pp. 713-724

Dornbusch, R. (1987): Exchange rates and prices, in: American Economic Review, Volume 77, pp. 93-106.

Dubravko, M. / Marc, K. (2002): A note on the pass-through from exchange rate and foreign price changes to inflation in selected emerging market economies, in: BIS Papers #8, Bank for International Settlements, pp. 69-81.

Gagnon, J. / Knetter, M. (1992): Markup adjustment and exchange rate fluctuations: evidence from panel data on automobile exports, NBER Working Paper #4123, National Bureau of Economic Research, Cambridge MA, USA.

Gali, J. / Monacelli, T. (2005): Monetary policy and exchange rate volatility in a small open economy, in: Review of Economic Studies, Volume 72, pp. 707-734.

Holden, S. (2002): The costs of price stability – downward nominal wage rigidity in Europe, NBER Working Paper #8865, National Bureau of Economic Research, Cambridge MA, USA.

Holden, S. / Wulfsberg, F. (2004): Downward nominal wage rigidity in Europe, CESifo Working Paper #1177, CESifo, Munich, Germany.

Holzer, H. / Montgomery, E. (1993): Asymmetries and rigidities in wage adjustments by firms, in: Review of Economics and Statistics, Volume 75, pp. 397-408.

Hooper, P. / Mann, C. (1989): Exchange rate pass-through in the 1980s: the case of U.S. imports of manufactures, in: Brookings Papers on Economic Activity, Volume 1, pp. 297-337.

Hufner, F. / Schroder, M. (2002): Exchange rate pass-through to consumer prices: a European perspective, Discussion paper #0220, Centrum for European Economic Research, Germany.

Itskhoki, O. (2004): Asymmetric price rigidity and the optimal rate of inflation, NES Working Paper #BSP/2004/075E, New Economic School, Moscow, Russia.

Korhonen, I. / Wachtel, P. (2005): A note on exchange rate pass-through in CIS countries, presented at BOFIT/CEFIR workshop on Russian Macroeconomic and Financial Issues, March 2005, Moscow, Russia.

Krugman, P. (1987): Pricing to market when the exchange rate changes, in: Real-Financial Linkages Among Open Economies, edited by S. Arndt and J. Richardson, MIT Press Cambridge, MA, USA, pp. 49-70.

Lewis, M. (2003): Asymmetric price adjustment and consumer search: an examination of retail gasoline market, Center for the Study of Energy Markets Working Paper #120, University of California Berkley, CA, USA.

Obstfeld, M. (2001): International macroeconomics: beyond the Mundell - Fleming model, NBER Working Paper #8369, National Bureau of Economic Research, Cambridge MA, USA.

Obstfeld, M. / Rogoff, K. (2000), The six major puzzles in international macroeconomics: is there a common cause? in: NBER Macroeconomics Annual, National Bureau of Economic Research, Cambridge MA, USA, pp.: 339-390.

Ohno, K. (1990): Export pricing behavior of manufacturing: a US – Japan comparison, International Monetary Fund Staff Papers, Volume 36, pp. 550-579.

Parsly, D. / Popper, H. (1998): Exchange rates, domestic prices and central bank actions: recent US experience, in: Southern Economic Journal, Volume 64, pp. 957-972.

Peltzman, S. (2000): Prices rise faster than they fall, in: Journal of Political Economy, Volume 108, pp. 466-502.

Phillips, R. (1988): The pass-through of exchange rate changes to prices of imported manufactures, A.N.U. Centre for Economic Policy Research Discussion Paper #197, Australian National University, Canberra, Australia.

Rotemberg, J. / Woodford, M. (1999): Interest rate rules in an estimated sticky price model, in: Monetary Policy Rules, edited by J. Taylor, University of Chicago Press, Chicago, Il, USA.

Shmykova, S. / Sosunov, K. (2005): The responsiveness of consumer prices to exchange rate in Russia, in: HSE Economic Journal, Volume 1, pp. 3-16 (in Russian).

Sosunov, K. / Zamulin, O. (2005): Monetary policy in a resource-based economy: the case of Russia, presented at BOFIT/CEFIR workshop on Russian Macroeconomic and Financial Issues, March 2005, Moscow, Russia.

Vdovichenko, A. / Voronina, V. (2004): Monetary policy rules and their application in Russia, EERC Working Paper #04/09, Economics Education and Research Consortium, Moscow, Russia.

Verbrugge, R. (1998): A cross-country investigation of macroeconomic asymmetries, Economics Working Paper #9809017, Virginia Polytechnic Institute and State University, Department of Economics, Virginia, USA.

Woodford, M. (1996): Control of the public debt: a requirement for price stability? NBER Working Paper #5684, National Bureau of Economic Research, Cambridge MA, USA.

Woodford, M. (2003): Interest and Prices: Foundations of a Theory of Monetary Policy, Princeton University Press, Princeton, USA.

Appendix 1

Table A1: The Structure of the Consumer Basket in Russia in 2006

All goods and services	**100**	**Services to population**	**23.55**
Foodstuffs	**42.71**	Everyday services	2.71
Meat and poultry	10.71	Passenger transport	3.31
Fish products	1.88	Communication	2.66
Butter	1.60	Housing and public utilities	8.90
Milk and diary products	2.84	Child care in pre-school institutions	0.28
Cheese	0.99	Education	2.02
Eggs	0.72	Cultural institutions	0.26
Cakes	2.33	Sanatoria, resorts and health care institutions	0.54
Tea and coffee	1.03	Public health	1.02
Granulated sugar	1.14	Other	1.85
Bread and bakery products	2.50		
Macaroni and groats	1.12		
Fruit and vegetables	3.96		
Alcoholic beverages	7.12		
Public catering	2.28		
Other	2.49		
Non-food goods	**33.74**		
Clothing and underwear	5.19		
Fur and fur products	0.56		
Knitwear	1.29		
Footwear	2.52		
Detergents	0.74		
Perfumes and cosmetics	1.36		
Haberdashery	0.79		
Tobacco products	0.83		
Furniture	2.17		
Electric appliances	2.18		
Publications	0.50		
Tv and radio sets	1.15		
Personal computers	1.13		
Means of communication	0.87		
Construction materials	1.83		
Vehicles	4.24		
Gasoline	1.91		
Medicine	1.43		
Other	3.05		

Does International Trade Transfer Technology to Emerging Countries? A Patent Citation Analysis[1]

Elif Bascavusoglu-Moreau, Imperial College London, UK[2]

1 Introduction

In 2005, according to statistics of International Monetary Found (IMF), the output of the emerging countries exceeds half of the world's total output.[3] As stated by the World Trade Organization (WTO), the liberalization in trade and investment regimes has played a central role in this expansion (see WTO 2003). Since neo-classical theory predicts that a higher rate of growth and wealth will result from a decrease in trade barriers and tariffs, openness implies higher productivity. The acknowledgement of international trade as one of the main channels of growth goes back to Adam Smith.

More recently, endogenous growth theory predicts that growth rates of countries are related through international trade linkages and associated embodied and disembodied knowledge spillovers, i.e. knowledge externalities (see Grossman / Helpman 1991). Knowledge is inherently non-rival in its use, and hence its creation and diffusion are likely to lead to spillovers and increasing returns. It is this non-rival property of knowledge that is at the heart of the theoretical models that predict endogenous growth from research and development (R&D) investments (see Romer 1990, Grossman / Helpman 1991 and Aghion / Howitt 1998). In this context, the development of a country depends heavily on its knowledge capital, which in turn is determined by the rate of national innovation and international technology diffusion. Three mechanisms have been identified to assess the impact of trade openness on technology diffusion (see Redding / Proudman 1998): the degree of international openness can affect the

[1] We are grateful to Prof. Silverman for providing data, and to Prof. Maureen Macintosh and the participants of Ateliers de la MSE (Paris, 2005) and FDI and Spillovers Workshop (Paris, 2005) for comments and suggestions.

[2] Business School, Imperial College London. Email: e.bascavusoglu@imperial.ac.uk

[3] We refer here to IMF' statistics adjusted by the Economic Intelligence Unit analysts, which include the newly industrialized countries such as South Korea, Taiwan, Hong Kong and Singapore (The Economist 2006). The argument behind this adjustment is that excluding these countries is equivalent to underestimating the eventual success of the developing economies in the catching-up process. We will come back to this debate in Section 4, when we discuss the definition of "developing" and "emerging" countries.

rate of domestic innovation, the quantity of transferred technology or the adoption rate of more advanced countries' technologies.

The empirical literature has long focused on the role of exports, given the exporting firms' high productivity growth (see Aw / Hwang 1995, Clerides et al. 1998 and Bernard / Jensen 1999). The positive impact of exports on learning effects has been demonstrated for emerging countries such as South Korea and China (see Kraay 1999 and Hahn 2004). Another branch of empirical research, initiated by Coe / Helpman (1995), has analyzed the knowledge capital incorporated in imported goods. The impact of these externalities on the host countries' growth has been largely verified (see Coe et al. 1997, Keller 2000 and van Pottelsberghe / Lichtenberg 2001). In the same context, multinational firms and foreign direct investment flows have also been considered as a channel of technology transfer to the host countries (see Blomström 1986, de Mello 1999 and Sjöholm 1999).

However, few studies have attempted to analyze the mechanisms by which the international trade transmits technological knowledge. The purpose of this paper is to achieve a better understanding of the interactions between international trade and technological diffusion, using a direct and precise measure, patent citations.

Whilst patent documents have been widely used in the economics of innovation, the use of patent citations is relatively recent. Initiated by Jaffe et al. (1993), the patent citations indicator has been used to measure the spatial distribution of the technological diffusion (see Jaffe / Trajtenberg 1998, Maurseth / Verspagen 2002, Bottazzi / Peri 2003 and Thompson / Fox-Kean 2005).

In this paper, following the work by MacGarvie (2005a, 2005b) and Peri (2005), we combine flows of bilateral trade with number of cited patents, in order to evaluate the interactions between embodied and disembodied knowledge. We expand previous studies by considering a North-South context and a sectoral level in the technology diffusion process. The objective of this paper is a better understanding of the technology transfer by trade linkages. Particularly, by assuming that patent citations reflect a direct process of learning, we seek to evaluate whether the emerging countries which are involved in international trade tend to cite their commercial partners.

We present an empirical evaluation of citations from 18 emerging countries to patents of 10 countries that we consider as "sources" of knowledge. Our study covers the period 1980-1998 and 18 manufacturing sectors. We attempt to evaluate first the impact of bilateral trade on the disembodied knowledge flows for the whole sample, and then, we distinguish sectors' R&D intensities.

This paper contributes to the previous literature in mainly three ways. Our principal concern is to assess the particularities of emerging countries as host countries in the technology diffusion process. For this purpose, we adopt and apply

Caballero and Jaffe's theoretical model (1993) to emerging countries. Secondly, in our empirical specification, we extent the original model by introducing cultural and historical proximities between commercial partners, for a better understanding of knowledge flows. Although the use of a common language as a vector of communication has been highlighted in the previous literature for developed countries (see Keller 2002, MacGarvie 2005a and Peri 2005), to the best of knowledge this paper is the first to consider historical proximities in a North-South context. Finally, in contrast with previous studies (see e.g. MacGarvie 2005a), we conduct an analysis at a sectoral level of manufacturing industry. In particular, we distinguish between high, medium and low technological intensities of sectors, in order to assess the interaction between knowledge diffusion and technological specialization.

The remainder of this paper is as follows. Section 2 presents a brief survey of literature on the relationship between international trade and growth. We outline in Section 3 the empirical model and the estimation method. Section 4 describes data and the variables. Our results are reported in Section 5. Section 6 concludes.

2 Related Literature

As the neo-classical theory predicts a higher rate of growth and wealth from the decrease of trade barriers and tariffs, openness implies a higher productivity.[4] International trade, especially exporting activity, has been considered to be one of the main channels of growth.

Empirical literature concludes that exporting firms differ from non-exporting firms in many aspects; they are more intensive in capital and technology and pay higher wages (see Bernard / Jensen 1999, p. 2). Cases studies, especially on South-Asian countries, underline the "learning by exporting" effects (see Rhee et al. 1984 and Hou / Gee 1995).[5] As a World Bank Report on South Asian Miracle puts out:

---

[4] According to the theoretical models, free trade avoids the efficiency losses associated with protectionism. The mechanisms by which the openness affects the growth are mainly: *(i)* widening of the market size; *(ii)* economies of scale, by avoiding an excess of entry on the markets; *(iii)* elimination of X-inefficiencies (Bhagwati 1988); *(iv)* rise of the incentives to innovate, resulting from an increased competition; *(v)* opening up to the new ideas and technologies. For empirical evidence, see Krueger (1980), Balassa (1985) and Bhagwati (1988).

[5] Arrow (1962) defines the notion of "learning" as an aptitude for a system to entertain and increase continuously its function, by considering its previous results, into a dynamic process of creating knowledge.

> "Buyers want low-cost, better-quality products from major suppliers. To obtain this, they transmit tacit and occasionally proprietary knowledge from their other, often OECD-economy suppliers" World Bank 1993, p.320 (cited by Clerides et al. 1998, p. 1).

While it is widely accepted that exporting firms are more productive, there is no evidence so far concerning learning by exporting. In fact, the direction of the causality relation between exporting and productivity is not so obvious. Are firms exporting because they are more productive or do they become more productive after exporting? This raises the problem of self selection, i.e. is it that exporters are more productive before entering in foreign markets.

At an aggregate level, exports and growth are positively correlated (see David 1992, Ben-David 1993, Edwards 1993, Sachs / Warner 1995 and Sebastian 1998). In fact, exports have been often considered as key to welfare creation, thus reflecting a mercantilist vision (see Girma et al. 2004).

Dollar (1992) finds that commercial distortions reduce growth, and hence, openness to trade is significant in explaining the growth of real per capita GDP. By analyzing the convergence of European countries, Ben-David (1993) shows that countries which converge are those involved in trade liberalization. Sachs and Warner (1995) analyze the impact of trade openness using a dummy variable and find that it accelerates growth. Edwards (1998) associates total factor productivity growth with nine different openness measures and concludes that more open countries had higher rates of growth. His results are robust to openness measures, estimation techniques and time periods.

However, some authors have serious reservations about these studies, suggesting a contingent relationship between exports and growth, depending heavily on countries' characteristics and methodological bias.[6] In order to overcome with this kind of problems, a branch of the literature has focused on micro econometric analysis.

The starting point of these firm level studies is the observed higher rate of growth of exporting firms. Nevertheless, there is still no consensus about the direction of the causality between high growth rates and exports. In a cross sectional study about Colombia, Morocco and Mexico, Clerides et al. (1998) find a learning by exporting effect only for Morocco, and a self selection effect for the whole sample. Studies by Aw / Hwang (1995, 2000) for Taiwanese firms, by Bernard / Wagner (1997) on German firms, by Bernard / Jensen (1999) on American firms, and by Isgut (2001) on Colombian firms are among others which find evidence of a self selection effect but no learning by exporting. Fi-

[6] See Rodriguez / Rodrik (1999) for a critical discussion of these studies.

nally, Delgado et al. (2002), in a study of Spanish firms, concludes that learning by exporting only concerns relatively young firms.

However, after controlling for self selection effects, some studies do find a positive learning effect from exports. Using a similar methodology to Clerides et al. (1998), both Bigsten et al. (2004) and van Biesebroeck (2003) find evidence of productivity gains by exports. In a study of Italian firms, Castellani (2002) shows that learning is associated with the export intensity. Kraay (1999) and Hahn (2004) also find evidence for higher productivity rates from exporting activities for Chinese and Korean firms respectively.

Endogenous growth theories provide the "missing link" between openness and growth via knowledge spillovers (see Lejour / Nahuis 2001). In this context, knowledge originating in a particular country or region increasingly transcends national boundaries and contributes to the productivity growth of other geographic areas, or at least, reduces duplication of the research effort.[7]

International trade can be a source of spillovers through demonstration effects when domestic firms learn the innovative content of imported goods. Coe / Helpman (1995), Coe et al. (1997) and Lichtenberg / van Pottelsberghe (1998) examine the influence of foreign trade partners' R&D on domestic total factor productivity. The empirical results confirm that foreign R&D influences domestic productivity and that the more countries are open to international trade, the more they benefit. Greenwood et al. (1997) attribute 60 percent of US long-term growth to embodied knowledge. Some authors have extended Coe and Helpman's framework, by including country characteristics (see Keller 2000), by restricting trade to capital goods (see Xu / Wang 1999), or by using a different estimation technique (see Kao et al. 1999).

The foreign direct investment (FDI) has also been suggested as a channel of embodied knowledge diffusion, by emphasizing three mechanisms; demonstration effects, labour mobility and linkages between buyers and suppliers.[8] The empirical literature, however, is ambiguous. While there seems to be evidence of spillover effects of outward FDI (see Hanel 1993 and van Pottelsberghe / Lichtenberg, 2001) as well as inward FDI (see Findlay 1978, Blomström 1986, Borensztein et al. 1998 and Balasubramanyam et al. 1996), there's no consensus about its magnitude.[9]

Empirical evidence on the effect of technological externalities on trade is rather limited. More often, international trade and/or international investment are considered as the carrier of international spillovers of knowledge and new

[7] See Grossman / Helpman (1991) for a review the endogenous growth theory.
[8] For an exhaustive survey for FDI spillovers, see surveys by Blomström / Kokko (1999), Cincera / van Pottelsberghe (2001) and Saggi (2002).
[9] See Haddad / Harrison (1993) and Aitken / Harrison (1999) for examples of the negative or null impact of FDI on home countries.

technology, without exploring the mechanisms of knowledge diffusion. This paper aims to fill this gap, using patent citations as a measure of disembodied knowledge flows.

Following Jaffe et al. (1993) and Jaffe / Trajtenberg (1998), we consider patent citations as a paper trail of knowledge flows. Like scientific papers, patent documents contain references to earlier patent documents;[10] we can then assume a knowledge flow from the cited patent to the citing one. Employing patent statistics as an output indicator of innovation allows patent citations to reflect the process of knowledge diffusion.[11]

Despite the noisy nature of the citation data, the latter have been used for many purposes as to assess the market value of patents (see Trajtenberg 1990, Harhoff et al. 1999 and Hall et al. 2005), to track the geographic boundaries of knowledge flows (see Jaffe et al. 1993, Thompson / Fox-Kean 2005, Maurseth / Verspagen 2002 and Bottazzi / Peri 2003), or to assess the impact of university (basic) research (see Jaffe / Trajtenberg 1996 and Sampat et al. 2003).[12]

Nevertheless, empirical research combining patent citations with trade and investment flows is rather scarce. Sjöholm (1996) finds a correlation between Swedish patent citations and bilateral imports, suggesting that imports contribute to international knowledge spillovers. Globerman et al. (2000) evaluate technology sourcing of Swedish multinational and small and medium sized enterprises (SME) and find that outward FDI increases citations. Brandstetter (2001) analyzes FDI and citation flows between USA and Japan, and shows a positive impact of FDI on knowledge spillovers. Using micro level data on French firms, MacGarvie (2005b) finds that both importers and exporters learn more from foreign technology compared to firms not involved in international trade. At a regional level, Peri (2005) compares knowledge and trade flows, and concludes that there is a lesser impact of distance on the former. Whether in a macro, meso or micro level, there are no studies evaluating the case of developing or emerging countries so far. The interaction between knowledge and trade flows has only been explored between industrialized countries. Even if the technology transfer literature highlights the role of imports in developing countries' growth, there's a lack of analysis on the mechanisms of how these spillovers are gener-

[10] For a discussion about the use of patent statistics as an innovation indicator, see Griliches (1991).

[11] As Griliches (1991) points out, the main difference between academic citations and patent citations is the existence of patent examiners, who have the possibility to add some cited patents if necessary.

[12] It's generally admitted that citations added by patent examiners bring some noise in data. Nevertheless, a recent inventor survey on USPTO patents from Jaffe et al. (2000) provide evidence that at least half of the citation flows correspond to some kind of knowledge flow, while about a one quarter of citation flows correspond to a very substantial knowledge flow. See also Duguet / MacGarvie (2005) for a survey of EPO patents.

ated by international transactions. This is the principal motivation of the present paper.

3 The Empirical Model and Estimation Method

3.1 Empirical Model

Our empirical specification is derived from the theoretical model developed by Caballero / Jaffe (1993). The authors combine an approach of creative destruction and knowledge spillovers in a growth model, in order to determine and measure the intensity and the impacts of knowledge spillovers on growth.

In this context, the probability that a patent N granted at year T will cite another patent n given at year t is given by the following:

(1) $$\alpha(n,N) = \delta e^{(-\beta(n,N)(T,t))}(1-e^{-\gamma(T-t)})$$

where β is the rate of obsolescence and γ, the rate of diffusion. The citation frequency rises with the diffusion of knowledge and decreases with the patent' obsolescence.[13]

In Caballero and Jaffe's analysis, the fact that a patent N at time T cites another patent n granted at t, is a proof that N_T uses the information contained in n_t. Hence, we can use the citation frequency in order to measure $\alpha(n,N)$. If $C_{T,t}$ is the number of citations from patents granted at time T to patents granted at time t, and P_T and P_t correspond respectively to the number of patents granted at time T ant t, the estimated citation probability would be given by:

(2) $$\alpha^*(n,N) = \frac{C_{T,t}}{P_T P_t}$$

The relationship between $\alpha(n,N)$ and $\alpha^*(n,N)$ is determined by the relationship between the number of citation and the number of ideas effectively used on the one hand, and, on the other hand, the relationships between the number of innovations and the number of patents. By assuming that these relationship can be represented by the parameter values φ and ψ, rerspectively, and by incorporating them into Equation (1), Caballero and Jaffe obtain the relation between the estimated citation probability and the probability of citation:

---

[13] The probability to have an idea of $(T - t)$ years old is given by $(1- e\ )$, if $\gamma \to \infty$ the diffusion is instantaneous. When $\gamma = 0$, this means that the previous ideas are not available, and hence, each inventor begin at zero (see Caballero / Jaffe 1993).

(3) $\alpha^*(n,N) = \phi_T \psi_T \psi_t \alpha(n,N)$

This last equation allows us the re-write Equation (1) as:

(4) $\alpha(n,N) = \phi_T \psi_T \psi_t \delta e^{(-\beta(n,N)(T,t))}(1 - e^{-\gamma(T-t)})$

Jaffe / Trajtenberg (1996, 1998) reformulate this citation probability as the ratio of the number of citations of a given patent to the number of potentially citing and cited patents in the same country/sector cohort. Equation (1) then becomes:

(5) $E[C_{IiTtj}] = (N_{IT})(N_{ijt})\alpha_{IiTtj}(e^{-\beta_{IiTtj}(T-t)})(1 - e^{-\gamma(T-t)}) + \varepsilon_{IiTtj}$

where C_{IiTtj} is the number of citations from a patent granted in country I at time T, to another patent granted in country i at time t and in sector j. N_{IT} and N_{ijt} correspond to the potential number of citing and cited patents, respectively. It is possible to rewrite Equation (5) as:

(6) $N_{IiTtj} \equiv \dfrac{C_{IiTtj}}{(N_{IT})(N_{ijt})} = \alpha_{IiTtj}(e^{-\beta_{IiTtj}(T-t)})(1 - e^{-\gamma(T-t)}) + \varepsilon_{IiTtj}$

By estimating Equation (6) for France, Germany, Great Britain, Japan and United States, Jaffe and Trajtenberg have shown that some countries cite each other's patents more often than other countries. MacGarvie (2005a) develops this finding by analyzing the determinants of these cross-country citations. She introduces a vector corresponding to potential channels for diffusion such as technological proximity, geographic distance, language barriers and trade. The objective of this paper is to take analysis of this topic forward, by conducting an empirical estimation at sectoral level and in a North-South context. For this purpose, we construct a vector δX_{IiTt}, which contains these bilateral characteristics and introduce it in our econometric specification.

3.2 Estimation Method

It is possible to estimate the specification in Equation (6), either by a non linear or a semi-parametric approach. However, the semi-parametric approach is less restricted regarding the form of citation function and allows us to consider the count nature of our data. For this reason we use a discrete probability model, the Poisson Regression Model (see Greene 1994). The non linear form of the citation function is introduced by having a separate parameter for each value of *(T −t).*[14]

So we consider an alternative specification of Jaffe and Trajtenberg:

$$(7) \qquad N_{IiTtj} = e^{\alpha_{(T-t)}\alpha_T\alpha_t\alpha_I\alpha_i\alpha_j\delta X_{IiTtj}}$$

where X_{IiTtj} reflects the bilateral characteristics of countries, and $\alpha_{(T-t)}$ varies following amount of time between T and t. By taking natural logarithms, equation (7) becomes:

$$(8) \qquad \ln(C_{IiTtj}) = \ln(N_{ITj}) + \ln(N_{itj}) + \delta X_{IiTtj} + \alpha_{(T-t)} + \alpha_T + \alpha_t + \alpha_I + \alpha_i + \alpha_j + \varepsilon_{IiTtj}$$

where N_{ITj} and N_{itj} are the number of granted patents in citing country I and cited country i, in sector j, respectively. C_{IiTtj} is the number of citations from citing country I at time T, to patents of cited country i at time t and for the sector j.

The Poisson regression model provides the standard framework to estimate count data.[15] When C_{it} denotes the number of citations, the Poisson model assumes that each C_{it} follows a Poisson distribution with parameter λ_{it}. The citation probability is hence expressed by:[16]

$$(9) \qquad \Pr[Y_i = C_i \mid x_i] = \frac{e^{-\lambda_i}\lambda_i^{C_i}}{C_i!}$$

the Poissin distribution specifies the expected value and variance of the model as a function of explanatory variables and parameters to be estimated:

$$(10) \qquad \begin{aligned} E[C_i \mid x_i] &= e^{x_i b} = \lambda_i \\ V[C_i \mid x_i] &= e^{x_i b} = \lambda_i \end{aligned}$$

As we can see from the above equations, the Poisson model assumes equidispersion, i.e. equality between expected value and the variance.

$$(11) \qquad E[C_i \mid x_i, \beta] = V[C_i \mid x_i, \beta] = \lambda_i$$

---

[14] In this approach, though, the cross-country differences are only explained by changes in the explanatory variables δX_{IiTt}.

[15] For a survey on the specification and estimation of count models, see Greene (1994) and Winkelmann / Zimmermann (1995).

[16] For the sake of simplicity, we do not consider the temporal and sectoral dimensions in following formulations.

This last property makes the Poisson Model very restrictive, and if it fails to hold this has the same implications as heteroscedasticity in a model of Ordinary Least Squares (OLS) (see Cameron / Trivedi 1998). Furthermore, the Poisson Model assumes homogeneity, given that the conditional expectation has a deterministic form that depends on the explanatory variables. Given the nature of our data, where we have both temporal and sectoral dimensions, the non-consideration of specific effects may lead to excessive dispersion. In the panel data context, this problem is resolved by using either a random effect approach or a fixed effect approach. If the specific effects are correlated with the explanatory variables, the random effect model fails to be consistent. We should therefore use a negative binomial model by introducing a random error term v_i:

$$(12) \quad E[C_i \mid x_i, v_i] = \exp(x_i, b)\exp(\varepsilon_i) = \lambda_i v_i$$

where $v_i = exp(\varepsilon_i)$ is a non-observable heterogeneity term. It reflects a specification error from omitted or non-observable exogenous variables with $E[v_i]=1$ and $V[v_i]=\sigma^2 v$.

This specification allows us to evaluate the implications of non observable heterogeneity without knowing the complete distribution of v_i, provided we know the moments of v_i:

$$(13) \quad \begin{aligned} &E[C_i \mid x_i, v_i] = e^{x_i b} E[v_i] = \lambda_i \\ &V[C_i \mid x_i] = E[E[C_i \mid x_i, v_i]] + V[E[C_i \mid x_i, v_i]] = \lambda_i (1 + \sigma_v^2 \lambda_i) \end{aligned}$$

We note that for $\sigma^2{}_v$, the variance of this distribution is greater than the one from the standard Poisson model. This allows us to interpret the excessive dispersion as a result of the omission of non observable heterogeneity.[17]

In our empirical specification, the rate of citation by the potentially citing patent N_{it} to the potentially cited patent N_{IT} is given by $E[C_{IiTt}|\lambda_{IiTt}]= \lambda_{IiTt}$. This rate depends on observable factors such as N_{IT}, N_{it} and X_{IiTt}. Hence, the conditional expectation of the dependant variable is given by:

---

[17] By assuming that vi is distributed by Gamma, the distribution of the Binomial Negative Law is given by (see Gourieroux / Trognon, 1984):

$$(14) \quad f(c \mid \lambda, \alpha) = \frac{\Gamma(c+\alpha^{-1})}{\Gamma(y+1)\Gamma(\alpha^{-1})} \left(\frac{\alpha^{-1}}{\alpha^{-1}+\lambda} \right) \left(\frac{\lambda}{\alpha^{-1}+\lambda} \right), \quad \alpha = \sigma_v^2 \geq 0$$

Note that this distribution is equivalent to the Poisson distribution if $\alpha = 0$. A likelihood test which examines the null hypothesis of α allows us to discriminate one of these two models. A value of α significantly different from 0 indicates an excessive dispersion, and therefore suggests that Negative Binomial Model is more appropriate.

(15) $E[C_{IiTt} \mid N_{IT}, N_{it}, X_{IiTt}] = \exp(\ln(N_{IT}) + \ln(N_{it}) + \ln(X_{IiTt}))$

But the Negative Binomial Model could also be insufficient to explain the frequency of zero citations.[18] In fact, it is possible that a country does not cite any patent from another country in the given sector and time period. This could lead to an excess of zeros in our sample. We should therefore consider alternative models, allowing for a generalization of the specification of the expectation and the variance. Initiated by Lambert (1992), the Zero Inflated Poisson (ZIP) and the Zero Inflated Negative Binomial (ZINB) Models have the property of correcting the excess zeros. These models are an extension of the Poisson Model, and assume that the citation decision has two steps, such that, the process that generates zeros and the positive values are different. C_i attains the value zero with a probability of φ_i, where C_i follows either a logit or probit model:

(16) $\varphi_i = \dfrac{\exp(\gamma_i z_i)}{1 + \exp(\gamma_i z_i)}$

here z_i represents the vector of the variables which affect the decision of not citing a patent.[19] In the second step, the probability of each count (including zeros) is determined by a Poisson or Binomial Negative Distribution. We hence have:

(17) $\Pr[C_i = 0] = \varphi_i + (1 - \varphi_i)\exp(-\varphi_i)$

(18) $\Pr[C_i = C \mid C > 0] = (1 - \varphi_i)\dfrac{\exp(-\varphi_i)\varphi_i^{C_i}}{C_i!}$

The Vuong (1989) test enables us to choose between the standard model and the model that corrects for excessive zeros. If the Vuong test confirms an excess of zeros, which is very probable given the nature of our sample, we proceed to a regression using the appropriate zero inflated model.

4 Description of the Data and Variables

4.1 Data and Descriptive Statistics

This study evaluates the role of bilateral imports and exports in knowledge spillovers to the developing countries at the sectoral level. The endogenous variable of the econometric model is the number of patent citations, a direct measure of disembodied knowledge flows.

[18] For each regression, we test the presence of excessive dispersion. If it is the case, a Negative Binomial Model is more appropriate then a Poisson Model.

[19] Given that we have no reason to suspect a difference between these two steps, we consider same vector of variables in the both steps ($x_i = z_i$).

We used two principal sources to construct an original database, which is used to evaluate the impact of the embodied knowledge flows on the disembodied knowledge flows. The first source is the NBER Patent and Citation Dataset, described in Hall et al. (2001). This dataset contains all the patents granted by U. S. Patent Office (USPTO) from 1963 to 2002 and all citations made by each patent to others from 1975 to 2002.[20] Our bilateral trade flows come from the NBER World Trade Data as described in Feenstra et al. (2005). This database presents the world trade flows at Standard International Trade Classification (SITC Rev.3) level for the period of 1962-2000. The other sources of data are presented in Appendix (A.3). We have used a number of correspondence tables to construct the final database which has aggregated data over 19 sectors.[21]

As we want to analyze the technology transfer in a North-South context, we should only consider Northern innovative countries with a certain stock of knowledge as "technology source" countries.[22] If we look at the total number of patents granted by USPTO, we can see that the innovative activities are concentrated in a number of countries (See Figure 1).[23] These are the same countries that invest in R&D (OECD 2003, 2005) and are classified among the high income countries according to the World Bank.[24] But a closer look at the evolution of granted patents over time reveals that some of these innovative activities only began in the early 1990 (Figure 2). Hence, countries like Taiwan, South Korea, Israel or Austria are not included among the technology source countries, even if they have a high growth rate of innovations. Hence, only United States, Japan, Germany, Canada, France, Switzerland, Sweden, Netherlands and Italy are considered as technology source countries. A final look at the distribution of citations by cited countries confirms our choice, as these 10 countries account for 72% of citations (Figure 3).

Our host countries are the emerging economies. As pointed out very briefly in the introduction, the category of emerging countries has no clear-cut definition. In order to distinguish between emerging and developing countries,

---

[20] The original database described in Hall et al. (2001) concerns only the period 1975-1999. We completed this database by the data available on Bronwyn Hall's personal homepage (http://emlab.berkeley.edu/users/bhhall/bhdata.html).

[21] See Appendix A.1 for the details of database construction.

[22] We consider knowledge stock at national as well as sectoral level. The choice of countries holds at both level of analysis. However, for the sake of clarity, figures are shown at the national level.

[23] These countries are United States, Japan, Germany, United Kingdom, France, Canada, Switzerland, Taiwan, Sweden, Netherlands, Italy, South Korea, Austria, Australia, Belgium and Israel.

[24] The high income classification corresponds to more then $ 9076 per capita. For more details, see World Bank (World Bank 2005).

we can refer to the definition of "developing countries" given by Arocena and Sutz:

> "When the transition from agrarian societies to industrial societies framed world history, "developing" countries were those unable to move along industrialization roads; consequently, the expansion of the industrial West was for them a source of subordination, and so they became in fact not "developing" but underdeveloped countries. Today, when we are living the transition to the knowledge society, the economy of developed countries is solidly based on science, technology, innovation and advanced education. "Developing" countries are "the rest", those unable to use knowledge – its generation, transmission and application – as a fundamental tool for economic growth and social improvement." Arocena / Sutz (2005, p. 1).

We interpret the term of emerging countries as referring to countries which already have the capacity to assimilate and use the technology developed elsewhere. Our sample is hence composed of 18 emerging countries, including some newly industrialized countries, as listed at the Appendix A.2.[25]

The following figures are derived from our original sample constructed by combining the USPTO and World Trade Databases.[26] Figure 4 highlights the evolution of the flows of citation and trade for the estimation period and the sample countries. One should note the relative stability of the citation flow, compared to the rise of trade flows. This confirms the relevance of our research question: whether trade flows are a determinant of knowledge transmission.

The sectoral distribution gives us some information about the composition of emerging countries' innovative activities (see Figure 5). The inter-sectoral distribution of citations flows seems rather homogenous except in four sectors.[27] In fact, 80% of the sectoral citations occur in the manufacture of textiles, paper products, electrical machinery, and professional and scientific equipment. We

---

[25] Our host countries are Argentina, Brazil, China, Czech Republic, Hong Kong, Hungary, Iceland, India, Israel, Korea, Malaysia, Mexico, New Zealand, Russian Federation, Singapore, South Africa and Venezuela. The major part of our sample is classified as middle and high income countries by World Bank except India, which his classified as a low income country.

[26] The final database used in this paper has thus [18x10x19 x18=] 61560 observations, of which 43% are zeros.

[27] See Appendix A.4 for the list of sectors.

can hence conclude that a very considerable part of the knowledge flows to developing countries occurs in middle-high technology intensive sectors.[28]

4.2 Variables and Expected Signs

Our independent variable is the number of citations made by the country *I* in each separate sector *j* and year *T*, from the country *i*, assuming that patent citations represent a link to pre-existing knowledge upon which the inventor builds. We limit the analysis to the period from 1980 to 1998, in order to reduce the truncation bias.[29] As we are concerned by the relationship between disembodied and embodied knowledge flows, all observations on citations of patents in the same country are removed.[30] We also take into account several other factors that could influence the disembodied knowledge flows, such as geographic, technological, and cultural distances.

Given that patent citations occur more between sectors using similar technologies, we use the technological proximity index developed by Jaffe (1986). The technological similarity between two countries *I* and *i* is given by the following equation:

$$(19) \quad \omega_{Ii} = \frac{\sum_{k=1}^{K} N_{Ik} N_{ik}}{\sqrt{\sum_{k=1}^{K} N_{Ik}^2 \sum_{k=1}^{K} N_{ik}^2}}$$

where $k = 1, 2, ..., K$ indicates sectors and *N* stands for the number of patents. The more similar the technological fields of the countries *I* and *i* are, the closer ω_{Ii} would be to unity. If the two countries have no patents in the same sector ω_{Ii} would be zero. We expect the technological proximity index to have a positive effect on the disembodied knowledge flows between two commercial partners.

The tacit nature of disembodied knowledge flows makes the geographic distance important for technology diffusion. It is widely accepted in the empirical literature that technological spillovers are geographically bounded (see Jaffe et al. 1993 and Audretsch / Feldman 1996). We use a geodesic distance measure

[28]The definition of high/medium/low technological intensity comes from Hatzichronoglou (1997), based on sectoral direct and indirect R&D intensity, and is presented in Appendix A.5.

[29] See Hall et al. (2001) for a discussion about the truncation problem of citation data.

[30] It is widely accepted that citation flows are more concentrated in intra-sectoral and intranational level (see Jaffe / Trajtenberg 1998). But in this paper we are principally concerned with the North-South technology diffusion. Furthermore, given the level of research and development investments and patenting activities in our sample, we believe that in our context, technology diffusion relies mainly on foreign knowledge.

from CEPII Distance Database.[31] We expect that distance acts as a barrier to the technology diffusion.

Finally, we believe that in the process of technological diffusion, cultural factors may be as important as the economic ones. In order to test this hypothesis, we construct a number of variables of cultural proximity, to evaluate the cultural and historical linkages which can affect the degree of communication between countries. The first is the use of a common language. Our dummy variable equals 1 if the two countries share a common language. The potential importance of language as a contributor to embodied and disembodied knowledge flows has several foundations (see Peri 2002). The transactions costs hypothesis of Williamson (1989) argues that communication across language barriers is more expensive, increasing the economic distance between potential partners not sharing a common language (see Eichengreen / Irwin 1996). We expect language affinities to provide an automatic channelling of information along linguistic lines (see Helliwell 1998). However, the complexity of culture can not be fully approximated by the language similarities alone (see Hussler 2004).[32] The degree of common cultural and historical links may also further the density of internationally shared knowledge and values. Hence we also construct another dummy variable concerning countries' colonial relationship and colonial link. Both of these variables are taken from CEPII Distance Database.

5 Results

5.1 Disembodied Flows, Trade and Proximities: An Overall View

Tables 1 and 2 show estimation results, all sectors pooled. The likelihood ratio test ($\alpha = 0$) has detected excessive dispersion, hence we use a Negative Binomial distribution rather then a Poisson distribution in our regressions. Furthermore, the Vuong test statistic which exceeds 1.96 in each regression, confirms the presence of excessive zeros. Therefore the regression method we use is then the Zero Inflated Negative Binomial (ZINB) Model.[33] Each estimation is associated with two different tables, i.e. two estimation steps. The first estimation models the process of zero citation from the innovators of citing country *I* to patents

[31] Geodesic distances are calculated following the great circle formula, which uses the geographic coordinates of the capital cities.

[32] See Hussler (2004) for the construction and use of other cultural proximity index.

[33] Each regression includes dummy variables for countries, sectors and years. We also assume that the observations are independent between the country pairs but not necessarily within the groups.

held by country *i* in each group of sector and year. The coefficients indicate the variation of the probability of being in the country group which doesn't cite the trade partner's patents. The second step shows the impact of the explanatory variables on number of citations.[34]

Table 1 presents the basic regression to evaluate the impact of bilateral trade on disembodied knowledge flows. The coefficients of total trade (i.e. exports plus imports) and imports are positive and significant.[35] However, the export variable is not significant in the first step. Hence, exports flows has no effect on the process of *not* citing the trade partner's patents (i.e. the zero flows), whereas its increase will raise the probability of citations. In the second step, however, the impact of exports is higher than that of imports. These results seem to confirm the ambiguity of previous studies concerning learning by exporting effect. Import flows appear to be the main driver of technology diffusion for emerging countries, conforming to the literature on technology transfer (see Coe et al. 1997). Meanwhile, for exporting firms, the impact of exports dominate that of imports, suggesting a self selection effect (see Aw / Hwang 1995, Clerides et al. 1998, Aw et al. 2000 and Isgut 2001). Finally, the first column of both estimations shows the foreign direct investment variable. The negative, although non significant, sign of this variable in the second step suggests a potential complementary relationship between trade and investment flows (see Lipsey / Weiss 1984 and Head / Ries 2001). We therefore choose to exclude the FDI variable from the analysis below. This omission leads to an increase in the coefficient of the total trade variable, which rises from 0.141 to 0.187.

The remaining explanatory variables have coefficients that either have opposite signs in the two steps, or fail to be significant in either step. In all specifications the largest coefficients are associated to the number of patents of citing and cited countries. We can interpret these variables as the propensity to cite. A one unit increase of the number of patents of the cited country *i* leads to a rise of citations of 2.30. A similar increase at the citing country *I*, leads to an increase of citations of approximately 1.80. Meanwhile, in both cases the resulting increase in citations is more than proportional to the increase in the number of patents, indicating a learning process. Countries with a higher level of inventive activities, i.e. with more patent applications, will be better placed to benefit from foreign innovations, confirming Cohen / Levinthal (1989). The coefficients we

[34] When we include the same variables in both equations, as in this case, the signs of the corresponding coefficients from the first step are often opposite to those or the same coefficients in the second step. This makes sense since the first stage estimation, which is a binary process, is predicting membership in the group that always has zero citations. So in the first stage, a positive coefficient implies lower productivity, whilst in the second stage, a negative coefficient indicates a lower productivity.

[35] The coefficients have opposite signs in the two steps.

find are higher than those found by MacGarvie (2005a) and Hussler (2004), but this may be due to the different levels of development and innovative activity of the countries analyzed in those studies.[36]

The results also show a high impact of technological proximity, confirming that diffusion is more likely between technologically similar countries and sectors (see Jaffe / Trajtenberg 1998, Orlando 2000, Peri 2002 and Hu / Jaffe 2003). Hence, we do not have evidence so far of different diffusion patterns between the North-North and the North-South contexts.

In order to have a more precise look on the mechanisms of knowledge flows, Table 2 presents the regressions in which different measures of proximity between trading countries have been introduced. The impact of imports is robust, having the same direction at the two steps. Moreover, the export variable also has the expected sign at the first step, contrary to the baseline specification. It appears that once we control for the proximity effect, the impact of import flows decreases.

The geographic distance is negative and significant, conforming to the geographic boundaries of knowledge flows (see Audretsch / Feldman 1996, Sjöholm 1996 and Bottazzi / Peri 2003). As expected, distance reduces the extent of transferred knowledge, whether in a North-North or a North-South context. Peri (2005) finds that 19% of regional knowledge flows disappear when passing country borders. These results are in line with Hussler (2004), who finds a negative effect of 0.23% of geographic distance on knowledge spillovers within Europe.[37] In a setting more similar to the present study, MacGarvie (2005a) finds a negative coefficient on the bilateral trade variable when geographic distance is introduced (among other distance measures). Whilst our results suggest a more pronounced negative effect of distance on disembodied knowledge flows (0.67 versus 0.15 in MacGarvie), our trade variables are still significant.[38]

Conversely, the cultural proximity variables seem to foster technological diffusion (see Lundvall 1992 and Taeube 2004). In all specifications, sharing a common language favours patent citations, confirming previous studies by Keller (2001) and MacGarvie (2005a). The impact of historical proximity, approximated by a former colonial relationship, is even stronger. It is natural to expect a

---

[36] MacGarvie's study evaluates the determinants of citations between Australia, Canada, France, Germany, Italy, Japan, Netherlands, United Kingdom and United States, whilst Hussler evaluates the geography of knowledge spillovers within Europe. Given the North-South context of our study, it is more plausible to have a learning effect from patent applications.

[37] However, we do not think that Peri's findings are an overestimation, given the disaggregated nature of his study.

[38] The correlation between trade and geographic distance is about 0.48, which allow us to introduce both variables in the regression. See Disdier and Head (2004) for an extensive analysis of effects of distance on bilateral trade flows.

privileged relationship between countries sharing a common history, given that the influence of former colonial powers lasts long after independence. But then again, we observe a decrease in the significance of the technological proximity variable, which is only significant in ZINB(5) where we only consider the impact of import flows. We believe that in the first estimations, this variable captured some other proximity measures than technological similarity. This result further stresses the important role of cultural, historical and geographic proximities on the technology diffusion process (see Hussler 2004).

5.2 Technological Intensity: Does it Make a Difference?

In this section, we analyze the role of trade in relation to disembodied knowledge flows in more depth, by distinguishing between sectors with low, medium and high technological intensity. Descriptive statistics have shown that most citations occur in low and medium technology intensive sectors (see Figure 6). The latter's share has increased from 36% to 54% during the period under consideration, to the detriment of the low technological intensity sectors' citations (which passed from 31% in 1980 to 14% in 1998), indicating that emerging countries become more specialized in technology intensive sectors over time.

In low technology sectors, we note a substantial decrease in the coefficients of the bilateral trade and import variables (compare Tables 1 and 3). The impact of exports is highest among the three trade variables, indicating again a learning by exporting effect. Export activities seem to foster disembodied knowledge flows, even in low-tech sectors. The coefficient of technological proximity also is much smaller than in the first specifications. It appears that the variables of common language and, particularly, colonial relationship determine the scope of disembodied knowledge flows, rather then the use of similar technologies. This lack of dependence on the technological intensity in sectors that are less intensive in R&D has been already emphasized by previous studies (see Olarreaga et al. 2003 and Schiff / Wang 2004). Olarreaga et al. (2003) found that the R&D content of trade does not affect the growth of total factor productivity in low R&D intensive industries in a North-South context. Learning in low technology sectors seems to take place through South-South trade (see Schiff / Wang 2004).

In sectors with medium technological intensity, there is a notable increase in the coefficients of the variables for trade and technological proximity. On the other hand, geographic distance no longer affects the probability to cite. It seems that trade flows transfer disembodied knowledge to emerging countries in these sectors. This transfer is higher, the more similar is the technology used in trade partners (see Kokko et al. 1994). From a certain threshold, distance does not seem to be an obstacle to knowledge transfers. This finding highlights the importance of the level of the technological capacity of emerging countries.

Finally, for the high technology sectors we find a decrease of the impact of trade, whereas the impact of technological proximity is rather high. Hence, we conclude that emerging countries patenting in high technology sectors are less dependent on their commercial partners in terms of technology transfer, than are countries specializing in sectors that are relatively less R&D intensive. However, the drop in the number of observations should be noted, indicating that for the moment only a few emerging countries have reached this stage of innovative capacity. Most of the sample countries in our sample remain specialized in medium technology intensive sectors, as indicated above.

This analysis regarding the sectors' technological intensity clearly shows the role of developing countries' absorptive capacity and technical level in the catching-up process. Our results indicate that technology transfer to emerging countries occurs mostly in the middle technology sectors. These findings are in line with the literature on the technological gap. Kokko et al. (1994) report that in Uruguay, technological spillovers exist only where the technological gap between local and foreign firms is of moderate size. In low tech sectors, the impact of trade flows on the diffusion of disembodied knowledge is small. Previous studies arrived a similar conclusions when studying the relationship between local firms' productivity growth and the size of the technology gap in developing (see Kokko 1994) or developed (see Imbriani / Reganati 1999) countries. On the other hand, in high technology sectors, developing countries no longer rely on foreign technology to be transferred by trade flows. This indicates that in order to benefit from commercial partners' knowledge, developing countries have to build their own technological abilities, confirming previous results on developed countries (see Castellani / Zanfei 2003). Once a threshold level has been reached and countries have developed a certain level of innovative capacity, knowledge seems to be transferred by other means than international trade.

6 Conclusions

The purpose of this paper was to investigate the mechanisms of technology transfer through trade flows in emerging countries. Using patent citations, which provide a direct and precise measure of innovative firms' learning process, we evaluated the role of international trade on disembodied knowledge diffusion in a North-South context.

Broadly speaking, the results show that trade flows transfer knowledge across borders. The more a country is involved in international trade, the more it tends to cite foreign patents. We can therefore conclude that the countries in our sample acquire and assimilate the knowledge incorporated in import and export flows from developed countries. Our results also show that technology diffusion by international trade is not a uniform process, and this enables us to highlight some particular aspects.

Our principal research question was to assess how emerging countries differ from industrialized countries in the knowledge diffusion process. For this purpose, we first identified the different effects of technological, geographical and cultural proximities on disembodied knowledge flows.

The first consequence of introducing the different proximity effects is the shift between the impact of import and export flows. Our results indicate a learning by exporting effect for emerging countries,[39] confirming previous studies. Exporter countries are more likely to cite their partner's patents than importers are.

Concerning the effects of the proximity variables, we obtain some interesting results. Cultural and historical proximities seem to foster disembodied knowledge flows, and their effect is more significant than technological proximity. This result relativates the role of technological distance and stresses the role played by more intangible proximities. The important role of communication skills (see Keller 2002 and MacGarvie 2005a) and cultural proximity (see Hussler 2004) as a determinants of cross-country citations has been already stressed for North-North diffusion. They seem to be even more important regarding emerging countries. The tacit nature of knowledge, combined with the potential lack of technological endowments in the host countries, emphasizes the extent of cultural linkages.

We also found that historical proximity, approximated here by colonial presence of Northern countries in the South, is particularly important for developing countries. Effectively, most of the developing countries have been colonized by today's industrialized economies. It seems that past colonial relationships continue to have an impact on disembodied and embodied knowledge transfers to Southern countries. To the best of our knowledge, the present study is the first to consider the role of historical linkages in the technology diffusion process.

But the most important factor of knowledge diffusion appears to be technological specialization, and thus, the technical capacity of the countries in our sample. Our findings change significantly when we differentiate with respect to technology intensities. In medium technology intensive sectors, where the emerging countries are mostly specialized, technological proximity appears to be more important, whereas the negative impact of geographical distance disappears. We therefore conclude that once emerging countries acquire a certain

[39] It should be noted that our analysis does not allow us to distinguish between learning by exporting effect and self selection. However, as we do not use firm level data, this distinction is not relevant for our analysis.

level of technical capacity in some sectors, they find it easier to benefit from foreign knowledge. The results of the regression for the high technology sectors confirm this finding, as they suggest that emerging countries are less dependent on their commercial partners.

This paper enriches the previous literature in several ways. Firstly, the use of patent citations allows us to evaluate the learning process in the dissemination of technology directly. Second, by distinguishing sectors' technological intensity and considering proximity effects, we reduce the potential biases associated with the analysis of trade flows. Finally, this paper provides a cross country evaluation of the knowledge flows in a North-South context and at a sectoral level, a subject unexplored in the literature. The most important contribution of this study is to establish that the role of cultural and historical factors should not be underestimated in the analysis of technology transfers.

References

Aghion, P. / Howitt, P. (1998): Endogenous Growth Theory, MIT Press, Cambridge, MA, USA.

Aitken, B. / Harrison, A. (1999): Do domestic firms benefit from direct foreign investment? Evidence from Venezuela, in: American Economic Review, Volume 89, pp. 605–618.

Arocena, R. / Sutz, J. (2005): Innovation systems and developing countries, DRUID Working Paper 02-05, DRUID, Copenhagen Business School, Department of Industrial Economics and Strategy/Aalborg University, Aalborg, Denmark.

Arrow, K. (1962): Economic welfare and the allocation of resources for invention, in: The Rate and Direction of Inventive Activity, edited by R. Nelson, Princeton University Press, Princeton, NJ, USA, pp. 609–625.

Audretsch, D. / Feldman, M. (1996): R&D spillovers and the geography of innovation and production, in: American Economic Review, Volume 86, pp. 630–640.

Aw, B. / Hwang, A. (1995): Productivity in the export market: a firm level analysis, in: Journal of Development Economics, Volume 47, pp. 313–332.

Aw, B. / Chung, S. / Roberts, M. (2000): Productivity and the turnover in the export market: micro-level evidence from the republic of Korea and Taiwan (China), in: World Bank Economic Review, Volume 14, pp. 65–90.

Balassa, B. (1985): Exports, policy choices, and economic growth in developing countries after the 1973 oil shock, in: Journal of Development Economics, Volume 18, pp. 23-35.

Balasubramanyam, V. / Salisu, M. / Sapsford, D. (1996): Foreign direct investment and growth in EP and IS countries, in: The Economic Journal, Volume 106, pp. 92–105.

Ben-David, D. (1993): Equalizing exchange: trade liberalization and income convergence, in: Quarterly Jounal of Economics, Volume 108, pp. 653-679.

Bernard, A. / Wagner, J. (1997): Exports and succes in German manufacturing, in: Weltwirtschaftliches Archives, Volume 133, pp. 134–157.

Bernard, A. / Jensen, J. (1999): Exceptional exporter performance: cause, effect, or both? in: Journal of International Economics, Volume 47, pp. 1–25.

Bhagwati, J. (1988), Export-promoting trade strategy: issues and evidence, in: World Bank Research Observer, Volume 3, pp. 27-57.

Bigsten, A. / Collier, P. / Dercon, S. / Fafchamps, M. / Gauthier, B. / Gunning, J. / Oduro, A. / Oostendorp, R. / Pattillo, C. / Söderbom, M. / Teal, F. / Zeufack, A. (2004): Do African manufacturing firms learn from exporting? in: Journal of Development Studies, Volume 40, pp. 115–141.

Blomström, M. / Kokko, A. (1999): How foreign investment affects host countries? Technical Report 1745, World Bank, Washington, DC, USA.

Blomström, M. (1986): Foreign investment and productive efficiency: the case of Mexico, in: Journal of Industrial Economics, Volume 35, pp. 97–110.

Borensztein, E. / De Gregorio, J. / Lee, J. (1998): How does foreign direct investment affect economic growth? in: Journal of International Economics, Volume 45, pp. 115–135.

Bottazzi, L. / Peri, G. (2003), Innovation and spillovers in regions: evidence from european patent data, in: European Economic Review, Volume 47, pp. 687–710.

Brandstetter, L. (2001): Are knowledge spillovers are international or intranational in scope? Microeconometric evidence from the U.S. and Japan, in: Journal of International Economics, Volume 53, pp. 53–79.

Caballero, R. / Jaffe, A. (1993): How high are the giants' shoulders: an empirical assessment of knowledge spillovers and creative destruction in a model of economic growth, NBER Macroeconomics Annual, MIT Press, Cambridge, MA, USA.

Cameron, A. / Trivedi, P. (1998): Regression Analysis of Count Data, Cambridge University Press, Cambridge, United Kingdom.

Castellani, D. (2002): Export behaviour and productivity growth: evidence from italian manufacturing firms, in: Weltwirtschaftliches Archiv, Volume 138, pp. 605-628.

Castellani, D. / Zanfei, A. (2003): Technology gaps, absorptive capacity and the impact of Inward investments on productivity of european firms, in: Economics of Innovation and New Technology, Volume 12, pp. 1–19.

Cincera, M. / van Pottelsberghe, B. (2001): International R&D spillovers: a survey, in: Cahiers Economiques de Bruxelles, Volume 169, pp. 3–32.

Clerides, S. / Lach, A. / Tybout, J. (1998): Is learning by exporting important? Micro-dynamic evidence from Colombia, Mexico, and Morocco, in: Quarterly Journal of Economics, Volume 113, pp. 903–947.

Coe, D. / Helpman, E. (1995): International R&D spillovers, in: European Economic Review Volume 39, pp. 859–887.

Coe, D. / Helpman, E. / Hoffmaister, A. (1997): North-South R&D spillovers, in: The Economic Journal, Volume 107, pp. 134–49.

Cohen, W. / Levinthal, D. (1989): Innovation and learning: the two faces of R&D, in: The Economic Journal, Volume 99, pp. 569-96.

Delgado, M. / Farinas, J. / Ruano, S. (2002): Firm productivity and export markets: a non-parametric approach, in: Journal of International Economics, Volume 57, pp. 397-422.

De Mello, L. (1999): Foreign direct investment-led growth: evidence from time series and panel data, in: Oxford Economic Papers, Volume 51, pp. 133–151.

Disdier, A. / Head, K. (2004): The puzzling persistance of the distance effect on bilateral trade, Development Studies Working Paper 186, Centro Studi Luca D'Agliano, Milano, Italy.

Dollar, D. (1992): Outward-oriented developing economies really do grow more rapidly: evidence from 95 LDCs, 1976-1985, in: Economic Development and Cultural Change, Volume 40, pp. 523-44.

Duguet, E. / MacGarvie, M. (2005): How well do patent citations measure flows of technology? Evidence from French innovation surveys, in: Economics of Innovation and New Technology, Volume 14, pp. 375–393.

Edwards, S. (1993): Openness, trade liberalization and growth in developing countries, in: Journal of Economic Literature, Volume 31, pp. 1358–1393.

Edwards, S. (1998): Openness, productivity and growth: what do we really know? in: The Economic Journal, Volume 108, pp. 383-98.

Eichengreen, B. / Irwin, D. (1996): The role of history in bilateral trade flows, NBER Working Papers 5565, National Bureau of Economic Research, Cambridge, MA, USA.

Feenstra, R. / Lipsey, R. / Deng, H. / Ma, A. / Mo, H. (2005): World trade flows: 1962-2000, NBER Working Paper 11040, National Bureau of Economic Research, Cambridge, MA, USA.

Findlay, R. (1978): Relative backwardness, direct foreign investment and the transfer of technology: a simple dynamic model, in: Quarterly Journal of Economics, Volume 92, pp. 1–16.

Girma, S. / Greenaway, D. / Kneller, R. (2004): Does exporting increase productivity? A microeconometric analysis of matched firms, in: Review of International Economics, Volume 12, pp. 855-866.

Globerman, S. / Kokko A. / Sjöholm F. (2000): International technology diffusion: evidence from Swedish patent data, in: Kyklos, Volume 53, pp. 17–38.

Gourieroux, C. / Monfort, A. / Trognon, A. (1984): Pseudo-maximum likelihood methods: applications to poisson models, in: Econometrica, Volume 52, pp. 701–720.

Greene, W. (1994): Accounting for excess zeros and sample selection in poisson and binomial regression models, Working paper No. EC-94-10, New York University, New York, USA.

Greenwood, J. / Hercowitz, Z. / Krusell, P. (1997): Long-run implications of investment specific technological change, in: American Economic Review, Volume 87, pp. 342–62.

Griliches, Z. (1991): Patent statistics as economic indicators: a survey, in: Journal of Economic Literature, Volume 28, pp. 1661–1707.

Grossman, G. / Helpman, E. (1991): Innovation and Growth in the Global Economy, MIT Press, Cambridge MA, USA.

Haddad, M. / Harrison, A. (1993): Are there positive spillovers from direct foreign investment? Evidence from panel data for Morocco, in: Journal of Development Economics, Volume 42, pp. 51–74.

Hahn, C. (2004): Exporting and performance of plants: evidence from Korean manufacturing, NBER Working Paper No.10208, National Bureau of Economic Research, Cambridge, MA, USA.

Hall, B. / Jaffe, A. / Trajtenberg, M. (2005): Market value and patent citations, in: Rand Journal of Economics, Volume 36, pp. 16-38.

Hall, B. / Jaffe, A. / Trajtenberg, M. (2001): The NBER patent citation data file: Lessons, insights and methodological tools, NBER Working Papers 8498, National Bureau of Economic Research, Cambridge, MA, USA.

Hanel, P. (1993): Inter-industry flows of technology: an analysis of the Canadian patent matrix and input-output matrix for 1978-1989, in: Cahiers de Recherche 93-06, Département d'Économique de la Faculté d'administration à l'Université de Sherbrooke, Quebec, Canada.

Harhoff, D. / Narin, F. / Scherer, F. / Vopel, K. (1999): Citation frequency and the value of patented innovation, in: Review of Economics and Statistics, Volume 81, pp. 511–515.

Hatzichronoglou, T. (1997): Revision of the high-technology sector and product classification, STI Working Paper, OECD, Paris, France.

Head, K. / Ries, J. (2001): Overseas investment and firm exports, in: Review of International Economics, Volume 9, pp. 108–22.

Helliwell, J. (1998): How much do national borders matter? Brookings Institution, Washington DC, USA.

Hou, C. / Gee, S. (1995): National Innovation Systems: A Comparative Analysis, Oxford University Press, New York, USA.

Hu, A. / Jaffe, A. (2003): Patent citations and international knowledge flow: the cases of Korea and Taiwan, in: International Journal of Industrial Organization, Volume 21, pp. 849–880.

Hussler, C. (2004): Culture and knowledge spillovers in Europe: new perspectives for innovation and convergence policies? in: Economics of Innovation and New Technology, Volume 13, pp. 523–541.

Imbriani, C. / Reganati, F. (1999): Productivity spillovers and regional differences: some evidence on the italian manufacturing sector, CELPE Discussion Papers 48, CELPE, University of Salerno, Italy.

Isgut, A. (2001): What is different about exporters: evidence from Colombian manufacturing, in: Journal of Development Economics, Volume 30, pp. 52-82.

Jaffe, A. (1986): Technological opportunity and spillovers of R&D: evidence from firms' patents, profits and market value, in: American Economic Review, Volume 76, pp. 984–1001.

Jaffe, A. / Trajtenberg, M. (1996): Flows of knowledge from universities and federal labs: Modelling the flow of patent citations over time and across institutional and geographic boundaries, NBER Working Papers 5712, National Bureau of Economic Research, Cambridge, MA, USA.

Jaffe, A. / Trajtenberg, M. (1998): International knowledge flows: evidence from patent citations, NBER Working Papers 6507, National Bureau of Economic Research, Cambridge, MA, USA.

Jaffe, A. / Trajtenberg, M. / Fogarty, M. (2000): Knowledge spillovers and patent citations: evidence from a survey of inventors, in: American Economic Review, Volume 90, pp. 215–218.

Jaffe, A. / Trajtenberg, M. / Henderson, R. (1993): Geographic localization of knowledge spillovers as evidenced by patent citations, in: Quarterly Journal of Economics, Volume 108, pp. 577-98.

Kao, C. / Chiang, M-H. / Chen, B. (1999): International R&D spillovers: an application of estimation and inference in panel cointegration, Center for Policy Research Working Papers 4, Center for Policy Research, Maxwell School, Syracuse University, New York, USA.

Keller, W. (2000): Do trade patterns and technology flows affect productivity growth? in: World Bank Economic Review, Volume 14, pp. 17–49.

Keller, W. (2001): Knowledge spillovers at the world's technology frontier, CEPR Discussion Papers 2815, Centre for Economic Policy Research, London, UK.

Keller, W. (2002): Geographic localization of international technology diffusion, in: American Economic Review, Volume 92, pp. 120–142.

Kokko, A. (1994): Technology, market characteristics, and spillovers, in: Journal of Development Economics, Volume 43, pp. 279–293.

Kokko, A. / Tansini, R. / Zejan, M. (1994): Productivity spillovers from FDI in the Uruguayan manufacturing sector, Working Paper 2, Stockholm School of Economics, Stockholm, Sweden.

Kraay, A. (1999), Exportations et performances économiques: Etude d'un panel d'entreprises chinoises, in: Revue d'Economie du Développement, Volume 1, pp. 183–207.

Krueger, A. (1980): Trade policy as an input to development, NBER Working Papers 0466, National Bureau of Economic Research, Cambridge, MA, USA.

Lambert, D. (1992): Zero-inflated poisson regression with an application to defects in manufacturing, in: Technometrics, Volume 31, pp. 1–14.

Lejour, A. / Nahuis, R. (2001): Openness, growth and R&D spillovers: uncovering the missing link? Research Memorandum 168, CPB Netherlands Bureau for Economic Policy Analysis, The Hague, Netherlands.

Lichtenberg, F. / van Pottelsberghe, B. (1998): International R&D spillovers: a comment, in: European Economic Review, Volume 42, pp. 1483–1491.

Lipsey, R. / Weiss, M. (1984): Foreign production and exports of individual firms, NBER Reprints 0558, National Bureau of Economic Research, Cambridge, MA, USA.

Lundvall, G. (1992): National System of Innovation: Towards a Theory of Innovation and Interactive Learning, Francis Printer, London, United Kingdom.

MacGarvie, M. (2005a): The determinants of international knowledge diffusion as measured by patent citations, in: Economics Letters, Volume 87, pp. 121–126.

MacGarvie, M. (2005b): Do firms learn from international trade? in: Review of Economics and Statistics, Volume 88, pp 46-60.

Maurseth, P. / Verspagen, B. (2002): Knowledge spillovers in Europe: a patent citations analysis, Scandinavian Journal of Economics, Volume 104, pp. 531–45.

Nicita, A. / Olarreaga, M. (2007): Trade, production, and protection database, 1976-2004, in: World Bank Economic Review, Volume 21, pp. 165-171.

OECD (2003): Science and Technology Indicators, Organisation for Economic Co-operation and Development, Paris, France.

OECD (2005): OECD Factbook, Organisation for Economic Co-operation and Development, Paris, France.

Olarreaga, M. / Schiff, M. / Wang, Y. (2003): North-South and South-South trade-related technology diffusion: an industry level analysis, CEPR Discussion Papers 3711, Centre for Economic Policy Research, London, United Kingdom.

Orlando, M. (2000): On the importance of geographic and technological proximity for R&D spillovers: an empirical investigation, Research Working Paper RWP00-02, Federal Reserve Bank of Kansas City, Missouri, USA.

Peri, G. (2002): Knowledge flows and knowledge externalities, in: CESifo Working Paper Series 765, CESifo, Munich, Germany.

Peri, G. (2005): Determinants of knowledge flows and their effect on innovation, in: Review of Economics and Statistics, Volume 87, pp. 308-332.

Redding, S. / Proudman, J. (1998): Productivity convergence and international openness, Bank of England working papers 77, Bank of England, London, United Kingdom.

Rhee, Y. / Ross-Larson, B. / Pursell, G. (1984): Korea's competitive edge: managing entry into the world market, World Bank, Washington D.C., USA.

Rodriguez, F. / Rodrik, D. (1999): Trade policy and economic growth: a skeptic's guide to cross-national evidence, Technical Report 7081, National Bureau of Economic Research, Cambridge, MA, USA.

Romer, P. (1990): Endogenous technological change, in: Journal of Political Economy, Volume 98, pp. 71–102.

Sachs, J. / Warner, A. (1995): Economic reform and the process of global integration, in: Brookings Papers on Economic Activity, Volume 1, pp. 1–118.

Saggi, K. (2002): Trade, foreign direct investment, and international technology transfer: a survey, in: World Bank Research Observer, Volume 17, pp. 191–235.

Sampat, B. / Mowery, D. / Ziedonis, A. (2003): Changes in university patent quality after the Bayh-Dole act: a re-examination, in: International Journal of Industrial Organization, Volume 21, pp. 1371–1390.

Schiff, M. / Wang, Y. (2004): On the quantity and quality of knowledge: the impact of openness and foreign research and development on North-North and North-South technology spillovers, Policy Research Working Paper 3190, World Bank, Washington D.C., USA.

Sebastian, E. (1998) Openness, productivity and growth: what do we really know? in: The Economic Journal, Volume 108, pp. 383–398.

Sjöholm, F. (1996): International transfer of knowledge: the role of international trade and geographic proximity, in: Weltwirtschafliches Archiv, Volume 132, pp. 97–115.

Sjöholm, F. (1999): Technology gap, competition and spillovers from direct foreign investment: evidence from establishment data, in: Journal of Development Studies, Volume 36, pp. 53–75.

Taeube, F. (2004): Proximities and innovation: evidence from the Indian IT industry in Bangalore, DRUID Working Papers 04-10, DRUID,

Copenhagen Business School, Department of Industrial Economics and Strategy, Aalborg University, Aalborg, Denmark.

The Economist (2006): Climbing back, The Economist, Issue 19/01/2006.

Thompson, P. / Fox-Kean, M. (2005): Patent citations and the geography of knowledge spillovers: a reassessment, in: American Economic Review, Volume 95, pp. 450–460.

Trajtenberg, M. (1990): A penny for your quotes: patent citations and the value of innovations, in: RAND Journal of Economics, Volume 21, pp. 172–187.

Van Biesebroeck, J. (2003): Exporting raises productivity in Sub-Saharan African manufacturing plants, NBER Working Papers 10020, National Bureau of Economic Research, Cambridge, MA, USA.

Van Pottelsberghe, B. / Lichtenberg, F (2001): Does foreign direct investment transfer technology across borders? in: Review of Economics and Statistics, Volume 83, pp. 490–497.

Vuong, Q. (1989): Likelihood ratio tests for model selection and non-nested hypotheses, in: Econometrica, Volume 57, pp. 307–334.

Williamson, O. (1989): Transaction cost economics, in: Handbook of Industrial Organization Volume 1, edited by R. Schmalensee and R. Willig , North-Holland, Amsterdam, Netherlands.

Winkelmann, R. / Zimmermann, K. (1995): Recent developments in count data modelling: theory and application, in: Journal of Economic Surveys, Volume 9, pp. 1–24.

World Bank (2005): World Development Indicators, World Bank, Washington DC, USA.

WTO (2003): World Trade Report, World Trade Organisation, Genève, Switzerland.

Xu, B. / Wang, J. (1999): Capital goods, trade and R&D spillovers in the OECD, in: Canadian Journal of Economics, Volume 32, pp. 1258–1274.

Appendix 1: Tables

Table 1: Disembodied Knowledge Flows and Bilateral Trade

First Step : Probability not to cite				
	ZINB(1)	**ZINB(2)**	**ZINB(3)**	**ZINB(4)**
Bilateral Trade	-0.235***	-0.114		
	(-4.08)	(-0.88)		
Imports			-0.514***	
			(-5.81)	
Exports				0.116
				(1.42)
FDI	2.479			
	(0.59)			
Technological Proximity		-0.551	-0.515	-0.436
		(-1.36)	(-1.43)	(-1.15)
Citing Country's Patents	-0.477***	0.129	-0.205*	0.156
	(-7.59)	(1.31)	(-2.13)	(1.71)
Cited Country's Patents	0.092	-1.380***	-1.066***	-1.393***
	(0.42)	(-16.58)	(-10.02)	(-17.74)
Constant	-13.811	6.509*	242.679*	259.702
	(-0.03)	(1.97)	(2.19)	(1.60)
Number of Observations	61560	61560	61560	61560
Likelihood Ratio Test	1145.14	1131.60	1094.19	1137.76
Prob>chibar2	0.000	0.000	0.000	0.000
Vuong Statistic	9.006	6.540	6.460	7.060

Table 1: Disembodied Knowledge Flows and Bilateral Trade *(cont.)*

Second Step : Probability to cite				
	ZINB(1)	**ZINB(2)**	**ZINB(3)**	**ZINB(4)**
Bilateral Trade	0.141***	0.187***		
	(14.04)	(16.94)		
Imports			0.068***	
			(4.03)	
Exports				0.142***
				(19.09)
FDI	-0.215			
	(-0.43)			
Technological Proximity		0.719***	0.715***	0.724***
		(11.46)	(10.51)	(11.70)
Citing Country's Patents	0.819***	0.874***	0.867***	0.840***
	(81.44)	(76.04)	(49.39)	(74.54)
Cited Country's Patents	0.589***	0.810***	0.803***	0.794***
	(17.43)	(38.63)	(37.78)	(36.23)
Constant	- 13.161***	- 13.601***	-17.913**	- 14.647***
	(-56.85)	(-57.28)	(-2.95)	(-3.48)
Number of Observations	61560	61560	61560	61560
Log-Likelihood	-29569.17	-29184.03	-30502	-30080.41
LR chi2	6590.217	6291.537	6250.611	6399.894
Prob>chibar2	0.000	0.000	0.000	0.000

Standard errors in brackets. *Significant at 10%; ** significant at 5%; *** significant at 1%

All variables are in logarithms, except the dependent variable

Table 2: Disembodied Knowledge, Trade and Proximities

First Step : Probability not to Cite			
	ZINB(4)	**ZINB(5)**	**ZINB(6)**
Bilateral Trade	-0.275***		
	(-5.37)		
Imports		-0.509***	
		(-6.50)	
Exports			-0.271***
			(-6.98)
Technological Proximity	-0.083	-0.661	-0.106
	(-0.06)	(-0.22)	(-0.07)
Distance	1.493***	1.477***	1.595***
	(13.52)	(10.80)	(13.70)
Common Language	-0.212	-0.359	0.105
	(-1.04)	(-1.29)	(0.56)
Historical Links	-2.377***	-2.666***	-2.449***
	(-7.85)	(-5.57)	(-7.57)
Citing Country's Patents	-0.515***	-0.582***	-0.552***
	(-8.37)	(-8.49)	(-8.64)
Cited Country's Patents	0.019	0.001	0.096
	(0.24)	(0.02)	(1.22)
Constant	10.623***	8.440***	10.657***
	(6.23)	(5.23)	(5.92)
Number of Observations	61560	61560	61560
Likelihood Ratio Test	571.34	632.45	591.76
Prob>chibar2	0.000	0.000	0.000
Vuong Statistic	7.503	8.005	8.305

Table 2: Disembodied Knowledge, Trade and Proximities *(cont.)*

Second Step : Probability to Cite			
	ZINB(4)	**ZINB(5)**	**ZINB(6)**
Bilateral Trade	0.182***		
	(13.72)		
Imports		0.102***	
		(7.43)	
Exports			0.114***
			(12.83)
Technological Proximity	0.840	2.030*	0.216
	(1.23)	(2.41)	(0.33)
Distance	-0.705***	-0.573***	-0.666***
	(-20.86)	(-16.34)	(-19.46)
Common Language	0.397***	0.305***	0.353***
	(12.17)	(9.71)	(11.31)
Historical Links	0.645***	0.403***	0.600***
	(9.22)	(5.64)	(8.86)
Citing Country's Patents	0.818***	0.838***	0.783***
	(58.60)	(53.86)	(56.29)
Cited Country's Patents	0.992***	0.967***	0.997***
	(73.56)	(69.97)	(83.73)
Constant	-8.564***	-11.358***	-9.144***
	(-21.73)	(-28.00)	(-24.12)
Number of Observations	61560	61560	61560
Log-Likelihood	-29410.4	-30131.46	-29718.62
LR chi2	6992.02	6877.18	7054.46
Prob>chi2	0.000	0.000	0.000

Standard errors in brackets. *Significant at 10%; ** significant at 5%; *** significant at 1%

All variables are in logarithms, except the dependent variable

Table 3: Sectors with Low Technological Intensity

First Step : Probability of not to Cite			
Bilateral Trade	-3.508***		
	(-4.26)		
Imports		-1.079*	
		(-2.33)	
Exports			-0.672***
			(-4.95)
Technological Proximity	5.573	-2.089	-2.838*
	(0.18)	(-0.13)	(-2.03)
Distance	2.109***	1.068*	0.835*
	(3.59)	(2.31)	(2.49)
Common Language	0.222	-3.995**	-1.540
	(0.29)	(-2.63)	(-1.89)
Historical Links	-1.592***	-1.146	-1.225
	(-1.16)	(-1.31)	(-1.88)
Citing Country's Patents	0.562	-1.788***	-1.475***
	(1.58)	(-3.80)	(-4.83)
Cited Country's Patents	-1.466***	-1.283***	-1.174***
	(-3.67)	(-4.68)	(-6.59)
Constant	-0.983	12.066	5.202
	(-0.08)	(1.80)	(1.32)
Number of Observations	22117	21405	21525
Likelihood Ratio Test	119.40	119.19	86.37
Prob>chibar2	0.000	0.000	0.000
Vuong Statistic	6.060	7.070	7.683

Table 3: Sectors with Low Technological Intensity *(cont.)*

Second Step : Probability to Cite			
Bilateral Trade	0.067***		
	(1.72)		
Imports		0.047*	
		(2.05)	
Exports			0.127***
			(2.75)
Technological Proximity	0.086***	0.062**	0.125***
	(5.23)	(3.04)	(5.46)
Distance	-0.064	-0.082*	-0.062
	(-1.84)	(-2.23)	(-1.86)
Common Language	0.215***	0.095*	0.214***
	(5.36)	(2.40)	(5.72)
Historical Links	1.912***	1.227*	1.955***
	(3.88)	(2.22)	(4.05)
Citing Country's Patents	0.937***	1.011***	0.951***
	(6.62)	(5.86)	(6.78)
Cited Country's Patents	0.977***	0.994***	0.958***
	(5.62)	(4.10)	(5.10)
Constant	-11.480***	-12.205***	-11.589***
	(-29.66)	(-27.90)	(-30.72)
Number of Observations	23037	21716	22074
Log-Likelihood	-8787.234	-8491.456	-8562.639
LR chi2	3419.149	3233.345	3391.156
Prob>chi2	0.000	0.000	0.000

Standard errors in brackets. *Significant at 10%; ** significant at 5%; *** significant at 1%

All variables are in logarithms, except the dependent variable

Table 4 : Sectors with Medium Technology Intensity

First Step : Probability to not to Cite			
Bilateral Trade	-3.009***		
	(-5.13)		
Imports		-1.460*	
		(-2.35)	
Exports			-3.472***
			(-5.83)
Technological Proximity	1.136	-2.133*	-0.176*
	(0.61)	(-0.05)	(-0.65)
Distance	0.363	0.163	0.629
	(1.36)	(0.51)	(1.90)
Common Language	-1.571***	-1.649**	-1.638***
	(-3.25)	(-1.68)	(-2.36)
Historical Links	-2.284***	-5.738***	-6.619***
	(-4.52)	(-4.50)	(-5.67)
Citing Country's Patents	-0.478*	-0.545*	-0.752***
	(-2.40)	(-2.12)	(-3.70)
Cited Country's Patents	-1.937***	-0.022	-0.254
	(-6.48)	(-0.01)	(-0.48)
Constant	9.002	-14.884	5.293
	(0.64)	(-0.60)	(0.73)
Number of Observations	22117	21405	21525
Likelihood Ratio Test	248.87	235.36	295.06
Prob>chibar2	0.000	0.000	0.000
Vuong Statistic	6.060	7.070	7.683

Table 4 : Sectors with Medium Technology Intensity *(cont.)*

Second Step : Probability to Cite			
Bilateral Trade	0.173**		
	(3.05)		
Imports		0.109***	
		(3.56)	
Exports			0.187***
			(6.49)
Technological Proximity	1.519*	2.355**	1.203*
	(1.55)	(3.28)	(2.55)
Distance	0.019	-0.005	-0.001
	(0.56)	(-0.14)	(-0.03)
Common Language	0.292***	0.275***	0.275***
	(7.96)	(6.91)	(7.41)
Historical Links	1.015***	1.062***	1.073***
	(3.71)	(2.97)	(1.93)
Citing Country's Patents	0.655***	0.629***	0.609***
	(4.95)	(6.99)	(6.67)
Cited Country's Patents	0.793***	0.709***	0.722***
	(3.43)	(3.79)	(1.71)
Constant	-12.098***	-12.256***	-11.549***
	(-27.35)	(-29.38)	(-26.93)
Number of Observations	22117	21405	21525
Log-Likelihood	-9477.743	-9223.987	-9379.857
LR chi2	4577.847	4539.764	4598.544
Prob>chi2	0.000	0.000	0.000

Standard errors in brackets. *Significant at 10%; ** significant at 5%; *** significant at 1%

All variables are in logarithms, except the dependent variable

Table 5: Sectors with High Technology Intensity

First Step : Probability to not to Cite			
Bilateral Trade	-0.210***		
	(-4.02)		
Imports		-0.291***	
		(-5.11)	
Exports			-0.042
			(-1.77)
Technological Proximity	-0.512**	-0.447**	-0.343*
	(-3.01)	(-2.85)	(-2.10)
Distance	0.294***	0.256***	0.289***
	(4.81)	(4.11)	(4.76)
Common Language	0.008	0.008	0.028
	(0.11)	(0.08)	(0.36)
Historical Links	-0.239	-0.222	-0.189
	(-1.84)	(-1.63)	(-1.44)
Citing Country's Patents	-0.905***	-0.980***	-0.920***
	(-2.76)	(-2.99)	(-1.99)
Cited Country's Patents	-0.979***	-0.963***	-0.982***
	(-2.07)	(-2.90)	(-2.25)
Constant	-8.179***	-8.650***	-8.975***
	(-11.57)	(-11.03)	(-13.15)
Number of Observations	10267	10164	10328
Likelihood Ratio Test	25.53	26.80	28.33
Prob>chibar2	0.000	0.000	0.000
Vuong Statistic	4.353	4.651	4.819

Table 5: Sectors with High Technology Intensity *(cont.)*

Second Step : Probability to Cite			
Bilateral Trade	0.073**		
	(3.05)		
Imports		0.109***	
		(3.56)	
Exports			0.087***
			(6.49)
Technological Proximity	1.519*	2.355**	2.203*
	(1.55)	(3.28)	(2.55)
Distance	0.019	-0.005	-0.001
	(0.56)	(-0.14)	(-0.03)
Common Language	0.092***	0.075***	0.075***
	(7.96)	(6.91)	(7.41)
Historical Links	0.015***	0.062***	0.073***
	(2.71)	(2.97)	(2.93)
Citing Country's Patents	0.955***	0.929***	0.909***
	(4.95)	(2.99)	(2.637)
Cited Country's Patents	0.893***	0.909***	0.922***
	(3.43)	(3.79)	(4.71)
Constant	-12.098***	-12.256***	-11.549***
	(-27.35)	(-29.38)	(-26.93)
Number of Observations	10267	10164	10328
Log-Likelihood	-4576.207	-4501.819	-4570.679
LR chi2	1186.349	1172.502	1172.818
Prob>chi2	0.000	0.000	0.000

Standard errors in brackets. *Significant at 10%; ** significant at 5%; *** significant at 1%

All variables are in logarithms, except the dependent variable

Appendix 2: Figures

Figure 1: Distibution of Patents of Innovating Countries

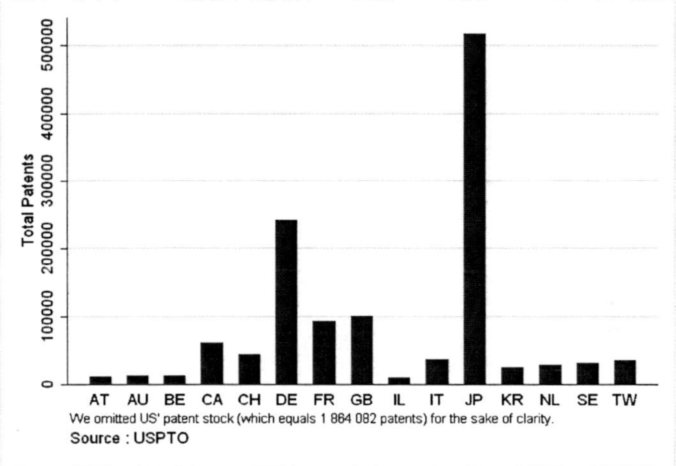

Figure 2: Evolution of Patent Applications by Innovating Country

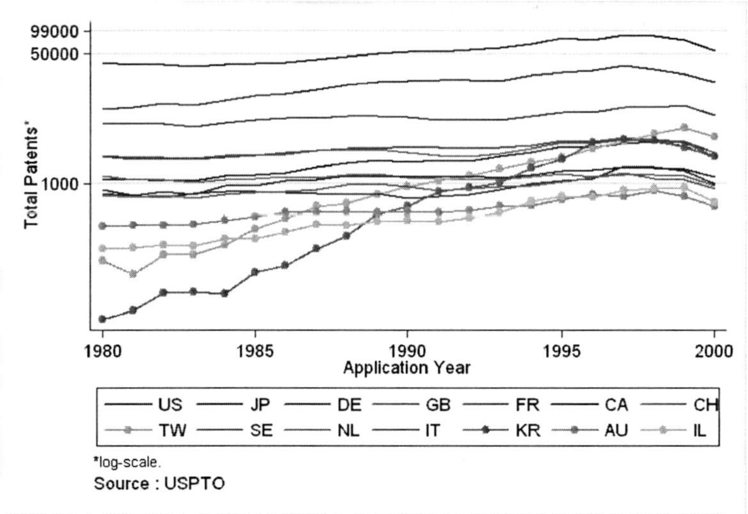

Figure 3: Citation Distribution of Emerging Countries

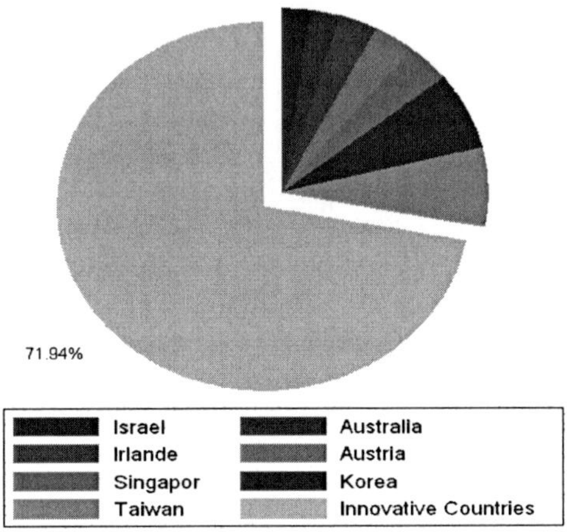

Figure 4: Evolution of Trade Flows and Citations

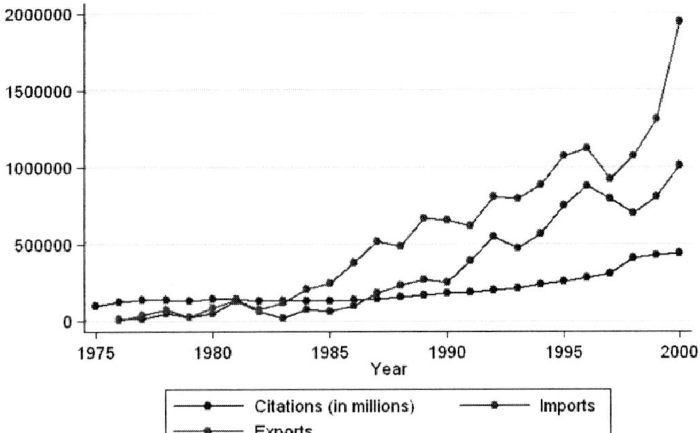

Source : Author's calculs from USPTO and NBER World Trade Databases

Figure 5: Sectoral Distribution of Patent Citations

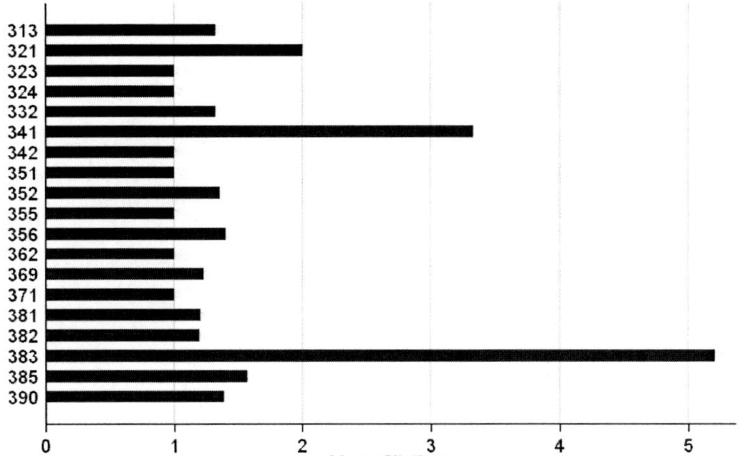

Source : Author's calculs from USPTO and NBER World Trade Databases

Figure 6: Citation Distribution According to Sectors' Technological Intensity

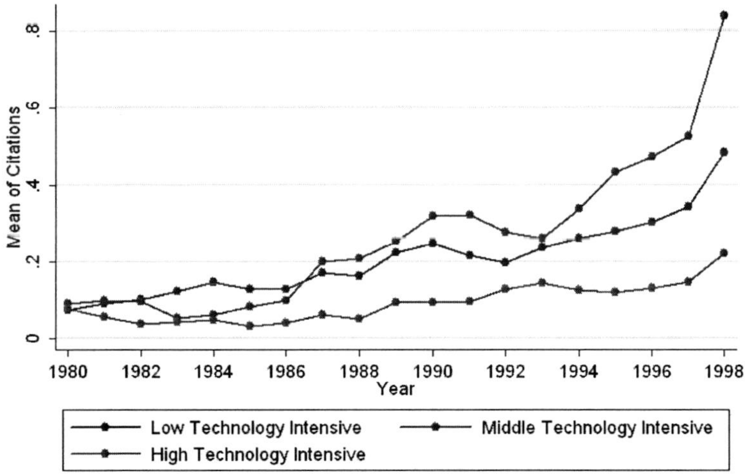

Source : USPTO

Appendix 3

A.3.1 Data Construction

Our primary source of data comes from NBER Patent and Citation Dataset[40] and UNIDO Trade and Production Database.[41] NBER data contains all the patents granted by U.S. Patent Office (USPTO) and all citations made by each patent to others, from 1975. The USPTO assign each patent to an original patent class. This United States Patent Classification (USPC) System consists about 400 main patent classes and 120.000 patent subclasses. In order to match patent citations over sectors and countries with UNIDO data, which is presented in International Standard Industrial Classification (ISIC Rev2), we needed to use several correspondence tables.

The first correspondence table was between USPC System and the International Patent Classification (IPC). We would like to thank Prof. Brian Silverman for providing these data. Once we had the IPC number for each patent on our database, we used a concordance that links the International Patent Classification (IPC) system to the U. S. Standard Industrial Classification (SIC) system at the four-digit SIC level, in order to have a SIC number for each citing and cited patent. This concordance table also comes from Prof. Silverman.[42] The next step was to link these SIC numbers to SIC Rev.2 Classification in order to match the two databases.

Using Jon Haveman's industrial concordance tables, we connected our 4-digit SIC numbers to 3-digit ISIC Rev.3 Classification System. Finally, the last step consisted to link ISIC Rev.3 Classification system to ISIC Rev.2, based on the United Nations' correspondence tables.

---

[40] See Hall et al. (2001) for details.

[41] See Nicita / Olarreaga (2007) for details.

[42] See Prof. Silverman's homepage (http://www.rotman.utoronto.ca/~silverman/ipcsic/documentation_IPCSIC_concordance.htm) for details.

A.3.2 Summary Statistics on the Countries

Country	Exports of goods and services (% of GDP)	Imports of goods and services (% of GDP)	FDI, net inflows (BoP, million US$)	GDP growth (%)	High-tech exports (% of manuf. exports)	Industry Value Added (% of GDP)	Trade in goods (% of GDP)
Argentina	10.89	11.52	10418.31	-0.79	9.04	28.06	18.12
Brazil	10.66	12.18	32779.24	4.40	18.61	27.97	18.90
China	25.87	23.20	38399.3	8.00	18.58	50.22	43.89
Czech Republic	64.46	67.54	4987.079	3.89	8.15	40.92	109.79
Hong Kong	145.50	141.91	61923.9	10.20	23.28	14.22	252.01
Hungary	74.88	78.73	1694.3	5.20	26.42	33.10	128.51
Iceland	34.99	42.10	155.3281	5.60	12.26	26.64	53.23
India	13.89	14.65	2496.042	3.94	5.01	26.60	20.53
Israel	40.40	45.43	5077	7.53	25.09	59.84	n.a.
Korea	40.82	37.67	9283.4	8.49	34.82	36.19	65.00
Malaysia	124.41	104.46	3787.6	8.86	59.53	50.73	199.50
Mexico	31.00	32.94	16597.6	6.60	22.40	28.01	60.05
New Zealand	35.94	34.22	3369.842	2.66	10.16	25.29	52.09
Russian Federation	44.06	24.03	2713	10.00	13.53	37.95	57.84
Singapore	n.a.	n.a.	17219.54	297.73	9	62.56	37.05
South Africa	28.86	25.86	968.831	4.15	6.97	31.13	46.62
Venezuela, RB	28.45	16.32	4701	3.69	2.83	40.47	39.60

Source: World Development Indicators - World Bank

A.3.3 Description of ISIC Rev.2 Sectors

ISIC Code	Description
313	Beverages
321	Textiles
323	Leather products
324	Footwear except rubber or plastic
332	Furniture except metal
341	Paper and products
342	Printing and publishing
351	Industrial chemicals
352	Other chemicals
355	Rubber products
362	Glass and products
369	Other non-metallic mineral products
381	Fabricated metal products
382	Machinery except electrical
383	Machinery electric
385	Professional and scientific equipment
390	Other manufactured products

Source: United Nations Statistics Division - UN

A.3.4 Description and Sources of Variables

Bilateral Trade	Bilateral flows of imports and exports NBER World Trade Database - NBER ISIC Rev3, 1960-2000
Patent Citations	Number of citations per country and sector NBER Patent and Citations Database - NBER 1963-1999
Technological Proximity	Index of technological proximity by Jaffe et al. (1986) between citing and cited countries NBER Patent and Citations Database - NBER 1963-1999
Geographic Distance	Geodesic distance between capitals Distance Database- CEPII
Language	Share (or not) of a common language between two countries (Official or national language, or language spoken by at least 20\% of the country) Distance Database - CEPII
Colonial Presence	Presence colonial (or not) of technology source country in the developing country, for a long time and with a substantial participation in the colonized country's government. Distance Database- CEPII

All variables are converted in constant dollar.

A.3.5 Classification of the Sectors According to their Sectoral Intensity

High Technology	**ISIC Rev2**
Aerospace	3845
Computers, Office Machinery	3825
Electronics-communication	3832
Pharmaceutical	3522
Middle-High Technology	
Scientific Instruments	385
Motor Vehicles	3843
Electrical machinery	383-3832
Chemicals	351+352+3522
Other Transport Equipment	3842+3844+3849
Non-Electrical Machinery	382-3825
Middle-Low Technology	
Rubber and Plastic Products	355+356
Shipbuilding	3841
Other Manufacturing	39
Non-Ferrous Metals	372
Non-Metallic Mineral Products	36
Fabricated Metal Products	381
Petroleum Refining	351+354
Ferrous Metals	371
Low Technology	
Paper Printing	34
Textile and Clothing	32
Food, Beverages and Tobacco	31
Wood and Furniture	33

Source: Hatzicronougou (1997)

Changes in Estonian Export Product Variety

Laura Ruud, Tartu University, Estonia[1]

1 Introduction

Estonia is considered to be a successful catching-up economy that has efficiently reallocated its production factors after the changes in economic and political environment in the beginning of 1990s. One of the important contributors to the fast adjustment has been the reorientation of exports to new markets. However, the sustainability of the current strong export growth, including the changes in export structure, has remained open to debate.

Recent studies have confirmed "the role of export variety fostering economic growth of the East European transition economies" (see Funke / Ruhwedel 2005). Special attention is paid to the export product variety in capital-intensive industries which – together with investment – is seen as a central element in export-led growth models (see Ventura 1997).

The available estimates of product variety of Estonian exports are based on relatively aggregated level analyses and hide some facts that are essential for an adequate assessment of recent developments. Bearing in mind the importance of export product variety in export-led growth, a more detailed understanding of recent developments in Estonian exports could provide us with better basis for the policy decisions. This is particularly true for the formulation of the balanced sectoral and entrepreneurship policy, supporting economic growth.

The objective of the current analysis is to estimate the changes in product variety in Estonian manufacturing exports over the period 1994–2004. The focus is on sectoral and destination country effects, taking into account the technology intensity of industries. In order to efficiently exploit the detailed information of product-level export data, the econometric analogue of the traditional shift-share approach has been applied.

The remainder of this paper is structured as follows. Section 2 provides an overview of recent results in the field of product differentiation in foreign trade. The third section introduces the methodology applied, whereas the data and the general development of Estonian exports are outlined in sections 4 and 5 respectively. The hypotheses and the model are described in the Section 6. Section 7 presents the estimation results, followed by concluding remarks in Section 8.

---

[1] Reseacher (MA) at Faculty of Economics and Business Administration, Tartu University. E-mail: laura.ruud@ut.ee

2 Theory and Recent Empirical Findings

Product differentiation in foreign trade has been analysed mainly in the context of the New Trade Theory that takes into account market imperfections, mostly referring to monopolistic competition in international trade (see Helpman 1988 and Borkakoti 1998). After the opportunities of inter-industry specialisation have been exploited (e.g. specialisation in textiles or machinery), intra-industry specialisation in similar products (e.g. specialisation in sports cars or passenger cars) takes over in further integrating international trade (Balassa 1966). The trade partners specialise in similar products belonging to the same industry in order to differentiate the exported products from the production of the destination country. Intra-industry specialisation can be estimated generally in two ways (Segnana / Bianco 2004), based on:

- the variety of products or
- the quality of products.

Product differentiation in foreign trade generally refers to specialisation in the trade of similar products with similar quality, increasing the heterogeneity of products. According to Greenaway et al. (1994) trade in similar products of similar quality is referred to as horizontal intra-industry trade while the trade in similar products of differentiated quality is called vertical intra-industry trade.

The specialisation in quality is measured in comparison to the trade partner, i.e. countries trade either similar quality products or different quality products. The specialisation in variety can be measured in comparison to a trade partner (e.g. CES production function approach, see Feenstra 1994), but also as a count-based approach for one country (number of products produced, exported or imported).

There are no established theoretical frameworks explaining export variety except for the intra-industry trade approach. In recent studies export variety has been analysed mainly in the context of its impact on economic growth, as in Ventura (1997) and Jones (1998). Ventura (1997) shows in his theoretical setup how economic growth is driven by physical capital accumulation and that countries specialise according to comparative advantage, explaining export-led growth. He also notes that exporting manufacturers specialising in capital-intensive sectors may have played a key role in the rapid East Asian growth process. As Funke / Ruhwedel (2005) conclude: "despite of diminishing returns to capital, the rate of return to capital was prevented from dwindling to very low values a result of this specialisation".

Jones (1998) also acknowledges that countries investing more strongly in physical capital tend to be richer. A simple semi-endogenous growth model is provided in which economies become more productive as a widening of the spectrum of available products occurs. The model emphasizes the importance of product variety since the steady state income level depends on the degree of product variety. In the model, increased product variety accelerates per capita income levels by more fully realising dynamic economies of scale. Similarly, Feenstra / Kee (2006) introduce a growth model with similar aspects as the Melitz (2003) monopolistic competition model. They show that in the presence of monopolistic competition and heterogeneous firms relative export variety enters positively in the GDP function. According to empirical estimations by Feenstra / Kee (2006) a doubling of export variety leads to a 3.4% increase in the country's productivity. Another interesting finding is by Hummels / Klenow (2005) who show that when decomposing trade growth into:

a) new products exported and
b) existing products exported in larger amounts,

new products account for two-thirds of the increase in exports of larger economies and one-third of their increase in imports.

For Estonia, intra-industry specialisation has been estimated in the context of matching exports and import flows[2] in trade with the European Union (EU) (see Gabrisch / Segnana 2003, Backé / Thimann 2004 and Ehrlich 2004), applying the methodology of Grubel and Lloyd (1975). The share of matching trade in total Estonian trade with the EU remains below the EU average.

Export variety has received less attention than matching trade flows. For Eastern European transition economies export variety has been measured relative to the export variety in the U.S., based on CES production function approach (Funke / Ruhwedel 2005). The results for 14 Eastern European countries show that export variety in Estonia lags far behind that in Czech Republic, Hungary, Poland and even Russia and Lithuania, but is leading Latvia. As an alternative measure, Funke / Ruhwedel (2005) apply product counts. Denoted as "the simple count-based measure", this alternative method leads to a similar ranking of the countries, except for indicating a higher diversity in Estonian exports compared to Lithuanian exports. Both measures show a gradual annual increase in export variety over in 1990s, with the exception of the peak in 1995 and the following slight decrease in 1996. The authors also distinguish between capital intensive and labour intensive goods, and find much higher export variety in capital intensive goods in Estonia. For labour intensive

[2] Intra-industry trade is defined as two-way trade (exports and imports) in the same product categories between two trade partners. For example, if a country both exports and imports electronic products, the trade (the sum of electronic products' exports and imports) is categorised as intra-industry trade.

goods, a huge drop in export variety was registered for Estonia in 1998 with a gradual increase afterwards, reflecting the impact of the Russian crisis.

These studies, however, still remain at a relatively aggregated level in their approach to product variety. The following analysis takes a more detailed approach to distinguish the sources of the increase of product variety in Estonian exports.

3 Methodology

In the current analysis, a change in exports product variety is defined as the increase or decrease in the number of different exported products belonging to a certain industry. In addition to differentiation of exported products, the variety of destination countries plays an important role. The larger the number of destination countries certain products are exported to, the larger the market share of the respective exporter and the larger the export volumes (ceteris paribus). We may observe an increase in the variety of exported products of a certain industry or we may find an increase in the number of exported products to a certain destination country. To quantify the role of industries (overall increase in the number of exported products belonging to a certain industry) and the role of destination countries (overall increase in the number of different products exported to a certain destination country) the application of the econometric analogue of the shift-share approach seems reasonable.

The shift-share approach has originally been applied in regional studies in order to differentiate sectoral, regional and/or temporal effects (see e.g. Blien / Wolf 2002). In regional studies, the shift-share approach is applied mainly in employment studies (Blien / Wolf 2002 on Germany and Patterson 1991 on New Zealand) and wage differentiation studies (Gera / Grenier 1994 on Canada and Kahn 1998 on several European developed economies). In the current paper, a similar approach has been applied. The increase in the number of different exported products belonging to a certain industry can be interpreted as a sectoral effect, whereas the increase in the number of different products exported to a certain destination country can be seen as a regional effect. Distinguishing the respective increases over several time periods, we can also measure effects for each time period, affecting all industries and destination countries (temporal effects).

The econometric analogue of the shift-share approach has been developed in order to determine the statistical significance of the respective effects. In addition, the regression-based approach enables us to add additional explanatory variables to the model.

The basic model is constructed as a regression model where the explanatory variables are the dummy-variables having the value one for a certain industry, region (destination country) or time period, and the value zero for all the other observations (see Patterson 1991). The variable under analysis – the increase in the number of exported products – has up to three dimensions: each exported product belongs to a certain industry and it is exported to a certain destination country in a certain time period. In order to capture all three dimensions, three sets of dummy-variables are included to the model in the full econometric analogue of the shift-share approach: sectoral, regional and temporal sets of dummy-variables. This leads to:

(1) $$Y_{irt} = \beta_i \cdot d_{irt} + \kappa_r \cdot \hat{d}_{irt} + \lambda_t \cdot \tilde{d}_{irt} + \varepsilon_{irt},$$

where the notations are as follows:

- Y_{irt} – the increase in the number of exported products belonging to industry i and exported to country r in time period t;
- β_i – the coefficient of the dummy-variables d_{irt} obtaining the value 1 if a certain observation expresses the exported product belonging to the sector i and obtaining the value 0 otherwise; i=1….I, where I denotes the total number of industries included to the analysis;
- κ_r – the coefficient for the dummy-variables $\hat{d}_{irt}$ obtaining the value 1 if a certain observation expresses the product exported to the country r and obtaining the value 0 otherwise; r=1…R, where R denotes the total number of destination countries included to the analysis;
- λ_t – the coefficient for dummy-variables $\tilde{d}_{irt}$ obtaining the value 1 if a certain observation expresses the export of the product in time period t and obtaining the value 0 otherwise; t=1…T, where T denotes the total number of time periods included to the analysis;
- ε_{irt} – the residuals.

In order to simplify the interpretation of the estimation results, the authors of regional studies have suggested restricted least squares estimation (see Blien / Wolf 2002). Restricted least squares estimation or constrained least squares regression (Patterson 1991) makes it possible to directly estimate the impact of each industry, region or time period on the observed variable. The estimation method of ordinary least squares (OLS) does not enable direct estimation of all the effects simultaneously as the effects are measured with respect to the omitted dummy-variable as the reference value. All dummy-variables cannot be included in OLS-estimation as it leads to perfect multicollinearity.

Restricted least squares estimation allows for inclusion of all the dummy-variables into the model and to escape the perfect multicollinearity problem (Greene / Seaks 1991). It makes it possible to explicitly impose restrictions of the hypothesis in the regression, resulting in a restricted least squares estimator (Greene 1997). To escape perfect multicollinearity, the sum of all dummy variables belonging to the same category (either industry, destination country or time period effects) is restricted to be equal to zero (see Patterson 1991 and Blien / Wolf 2002):

(2) $\beta_1+\beta_2+\ldots+\beta_I = 0$

(3) $\kappa_1+\kappa_2+\ldots+\kappa_R = 0$

(4) $\lambda_1+\lambda_2+\ldots+\lambda_T = 0.$

For the econometric quantification of industry, destination country and time period effects, the estimation procedure follows traditional panel data estimation, where the sums of the coefficients of dummy-variables are restricted to equal to zero for each category. The application of restricted least squares estimation is not limited to models with several sets of dummy-variables, nor do the restrictions have to be equal to zero. However, in the current approach, the objective is to measure the industry and destination country effects of changes in export product variety. Therefore the restrictions are applied as explained by the equations (2)–(4).

4 Data

To estimate product variety in Estonian exports, disaggregated bilateral foreign trade statistics of Estonian exports are necessary. In Estonia the foreign trade statistics are collected based on customs declarations and, starting from May 2004 (since the membership of the European Union), also on questionnaires of National Statistics Estonia on foreign trade with the European Union member states. The current paper uses the internal disaggregated database of trade statistics available in Bank of Estonia.[3]

As the focus of the study is on differentiated products, it is important to limit the data to special trade (excluding trade with free economic zones included in general trade statistics) and normal trade (excluding re-exports) of manufactured products (Classification of economic activities in the European Community NACE Rev. 1.1 at 2-digit level the levels 15–36). The highest

[3] The database is the basis of compiling trade balance of balance of payment statistics, not accessible publicly.

available disaggregated product level is the 6-digit level of the Harmonised System (HS) classification that is used in the following analysis.

From the perspective of competitiveness and sustainable economic growth the changes in product variety of high-technology products is especially important. In order to estimate the relevance of changes in product variety of technology-intensive products in Estonian exports, the grouping of industries according to the Eurostat classification of manufacturing industries by technology intensity has been used. Eurostat classifies all manufacturing industries into four technology-intensity based groups (see also Appendix 1):

1) high-technology (aerospace, pharmaceuticals etc.),
2) medium-high-technology (electrical machinery, motor vehicles, etc.),
3) medium-low-technology (rubber and plastic products, non-metallic mineral products, etc),
4) low-technology (food, beverages and tobacco, textile and clothing, etc.).

The Eurostat classification of economic activities by technology intensity is based mainly on NACE 2-digit level aggregation. From chemicals (NACE 24) the pharmaceuticals (NACE 24.4) are classified as high-technology products, while the remaining chemicals are classified as medium-high-technology products. NACE 3-digit classification is also applied for transportation equipment, classifying aerospace (35.3) as high-technology, shipbuilding as medium-low-technology (35.1) and other transportation equipment as medium-high-technology industries.

Estonian foreign trade statistics are product-group based and are classified according to NACE 2-digit aggregation level but not according NACE 3-digit aggregation level. In order to follow the technology intensity classification of Eurostat, pharmaceutical (NACE 24.4), aerospace (NACE 35.3) and shipbuilding (NACE 35.1) products are distinguished by the verbal product description in trade statistics in the following analysis. Despite its subjectivity, this is the only possible approach the to NACE 3-digit industries product classification. As the descriptions on 6-digit aggregation level are relatively detailed the possible bias should not be very significant and therefore should not seriously influence the results of the analysis. The number of industries included in the analysis is 27, distinguished according to Eurostat's economic activities technology intensity based classification (NACE 2-digit and 3-digit).

Among destination countries, 108 and 161 different countries (including classifications "unknown") are distinguished in 1994 and 2004, respectively. Not all products exported in 1994 were also exported on 2004 and vice versa, the same applies for destination countries. Among destination countries, 213 countries are distinguished, exports registered either in 1994, in 2004, or in both years.

Product variety is measured on annual basis as changes across quarters or months can be affected by seasonal developments. In the following analysis the annual data of 1994 and 2004 are used, as Estonia has reliable foreign trade statistics starting from 1994 and the latest available full year data are from 2004.

5 General Developments in Estonian Exports

Estonia is a small open economy, merchandise exports constituting 60% of GDP in 2005[4] (53% in 2004) according to national accounts statistics. Over the last decade, the exports share in GDP has gradually increased, while, despite of some volatility, remaining above 45%, except for 1996 when export to GDP ratio dropped to 40%.

Normal exports in manufacturing (excluding re-exports) constitute the major share of total merchandise exports. They constitute over 70% of total Estonian merchandise exports in recent years, being generally about 60% over the decade, i.e. about 30% of GDP. Manufacturing exports have been relatively concentrated: three industries being responsible for more than 40% of total manufacturing exports, both in 2004 and 1994.[5] The food industry and wood and pulp industry and have been among the largest exporters over the last 10 years. Additionally, electronics-communication industry has become one of the main contributors to exports in recent years, while the relatively high share of the chemicals industry in 1994 has somewhat decreased over the years.[6]

In terms of export product variety, the ranking of industries does not overlap with the ranking in terms of export value. The most diversified in terms of HS 6-digit products has been the export of non-electrical machinery. Over the 10 years, the industry contributed up to 5% of total manufacturing export value. Of total number of HS 6-digit products exported, non-electrical machinery products constitute 11-12%, comparable to diversification of textiles, chemicals and food industries (see Figure 1).

Although the increase in export value of an industry can be related to introduction of new products exported, it does not mean that the largest exporting industries have the highest number of products exported. For example,

---

[4] Preliminary foreign trade statistics, subject to revisions.

[5] For relative proportions of industries in exports see also Appendix 2.

[6] Here and afterwards the trade statistics of 2004 are not directly comparable to the previous trade statistics, as since Estonian membership in the European Union (May 2004) the trade data collection has changed. However, as there are no more reliable trade statistics, the present estimates are based on the best available data.

in case of food industry the value of exports amounted to 25% of total manufacturing exports while food products constituted only 12% of total manufacturing products exported. Also, the exports of one of largest the exporters, the wood and pulp industry, have a relatively low diversification in products, wood and pulp products constituting 2% of total manufacturing products exported. The same applies for electronics-communication products, the share of which in total products exported has remained at 2% although its contribution to total manufacturing export value has increased to 16%.

Figure 1: Industries with the Highest Number of Exported Products in Estonia 2004 and 1994

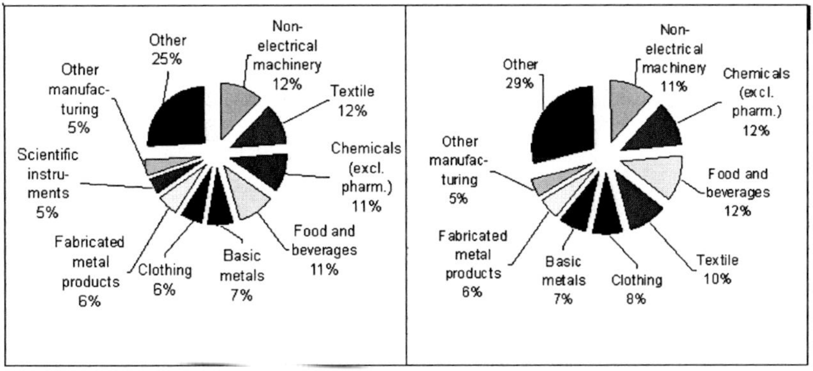

Source: Foreign trade database of Bank of Estonia, own calculations.

In terms of relative concentration, product diversification has been distributed somewhat more evenly across industries compared to export value (see also Appendix 2). In contrast to the remarkable changes in relative shares of industries in exporting value, there are no large changes over time in relative shares of products exported across industries. The total number of exported manufacturing products increased by 20% between 1994 and 2004. The largest absolute increase took place in the textiles industry. Large relative increases of exports product variety in electronics-communication and wood and pulp industries match the strong increases in export value of these industries, confirming the positive correlation between two growth rates.

In the distribution of export products according to technology-intensity based groups, the relative shares of four groups have remained relatively unchanged, confirming the results discussed above (see Figure 2). Products of low-technology intensity industries still account for 40% of total manufacturing products exported, while the share of such industries in export value has dropped from 50% to 40%. Low-technology intensity industries include food, textiles, clothing and other manufacturing products that are among the industries with the highest product diversification (see Figure 1), but also the wood and pulp industry with a relatively low product variety but a high contribution to export value (see Appendix 1).

Figure 2: Distribution of Export Products by Technology Intensity (Number of Products)

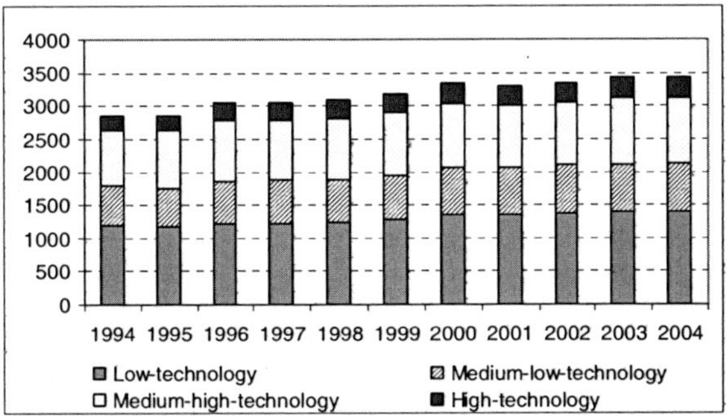

Source: Foreign trade database of Bank of Estonia, own calculations.

The share of the exported products of medium-high-technology intensity industries (including high product variety industries in Estonia: chemicals and non-electrical machinery) has remained 30%, while the share of products of medium-low-technology intensity industries (incl. basic metals and fabricated metal products) still constitutes 20%. The share of high-technology intensity products (incl. scientific instruments) has remained at about 10%. In the trade statistics, some slight decrease in low-technology products and a slight increase in high-technology intensity products can be distinguished over the years (about 1 percentage point), but as this can also be due to small errors in data collection, so no firm conclusions can be drawn.

Across the destination countries the relative shares of the countries or country groups for the exported products cannot be distinguished, as one product can be exported to several destination countries. However, in terms of export value, Estonian exports are strongly affected by the reorientation from Eastern neighbours (Russia, Ukraine) to the European Union members (Finland, Sweden). Exports to the EU-15 have increased from 40% of total manufacturing exports to 60%, the share of new European member states (NMS) has remained around 20%.

Ranking the industries according to their exported products variety and taking into account the respective number of destination countries, leads to results that differ somewhat from the distribution of industries based on the number of products exported. Adding up the number products exported to all destination countries (allowing products to overlap across destination countries) for each industry, the food industry acquires the first position, indicating the highest product variety, adjusted for the number of destination countries. The changes in the positions of other industries remain relatively small.

In the following analysis the emphasis is on the variable indicating the change in the number of products belonging to a certain industry and exported to a certain destination country, related to changes in the product variety adjusted for the number of destination countries. That is, the variable under analysis increases both when a new product is introduced (not available in the total product range in the previous period) and when the previously available product is exported to the certain destination country in the later period (but not exported in the previous period).

6 Hypotheses and Models

The objective of the current analysis is to estimate Estonian manufacturing specialisation over the period 1994–2004. The aspects of interest are the change in the number of manufacturing products exported across destination countries and the impact of reorientation of exports from Eastern countries to Western neighbours, especially to the European Union countries. We could expect that Estonia has developed towards more technology intensive exports and that the increased international integration has forced it to specialise on more heterogeneous exports, especially in foreign trade with its main trade partners. The hypotheses for testing are the following:

1) over 10 years, export specialisation has increased more in high-technology products compared to low-technology products;
2) export specialisation has increased more in the direction of the main trade partners and countries belonging to the European Union compared to the other countries.

The hypotheses are tested by applying an econometric shift-share type estimation technique, estimating the impact of industry and destination country effects. The number of time periods is restricted to one and therefore no temporal effects are measured.

The measurement unit is the increase in the number of 6-digit level products belonging to the industry *i* (NACE 2-digit level) and exported to destination country *r* over the time period 1994 to 2004. For industry effects, 27 industries are distinguished based on technology intensity. They are aggregated into four larger groups: high-technology (HT), medium-high-technology (MHT), medium-low-technology (MLT) and low-technology (LT) industries. Among destination countries 213 countries are distinguished that are grouped in two ways:

1) 10 main export partners in 1994 and 2004, respectively (altogether 12 countries), and the other countries (r=1…13),
2) four main country groups in terms of exports (r= 1…4):
   - European Union member states before May 2004 (EU-15),
   - new European member states after May 2004 (NMS),
   - countries belonging to the Commonwealth of Independent States (CIS),
   - other countries.

The country groups are formed in order to capture all relevant effects. The data coverage does not enable us to estimate the effects on all the 213 destination countries due to an insufficient number of degrees of freedom.

Taking into account the industry and country groupings, two modifications of the above-introduced model are estimated:

(5) $$Y_{ir} = \beta_i \cdot d_{ir} + \kappa_r \cdot \hat{d}_{ir} + \varepsilon_{ir}, \quad i=1...27,\ r=1...13$$

(6) $$Y_{ir} = \beta_i \cdot d_{ir} + \kappa_r \cdot \hat{d}_{ir} + \varepsilon_{ir}, \quad i=1...4,\ r=1...4$$

The first equation, Equation (5), denotes the model with 27 manufacturing industries and 13 destinations (10 main export partners in 1994 and 2004 and the other countries). The second equation, Equation (6), captures the effects of four groups of industries grouped according to technology intensity and the effects of four country groups (EU-15, NMS, CIS and the other countries).

There are relatively many observations where the exports of some industry products to some destination country are zero either in 1994 or 2004 or both years. In order to include as many observations as possible, the growth of the number of 6-digit level products belonging to a certain industry is measured as follows:

(7) $$G_{ir} = \frac{N_{ir}^{t} - N_{ir}^{t-1}}{\frac{N_{ir}^{t} + N_{ir}^{t-1}}{2}}$$

where G_{ir} denotes the growth rate of the number 6-digit level products belonging to the industry i and exported to the country r. N_{ir} indicates the respective number of products in the years t (2004) and t-1 (1994). The use of this growth rate was suggested by Davis et al. (1996) and has been applied also by Kolko (2002) and Bellini et al. (2003).

The data for the model can be interpreted as a 213x27 matrix with 213 destination countries and 27 industries. The aggregated groups of industries (HT, MHT, MLT and LT) and destination countries (EU-15, NMS, CIS and other countries, or the 10 main trade partners and other countries) are distinguished by respective dummy-variables. The models are estimated with STATA 8.2.

7 Estimation Results

The regression analysis covered 1808 observations of changes in the number of HS 6-digit level products belonging to one of the manufacturing industries i and exported to one of the destination countries r over the periods 1994 and 2004. More than two thirds of the potential observations (213 destination countries and 27 industries) were dropped due to the missing exports in both the base year and the end year.

The estimation results for the industry effects show that about half of the industries have a significant effect on the increase in product diversification in manufacturing exports, i.e. the increase in the number of products exported (see Table 1). The effect is mainly positive. At the same time the estimation results show that the effects of technology intensity based groups of industries (Equation (6)) are all statistically significant except for medium-low-technology industries.

The results of industry effects from the two different models (Equation (5) and Equation (6)) are consistent for the case of medium-high-technology and low-technology industries, where the significant positive effect dominates. The results for medium-low technology and high-technology industries are not very consistent, especially for high-technology industry where the first model (Equation (5)) suggests a statistically insignificant effect but the second model (Equation (6)) suggests a statistically highly significant negative impact. Due to varying results of the two models, the increase in product variety in high-technology industry exports cannot be confirmed. However, with higher confidence the statistically significant increase in the product variety in low-technology industries exports can be observed.

The estimation results for destination country effects show high statistical significance of all three regions analysed (see Table 2). Product variety in exports to the EU-15 has increased as expected, product variety has also increased in exports to the countries not included to any country group. With overall exports decreased to CIS countries, the product variety in exports to CIS countries has also decreased. Somewhat surprisingly, the product variety of exports to new European Union member states has decreased compared to 1994.

Table 1: Estimation Results of Industry Effects

Industry group	Industry coefficients (Eq. 6)	Number of industries with statistically significant impact (Eq. 5)[7]	Number of industries with statistically insignificant impact (Eq. 5)	Total number of industries
High-technology	-0.186***[8]	1(1)[9]	4	5
Medium-high-technology	0.114**	4(4)	3	7
Medium-low-technology	-0.054	3(2)	3	6
Low- technology	0.126***	5(4)	4	9
Total		14(11)	13	27

Source: Own calculations.

Table 2: Estimation Results of Destination Country Effects

Country group	Coefficients of country regions (Eq. 6)	Countries with statistically significant impact (Eq. 5)[10]	Countries with statistically insignificant impact (Eq. 5)
EU-15	0.394***	Finland(-)[11] United Kingdom(+) Denmark(+)	Sweden (-) Germany(-) Netherlands(+)
NMS	-0.381***	Latvia(-)	Lithuania(-) Hungary(-)
CIS	-1.156***	Russia(-) Ukraine(+)	
Others	1.142***	Norway (+) Others (+)	
Total		14(11)	13

Source: Own calculations.

[7] At least 10% significance level.
[8] *** significant at 1% level, ** significant at 5% level.
[9] The number in brackets indicates the number of positive coefficients.
[10] At least 10% significance level.
[11] (-) denotes negative impact on specialisation, (+) denotes positive impact on specialisation.

Due to technical reasons, it was not possible to estimate the country effects of all destination countries, therefore only the effects of the 10 main export partners are available. The decrease in product variety in exports to Russia is consistent with overall reduction of exports to it. At the same time, the decrease in product variety in exports to Finland and Sweden, the main trade partners of Estonia in recent years, is relatively unexpected. The results contradict the hypothesis that increasing integration of two economies leads to higher product diversification in order to exploit the benefits of intra-industry trade. The reduction in exports product variety to the main trade partners, Finland and Sweden, may be related to exploiting the benefits of economies of scale. However, a detailed analysis across industries is required to draw more solid conclusions.

Assuming the rational behaviour of exporters, the above estimation results reflect the consequences of rational choices in the economic situation in 2004 relative to 1994. Mainly due to institutional reasons (introduction of trade agreements with the EU, high customs tariffs for exports to Russia and the Russian financial crisis) the exports were re-oriented to European countries, i.e. to the countries that have relative advantage in producing and exporting capital-intensive (and technology-intensive) goods. Due to its relative advantage in labour-intensive goods arising from lower labour costs, Estonian exporters invested mainly in labour-intensive (also low-technology intensive) industries that resulted in a statistically significant increase in exported products of low-technology intensive industries.

While the difference of labour costs in Estonia and its main trade partners decreases over time and the capital abundance increases through extensive investments, the main investments should shift to more technology-intensive industries. The respective shift is somewhat confirmed by the statistically significant increase in exported products of medium-high-technology intensive industries (chemicals, non-electrical machinery). The statistically significant decrease in the number of exported products of high-technology intensive industries may indicate the currently rational shift towards low-technology intensive industries, exploiting efficiently the advantage of (still) relatively low labour costs. The current results from the comparison of the years 2004 and 1994 show that by 2004, the relative advantage of Estonia in low-technology industries was still highly significant.

In the coming years, when the advantage of relatively low labour costs diminishes or disappears, investments and, therefore, export product diversity are expected to increase mainly in higher-technology intensive industries. Concerning the importance of sustainable export growth for the economic development of a small open economy, governmental institutions could favour initiatives of product development in high-technology intensive industries. This would ensure the presence of mature products by the time the relative advantage of labour intensive industries has disappeared. The role of the government could be most relevant in providing information and easing possible market rigidities. The current analysis quantifies sectoral and regional effects of changes in product variety, allowing the assessment of the statistical significance of the effects. In order to verify the proposed reasons for the described developments additional explanatory variables need to be tested. This could be done by extending the current model.

8 Conclusions

Developing and deepening trade relations are expected to lead to higher diversification of products in foreign trade, including exports. Measuring product diversification as the increase in the number of exported products belonging to a certain industry, the estimation results of industry and destination country effects show relatively mixed results for Estonian exports.

The estimation results indicate that Estonian exports do not show an increase in product diversification or product variety in high-technology industries but rather in low-technology industries. This can be considered as being consistent with the Estonian relative advantage in labour intensive or low-technology intensive industries compared to its main trade partners' capital abundance. In order to remain competitive, Estonian exports are expected to move towards increasing investments in (and accompanying product variety of) high-technology intensive industries, as the available capital is expected to increase over time.

The estimated destination country effects show that the product variety in exports to the main trade partners markets has not increased but rather decreased, opposite to what could be expected after more than 10 years of intensive trade relations with Estonia's Nordic neighbours. The decrease in product variety may be related to the exploitation of economies of scale, but this needs a more detailed analysis.

After describing the changes in export product variety, the reasons for the current patterns need to be determined. They could be tested by adding explanatory variables to the currently applied regression analysis. For policy purposes the possibilities of influencing product variety need to be tested. The analysis confirms that at least by 2004, the export variety reflected product development concentrating on low- rather than high-technology intensive products. In order to ensure a sustainable growth of exports, the government could favour the development high-technology intensive products. Until 2004, production factors seem still to be engaged mainly with short-term perspective activities and the potential effect of directive government policies has remained high. The role of policies could be especially important in providing more information and reducing market distortions.

References

Backé P. / Thimann C. (2004): The acceding countries' strategies towards ERM II and the adoption of the euro: an analytical review, European Central Bank Occasional Paper No 10, European Central Bank, Frankfurt am Main, Germany.

Balassa, B. (1966): Tariff reductions and trade in manufactures among industrial countries, in: American Economic Review, Volume 56, pp. 466–473.

Bellini, E. / Ottaviano, G. / Pinelli, D. (2003): The ICT revolution: opportunities and risks for the Mezzogiorno, Working Paper No. 86, Fondazione Eni Enrico Mattei, Milan, Italy.

Blien, U. / Wolf, K. (2002): Regional development of employment in eastern Germany: an analysis with an econometric analogue to shift-share techniques, in: Papers in Regional Sciences, Volume 81, pp. 391–414.

Borkakoti, J. (1988): International Trade, Causes and Consequences: An Empirical and Theoretical Text, Macmillan Press Ltd., Hong Kong.

Davis S. / Haltiwanger, J. / Schuh, S. (1996): Job Creation and Destruction, MIT Press, Cambridge, MA, USA.

Ehrlich, L. (2004): Eesti integratsioon Euroopa Liiduga tööstusharusisese kaubavahetuse järgi, in: Economic Policy Perspectives of Estonia in the European Union, Reports-papers of the XII Scientific and Educational Conference, Tartu-Värska, 1.–3. July 2004, edited by M. Tallinn, Berliner WirtschaftsVerlag, Berlin, Germany, pp. 425–432.
In Estonian: Estonian integration to the EU according to intra-industry trade.

Eurostat (2006): Economic, Science & Tech. and Employment statistics, Eurostat Metadata in SDDS format: Base Page, Luxembourg. [http://europa.eu.int/estatref/info/sdds/en/htec/htec_base.htm]

Feenstra, R. (1994): New product varieties and the measurement of international prices, in: American Economic Review, Volume 84, pp. 157–177.

Feenstra, R. / Kee, H. (2006): Export variety and country productivity: estimating the monopolistic competition model with endogenous productivity, World Bank Policy Research Group and University of California, Davis, CA, USA.

Funke, M. / Ruhwedel, R. (2005): Export variety and economic growth in East European transition economies, in: Economics of Transition, Volume 13, pp. 25–50.

Gabrisch, H. / Segnana, M. (2003): Vertical and horizontal trade patterns of intra-industry trade between EU and candidate countries, IWH Sonderheft 2/2003, Institute für Wirtschaftsforschung, Halle/Saale, Germany.

Gera, S. / Grenier, G. (1994): Interindustry wage differentials and efficiency wages: aome Canadian evidence, in Canadian Journal of Economics, Volume 27, pp. 81–100.

Greenaway, D. / Hine, R. / Milner, C. (1994): Country-specific factors and the pattern of horizontal and vertical intra-industry trade in the UK, in: Weltwirtschaftliches Archiv, No. 130.

Greene, W. (1997): Econometric Analysis, 3rd edition, Prentice Hall, Englewood Cliffs, NJ, USA.

Greene, W. / Seaks, T. (1991): The restricted least squares estimator: a pedagogical note, in: Review of Economics and Statistics, Volume 73, pp. 563–567.

Grubel, H. / Lloyd, P. (1975): Intra-Industry Trade: The Theory and Measurement of International Trade in Differentiated Products, Wiley, New York, USA.

Helpman, E. (1988): Imperfect Competition and International Trade: Evidence from Fourteen Industrial Countries, in: International Competitivness, edited by A. Spence and H. Hazard, Ballinger Publishing Company, Cambridge, MA, USA, pp. 197–220.

Hummels, D. / Klenow, P. (2005): The variety and quality of a nation's trade, in: American Economic Review, Volume 95, pp. 704–723.

Jones, C. (1998): Introduction to Economic Growth, W.W. Norton, New York, USA.

Kahn, L. (1998): Collective bargaining and the interindustry wage structure: international evidence, in: Economica, New Series, Volume 65, pp. 507–534.

Kolko, J. (2002): Silicon mountains, silicon molehills: geographic concentration and convergence of Internet industries in the US, in: Information Economics and Policy, Volume 14, pp. 211–32.

Melitz, M. (2003): The impact of trade on intra-industry reallocations and aggregate industry productivity, in: Econometrica, Volume 71, pp. 1695–1725.

Patterson, M. (1991): A note on the formulation of a full-analogue regression model of the shift-share method, in: Journal of Regional Science, Volume 31, pp. 211–216.

Segnana, M. / Bianco, A. (2004): Openness, domestic production and catch-up of EU accession countries: sectoral versus intra-sectoral results, first draft, presented at the Workshop on "EU integration and the prospects for catch-up development in CEECs", 29–30 May 2004, Budapest, Hungary.

Ventura, J. (1997): Growth and interdependence, in: Quarterly Journal of Economics, Volume 112, pp. 57–84.

Appendix 1: Classification of Industries According to Technological Intensity

Technological intensity group	*NACE*[12] Rev. 1.1 industries
High-technology	Aerospace (*NACE* 35.3) Pharmaceuticals (24.4) Computers, office machinery (30) Electronics-communication (32) Scientific instruments (33)
Medium-high-technology	Electrical machinery (31) Motor vehicles (34) Chemicals (excl. pharmaceuticals) (24 excl. 24.4) Other transport equipment (35.2+35.4+35.5) Non-electrical machinery (29)
Medium-low-technology	Coke, refined petroleum products and nuclear fuel (23) Rubber and plastic products (25) Non-metallic mineral products (26) Shipbuilding (35.1) Basic metals (27) Fabricated metal products (28)
Low-technology	Other manufacturing and recycling (36+37) Wood, pulp, paper products, printing and publishing (20+21+22) Food, beverages and tobacco (15+16) Textile and clothing (17+18+19)

Source: Eurostat.

[12] *NACE* – Classification of economic activities in the European Community.

Appendix 2: Distribution of Export Indicators Across Industries

Industry	Number of products exported		Value of exports		Number of products exported by destination countries	
	2004	1994	2004	1994	2004	1994
Non-electrical machinery	12%	12%	5%	3%	10%	10%
Textile	12%	10%	7%	8%	9%	8%
Chemicals (excl. pharmaceuticals)	11%	12%	5%	9%	8%	9%
Food and beverages	11%	12%	9%	25%	18%	14%
Basic metals	7%	7%	6%	8%	4%	4%
Clothing	6%	8%	3%	4%	7%	9%
Fabricated metal products	6%	6%	3%	2%	7%	6%
Scientific instruments	5%	4%	2%	1%	4%	3%
Other manufacturing	5%	5%	7%	6%	5%	6%
Rubber and plastic products	4%	3%	3%	2%	5%	4%
Non-metallic mineral products	4%	4%	2%	4%	3%	4%
Electrical machinery	4%	3%	4%	1%	5%	3%
Paper products	3%	3%	2%	1%	2%	3%
Electronics-communication	2%	2%	16%	1%	3%	2%
Wood and pulp	2%	2%	16%	9%	3%	3%
Leather products	2%	2%	1%	1%	2%	3%
Motor vehicles	1%	2%	6%	8%	2%	3%
Computers, office machinery	1%	1%	0%	1%	1%	1%
Pharmaceuticals	1%	1%	0%	0%	1%	1%
Printing and publishing	1%	1%	1%	0%	1%	1%
Other transport equipment	1%	1%	0%	1%	1%	0%
Coke, refined petroleum products and nuclear fuel	0%	0%	2%	4%	1%	0%
Shipbuilding	0%	0%	1%	2%	0%	1%
Aerospace	0%	0%	1%	1%	0%	0%
Tobacco	0%	0%	0%	0%	0%	0%
Total	100%	100%	100%	100%	100%	100%

Source: Foreign trade database of Bank of Estonia, own calculations.

Small Firms and Diverging Regions: The Case of Poland

Alan Mulhern, Kingston University, UK.

1 Introduction

The Polish economy has developed powerfully since the 1989 Transitional Economic Programme commenced. A significant contribution to Polish performance has been the small business stratum. Accompanying this development have been growing regional disparities in macroeconomic performance. This paper wishes to test a hypothesis that regions with differences in GDP per capita will also have different levels of development of the small firm stratum. Small firm development is conceived of as a range of variables that include quantitative macro-features of the stratum as a whole in a region (e.g. small firm numbers and employment levels) and qualitative micro-features of small firms (i.e. a range of organisational, behavioural and performance variables). It is expected that more developed regions within Poland will have not only a greater quantitative development in the numbers of small firms and their employment levels, but also a greater qualitative development of the stratum at the micro level of individual small firms[1]. Greater quantitative development of small firms in the more developed region would not be a surprising finding.[2] However differences in the qualitative development levels of small firms across regions is quite another matter. Literature (especially with statistical analysis) showing regional differentiation of small firms with an emphasis on their organisational, behavioural and performance differences is unknown to the author.

---

[1] Other countries will have different evidence, e.g. that economic development will have an inverse relationship with the number of small firms as economies of scale benefit larger firms - we see this particularly at a European level where the north, generally having a higher GDP per capita than the south, has a lower SME population density. In the case of Poland, however, we have been observing a dismantling of its state run sector and an explosion of small firms which have been a major engine of growth.

[2] Although such data is not readily available in Poland it is for certain other selected countries. An inspection of a key small firm web site such as that of the UK's Department of Trade and Industry regional section (http://stats.berr.gov.uk/ed/sme/smestats2005-regspr.pdf) shows the existence of regional differences in the numbers and employment levels of small firms across national space. There is generally a positive correlation between such quantitative measures and regional GDP per capita.

Information at the level of small firms in the regions in Poland is extremely limited. For example, quantitative data on the numbers and employment levels of firms of different size at the regional level is very difficult to obtain.[3] Certainly there is no data on the qualitative functioning of small firms across regions. The purpose of this paper is to use original survey material in order to examine such macro and micro differences in the Polish small firm stratum. Why is this research useful and is it new? Firstly this investigation will provide information in a specific country, Poland, showing a correlation between small firm and regional development, both of which are of considerable importance at the national and the EU level. Regional disparities have widened in Poland and this issue occupies the minds of policy makers at the highest level. The same applies to the small firm issue since the promotion of small firm start up, survival and growth is considered vital for employment and prosperity. Showing an interrelationship between both these areas will be provocative for policy makers. Polish unemployment, situated at 19% of the labour force between in 2002, was the highest in the OECD and its regional labour markets have proved to be tight - for example lack of housing in the regions proved to be a considerable obstacle to regional migration (Deichmann / Henderson 2000). Secondly these questions - unemployment, regional development and small firms - are also of considerable importance at the EU level. Poland's accession to the EU has brought these issues into the European arena. Thirdly an empirical relationship between the level of small firm development and regional development can provoke fresh theoretical thinking.[4] This paper will suggest some theoretical reasons why small firm differences should exist at the regional level.

The structure of this paper is as follows. Section 2 gives the broad background of the two chosen regions used for the survey. Section 3 outlines the survey and describes briefly the general characteristics of Polish small firms emerging from it. Section 4 describes the regional differences in small firms that exist between our two sample regions Pomorskie and Lubelskie. Section 5 reflects on the results and explores theoretical and policy implication. Section 6 concludes.

---

[3] Such information is not available on web sites of the central government statistical agency.

[4] The theory of the firm has little if anything to say on this issue. The Structure-Conduct-Performance model has given us the basis for understanding that firms in different market structures have different conduct and performance features. However there is no application of this theory to regional differences in small firm development - especially of a qualitative nature. Neither does regional economics provide us with insight into this question. Other developments of the theory of the firm e.g. managerial economics, behavioural theories or transactional theory offer little of interest on this topic.

2 Two Contrasting Regions

In order to understand regional differences in small firms in Poland we examine two contrasting areas. The region[5] of Lubelskie is in southeast Poland and borders on the Ukraine. Industrialisation is lighter than in the developed Polish regions and there is a preponderance of large firms in the industrial structure indicating the presence of older industries. Agriculture plays a significant part in the region employing 30% of the workforce, many of whom are under-employed yet trading in the informal sector. Lubelskie is by no means in the last economic rank of Polish regions yet it belongs in that group that has been called Poland B - regions generally east of the Vistula, less developed, more agricultural and bordering the former Soviet Union. Pomorskie, by contrast, is a more developed and industrialised region in northwest Poland and closer to the EU - representative of what has been called Poland A.[6] The two regions have virtually the same population numbers (2.2 million) yet Pomorskie is 50% more urbanised. Besides having an industrial sector 120% larger, Pomorskie's industrial labour productivity is 40% higher than that of Lubelskie's.[7] There is a significant and growing difference between the GDP per capita of Poland A and Poland B (see Figure 1). Unsurprisingly, Pomorskie, which has a 20% higher average wage in its industrial private sector, experiences positive net migration from within Poland while Lubelskie has negative net migration. Important regional differences in small firm development were expected to emerge from surveys of two such contrasting areas.

To demonstrate that these regional macroeconomic differences between Poland A and B are not trivial Figure 1 illustrates that in 1995 the gap between their averaged GDP per capita was 30% but by 2000 it had widened to 40%. Pomorsksie and Lubelskie are clearly located within contrasting economic spaces. Serious divisions in Poland were increasing prior to EU accession and look likely to continue. The Polish Foundation for SME Promotion and Development (2000) comments:

> "Intensified polarisation of regions has been observed in Poland since 1989. It is likely that (EU) integration processes will increase the competitive power of the largest urban

[5] Called voivodships in Poland.

[6] This division into Poland A and B is used, for example, by The Polish Agency for Enterprise Development (2001, p. 63) and the Polish Foundation for SME Promotion and Development (Piasecki et al. 1998, p. 122). There are other more complex models of Polish space but the purpose of this paper is not to examine Polish regional structure but rather to examine small firm differences in two contrasting regions.

[7] These and later figures are taken or calculated from official government statistics, Central Statistical Office: http://www.stat.gov.pl/gus/index_ENG_HTML.htm.

agglomerations (being places where contacts with abroad are concentrated) and border regions, especially in the western border zone...." (p. 121)

Before proceeding to demonstrate a wide range of these regional differences in small firm development we briefly outline the nature of our primary data as well as the general, shared characteristics of small firm in both these regions.

Figure 1: Poland A and Poland B

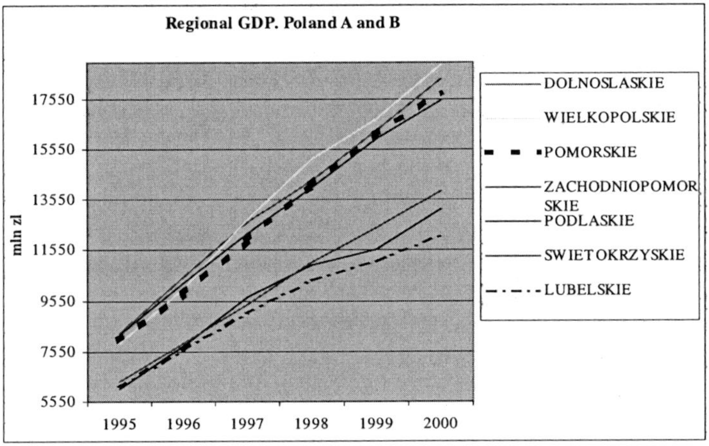

Note: We have averaged the regional GDPs of three provinces representative of Poland A and four provinces representative of Poland B - a sample suggested by The Polish Agency for Enterprise Development (Dzierzanowski / Stachowiak 2001). The regions (vivoidships) representing Poland A are: Dolnośląskie, Wielkopolskie, Pomorskie, Zachodniopomorskie while those representing Poland B are: Podlaskie, Swiętokrzyskie, Lubelskie.
Source: Central Statistical Office, Warsaw: author's calculations.

3 General Characteristics of Lubelskie and Pomorskie Small Firms

A survey[8] of Polish small firms was completed in 1999 in Lubelskie and Pomorskie. A proportionate stratification sampling method was used across the

[8] The survey was financed by the European commissions PHARE ACE PROGRAMME 1997, Contract Number p97-8123-R and organised by Professor Subrata Ghatak of Kingston University.

sectors of industry, trade, construction, transport and services.[9] The sample consisted of 5% of the small firm population in both areas. A small firm was defined as employing between 10-49 workers and thus excluded the myriad of micro firms and the considerable number of medium sized firms in the regions.[10] Separate reports[11] on the small firm picture in Lubelskie on the one hand and Pomorskie on the other were completed. Statistical investigations were also carried out testing for optimism in the small firm stratum.[12] An examination of the regional differences between small firms, the object of this paper, remained to be carried out. Let us firstly briefly outline the overall picture of small firms in the two regions that emerged from the surveys. This will allow us to then better focus on their regional differences.

Examination of the survey material for both Pomorskie and Lubelskie shows that Polish small firms are overwhelmingly young, private sector firms and owned by sole proprietors.[13] Most are self-financing and object to high cost bank loans. They tend to be locally focussed with few export outlets and low in national presence. Most describe themselves as of medium level technology. Few engage in franchising, subcontracting and licensing, especially in less developed regions. Trade union membership is low and there is little investment in training and human capital. Little emphasis is put on management training. Nevertheless they have considerable optimism. Profits and investments were positive for most of the decade though with some deceleration in the latter part. A significant number of firms engaged in recent restructuring. The majority were optimistic concerning their prospects on EU accession and anticipated greater demand and production. Surprisingly they did not fear foreign competition or capital mobility. Many small firms expressed confidence in the prices and quality of their products and were also optimistic concerning expansion in the 1999-2001 period stressing their good knowledge of the market and the high quality of their employees. However disadvantages in marketing and new technologies were evident. Anomalies were also evident - e.g. high expectations concerning the EU coexisted with little preparation for it and even with some protectionist sentiment. Small firm's belief in their employees was reassuring yet there was little investment in the training of their workforce. The surveys indicate optimism reflecting the impressive expansion of the 1990s.

[9] Agricultural small firms were excluded since the inclusion of small farmers would give a misleading impression of recent development in the country.

[10] Data from micro firms was not regarded as reliable as that of small firms - there was an aversion to revealing information that could complicate their position with the authorities.

[11] Blawat et al. (2001) for Lublin / Szreder (2001) for Gdansk.

[12] Ghatak et al. (2001), Ghatak et al. (2003).

[13] Poland has a far higher percentage of sole-proprietorship than other EU countries. It also has a longer age profile, less limited companies and more private sector companies than the Baltic States.

However examination of publications, within and outside of Poland (Central Statistical Office Warsaw, and Smallbone et al. 2001) which have analysed the small firm stratum, shows a picture of a comparatively under-powered small and medium firm stratum that faces considerable difficulties within the EU. The optimism of the Polish small firm stratum is almost certainly indicative of expectations of advantages (FDI and EU funding for example) from joining the EU.

4 Differences between Small Firms in Lubelskie and Pomorskie

Strengthening our expectation that the regional differences in per capita GDP will be reflected in regional differences in small firm development, the Polish Foundation for SME Promotion and Development note that…

> "The high level of economic development in some areas - in terms of GDP per capita - seems side by side with industrialisation, one of the most important factors conducive to concentration of large number of small and medium units." (Piasecki et al. 1998, p. 90)

The Polish Foundation for SME Promotion and Development, while pointing out that the divisions between Poland A and B were widening, noted that SME numbers were growing faster in Poland A than Poland B (Piasecki et al. 1998, p. 63). Clearly macro differences in regional small firm development (e.g. the numbers of firms and employment levels) are operative in regions of differing levels of development.

Our survey of two regions, Pomorskie and Lubelskie, confirmed these quantitative differences. The survey chose 5% of the small firm population in both regions - 239 firms from Pomorskie and 135 from Lubelskie. The small firm population in the regions was 7480 firms in total with 4780 in Pomorskie and 2700 in Lubelskie. Pomorskie, the more developed region, had 70% more small firms than Lubelskie. Total employment in the small firms stratum in the two regions is calculated at 86,040 in Pomorskie and 48,600 in Lubelskie (a 77% difference). The uniqueness of this research is to show that a wide range of qualitative differences in small firms exist in regions of different levels of development.

Substantial differences at the micro level of the organisation (behaviour and performance features) of small firm exist between the two regions. The original questionnaire of the survey contained fifty-eight questions. For the purpose of the test 13 variables were chosen on both practical and theoretical grounds. Not all variables from the original 58 questions were suitable for measurement and inclusion in this test. There were some variables from which clear measurable data was inherently difficult to extract. Some of the questions duplicated one another while others did not lend themselves to classification of regional differences. A number of variables (8) had to be excluded from the test because, although they appeared likely candidates for inclusion, they nevertheless failed the statistical criterion for inclusion (see footnote to Table 1). The choice of our 13 variables was based upon economic reasoning concerning the likely variables that would highlight regional differences in small firm development and which would reflect regional macroeconomic differences. This economic reasoning centred around the belief that the more developed region would produce more competitive dynamics in the small firm stratum (as it would do in all the firm size categories). This reasoning is explained in the following section. We therefore expected that all our variables would indicate significant differences between small firms in the two regions.

Table 1 in the appendix lists the answers to the questions firstly in the form of a percentage response. For example the question concerning the legal structure of the firm established that in our sample population 27% of the small firms in Pomorskie had limited company status compared to 19% in Lubelskie. In the test this proved to be a significant difference between the two regions. To test the significance of the reported difference in a variable between the two regions we used a Difference between Proportions Test and in Table 1 we report the results of this.[14] It was expected that Pomorskie would possess a more developed small firm private sector which could be measured across a range of variables illustrating organisational, behavioural and performance differences. We also expected to find a more dynamic Pomorskie small firm stratum (for example in the degree of change that is occurring within the firm and in their growth intentions).

All 13 of the chosen variables, except two, proved significant at the 99% level. The two exception, limited company status and connection to research

[14] More rigorous econometric methods (e.g. Probit and Logit models) proved to have a very high cost in terms of information loss, the model typically ending with only 162 observations out of the original 376, thus reducing the sample population considerably. The Difference in Proportions Test offered a solution to this information loss by not excluding an observation (i.e. a firm) simply because it failed to answer one question of the total questionnaire - unlike the Probit analysis which did exclude it. Thus the Probit model, despite its rigour, was "exclusionary" and did not give as broad picture of the characteristics of the population, while The Difference in Proportions Test, though less rigorous, proved more inclusive of information and therefore gave a broader picture of the population characteristics. See also comments to Table 1.

institutes, were however significant at the acceptable 95% level. Thus all the included variables proved significant. Here are the details.

Pomorskie has more firms *legally constituted* as limited companies - thus indicating that many of its firms have past beyond the elementary form of legal ownership (sole proprietorship and partnership). This indicates a higher level of small firm development since the transition to limited company status with its higher accounting standards implies greater corporate governance (Cowling 2003) and, of course, greater insulation from bankruptcy.

Network arrangements again showed the greater development level of Pomorskie small firms. Subcontracting (defined as existing when over 25% of total production proceeded from such a source) was considerably higher in Pomorskie, with 38% of its small firms reporting such arrangements (7 times greater than Lubelskie's). Subcontracting indicates greater integration with the local economy, greater levels of contact with foreign firms and methods, and interestingly, greater access to credit - since greater levels of "knownness" to other firms constitutes a reference for banks who can access these other firms for information on a firm applying for credit (Lyons / Bailey 1993). Networking arrangements in relation to both suppliers (defined as formal meetings discussing integrating arrangements between supplier and customer) and connection to research institutes was higher than expected with Pomorskie firms generally having over double the proportion of firms reporting such connections. The higher networking arrangements of Pomorskie small firms with suppliers implies a greater level of integration with the region's competitive dynamics.[15] The equally greater level of connection with research institutes implies a concern with innovation and technological development - both variables which prove significant below.

An important difference between the two regions appeared in the variables indicating *change in small firms*, all of which showed real differences in the test in favour of Pomorskie. The significantly higher levels of investment, innovation, and new technologies of small firms all clearly indicate a more dynamic small firm stratum in the Pomorskie area. Investment in fixed assets between 1998-1999 was at double the level in Pomorskie compared to Lubelskie. Innovation included new or improved products and/or new or improved methods of production. Greater change was once again observed in the Pomorskie region (49%) compared to Lubelskie (30%). The same story was evident for the introduction of new technologies. Clearly these greater levels of investment, technology and innovation are major contributors to economics growth and are part of the picture that help explain regional GDP per capita differences between the two regions. The qualitative differences between small firms in the two regions is striking.

[15] Power of suppliers is one of Porter's five forces.

Sources of financing investment [16]- greater numbers of Pomorskie firms (60%) were re-investing in 1998-1999 compared to Lubelskie (31%). This clearly indicates the greater dynamism of the Pomorskie sector. We expect this investment level to reflect both greater demand in the region and the competitive pressures that oblige firms to invest in order to obtain or maintain competitive advantage. Pomorskie firms are more than twice as likely to be investing from their own profits indicating higher profit levels and more confidence in the future. They are also investing more from their owner's capital surely indicating greater confidence and commitment to the future.

Table 1 shows that greater numbers of Pomorskie firms expected higher growth rates in excess of 5%. Clearly, despite the slowdown in the economy, more growth was expected in the more developed and better located (vis-à-vis the EU) region.

Finally Table 1 shows Pomorskie employees to be more *highly educated* - for example 33% have a university and post-secondary level education compared to Lubelskie's 19%. This variable proved in the test to be a real difference between the regions and is in accord with theoretical expectations that links growth to human capital (Barro / Sali-Martin 1995).

5 Reflections on the Results: Theory, Policy and Limitations

Of the 18 variables chosen for investigation 13 proved to have significant differences (at the 95% level) between the two regions. All of these were according to an expectation based on economic reasoning concerning competitive dynamics at the regional level. This reasoning is as follows. Within a given national economic space different regions have different levels of economic dynamism. Faster growing regions may have certain assets in their favour such as those of natural resources or geography. For example Pomorskie is in Western Poland and therefore nearer to the EU and Germany. It also has access to the Baltic which has allowed shipbuilding and trade to develop. These advantages lead to greater potential for economic growth. Greater levels of population density emerge in the faster growing regions and this is accompanied by rising levels of industrialisation and urbanisation. These produce agglomeration advantages and become externalities that affect further economic growth and development, constituting regionally shared productivity advantages. The evidence from the Pomorskie and Lubelskie regions is that there are different levels of urbanisation and industrialisation in the two regions

[16] Both regions, incidentally reported a comparably low level of bank loan contribution towards their investment. It is not that bank loans are difficult to get, but small firms complain of high interest rates. Excessive demands from the banks in terms of requirements and documentation are also complained about although to a far less extent

and there are also different levels of productivity.[17] So far the two regions would seems to fit a simple model of cumulative growth theory (Dixon / Thirlwall 1975). However growth and development takes place internally within the firms (micro level) as well as at the macro level of regions. Firms in the faster growing and more developed regions would be expected to be growing faster and to have greater productivity levels. To accomplish this they need to not simply invest more and respond to greater levels of demand but they need to be organised differently. Qualitative developments within the firm need to take place so that such productivity and growth differentials emerge. We expect that this will be a response to the competitive dynamics of the faster growing region. We have outlined these dynamics above within the context of a cumulative causation model. Other models could also be used to provide an explanation for relative competitive dynamics of different regions. In a Porter-5-forces-competitive-framework (Porter 1979) for example, we would expect that faster growing regions (especially those geographically close to the EU) would possess: greater rivalry (larger firm numbers including foreign firms) within a sector or niche; greater levels of potential entry (from domestic and foreign firms who assess the faster growing and more lucrative regions); greater levels of substitutes (potentially available from abroad and from foreign firms already in the region); greater levels of buyer power exerted upon smaller firms as larger firms (especially foreign entrants) enter a sector; and greater levels of seller's power exerted over smaller firms as larger firms grow larger (with economies of scale) in faster growing regions. Porter's model can complement the cumulative causation model since they both contribute to explain the greater competitive dynamics of the faster growing region. This research has shown how this can be translated into qualitative dynamics within the firm as it responds to its environment.[18]

Thus firms in the faster growing regions have more competitive pressure yet, as we have also observed, they have the potential for greater rewards if they meet the requirements of a faster moving and growing market. We can therefore understand why there should be qualitative differences in behaviour and performance between small firms in different regions.

A striking observation that emerges from the results is the heterogeneity of small firms - something we don't expect from the traditional theory of the firm or theory of market structures. Indeed many policy documents on the small firm speak of them as if there were a high degree of homogeneity. This paper shows

---

[17] We have quoted these figures in Section 1 above.

[18] Poland has dismantled much of its large state sector and relies upon SMEs . We expect and observe numerical differences between small firm numbers and employment between regions. However this paper also expect qualitative differences (in behaviour, conduct and performance) between small firm in regions of different economic development.

there are considerable differences between firms in more and less developed regions. These differences are not only in their numbers, employment and output levels but in internal organisation, behaviour and performance. If this is the case small firm policy should tailor itself towards these differences rather than impose generic solutions upon the stratum as a whole, a point also emphasized by Piasecka / Rainnie (2000). For example, information and training requirement of small firms in Pomorskie and Lubelskie may be at radically different levels, the former concerned with growth, taxation, export advise, information technology training, and European integration, the latter with lower levels of growth and even with simply survival. Curran / Blackburn (2000), in another context, have stressed the heterogeneity of small firms and have recommended that an industrial sector tailored approach to their needs.

There are limitations to this research. Firstly we are greatly constrained by lack of data and information on Poland's small firms. The primary data we use is not available from government institutions or web-sites. It has been collected privately and constitutes original data. It has been impossible to extend the analysis and testing to other Polish regions. However clearly this remains to be done. The same argument applies the desirability of time series information which would more clearly reflect the dynamics of a region over time. We have only been able to obtain the data on the internal variables in companies for one year. Our ability to generalise from our study is limited. An investigation would have to be carried out in other countries as well, to establish sound empirical conclusion on the relationship between small firms and regional development.

6 Conclusions

It is clear that substantial differences exist between small firms in the two regions in our study. In general Pomorskie had the greater development of the small firm stratum as well as greater expectations from the EU and future growth. This is evidenced by the level of the following variables: a higher level of the firm's legal status, a greater presence of foreign capital, more international orientation, greater network arrangements (such as sub-contracting), and formal collaboration with other Polish firms. Pomorskie has higher levels of R&D and innovation (including improved technologies with respect to new products and services), higher levels of human capital and a greater degree of external financial help and grants. Pomorskie's firms have greater experience of restructuring arrangements, a greater intention to increase output and higher levels of investment. By contrast small firms in less developed area of Lubelskie are smaller, overwhelmingly of sole proprietorship structure with a low technology level, they have very little networking and no developed form of financing - e.g. leasing. Their levels of education and training are below firms in the developed regions and their export activity is lower - in the eastern provinces there will probably be very little exported to the EU and what exists will be going east to the Ukraine and Belarus.

The scenario of Poland being regionally polarised in its development is still a real threat (Fiedorowicz 2005). Regional policy in Poland, however, is still in its infancy and many of the legal framework requirements are lacking for such a policy to be effective. However our research shows that different levels of development operate not only at a macro level but also at the micro level of small firms. Since small firms in the less developed regions of Poland have substantial differences from those in the more developed areas it implies that SME policy needs to be regionally differentiated within the country - a generic policy applied uniformly to the whole country would be a blunt instrument.

However the empirics of this paper are subject to a theoretical perspective. The hypothesis that such regional developmental difference in small firms reflects regional differences in macroeconomic development has received considerable support since evidence for a growing divergence between the less developed and more developed areas of Poland has been presented as summarized in Figure 1. It is suggested that this can be understood within a cumulative causation model of regional development. We thus can begin to flesh out what is absent from the literature of regions and small firms – an appreciation of the interaction between the dynamism of a region and the qualitative nature of its small firms.

References

Barro, R. / Sali-Martin, X. (1995): Economic Growth, McGraw-Hill, London, United Kingdom.

Blawat, F. / Ossowski, J. / Zieba, K. (2001): Small enterprises in the region of Lublin in Poland and their attitudes to European Union, in: Statistics in Transition: Journal of the Polish Statistical Association, Volume 5, pp. 570-584.

Central Statistical Office, Warsaw, Poland. Accessed 18.07.07. [http://www.stat-.gov.pl/gus/index_ENG_HTML.htm]

Cowling, M. (2003): Productivity and corporate governance in smaller firms, in: Small Business Economics, Volume 20, pp. 335-344.

Curran, J. / Blackburn, R. (2000): Panacea or white elephant: response to the DTI consultancy paper, in: Regional Studies, Volume 34, pp. 181-189.

Department of Trade and Industry, Regional Section, United Kingdom, Accessed 18.7.07. [http://stats.berr.gov.uk/ed/sme/smestats2005-regspr.-pdf]

Deichmann, U. / Henderson, V. (2000): Urban and regional dynamics in Poland, Working Paper No. 2457, World Bank, Washington DC, USA.

Dixon, R. / Thirlwall, A. (1975): A model of regional growth-rate differences on Kaldorian lines, Oxford Economic Papers, New Series, Volume 27, pp. 201-214.

Dzierzanowski, W. / Stachowiak (Eds.) (2001): Report on the Condition of the SME Sector in Poland for the Years 1999-2000, Polish Agency for Enterprise Development, Warsaw, Poland.

Fiedorowicz, K. (2005): The causes of regional growth dynamism: diversity in Poland, RSA, International Conference: "Regional growth agendas", Gateway 8, 28th -31st May, 2005, University of Aalborg, Aalborg, Denmark.

Ghatak, S. / Manolas, G. / Rontos, C. / Vavouras, I. (2001): Research on the profile of the successful Polish small enterprise in the European context using logit analysis, in: Statistics in Transition: Journal of the Polish Statistical Association, Volume 5, pp. 146-158.

Ghatak, S. / Mulhern, A. / Stewart, C. (2003): Determinants of intended expansion of Polish small firms, in: Journal of Policy Modelling, Volume 25, pp. 287-329.

Lyons, B. / Bailey, S. (1993): Small subcontractors in UK engineering: competitiveness, dependence and problems, in: Small Business Economics, Volume 5, pp. 101-109.

Piasecki, B. / Rogut, A. / Stawasz, E. / Johnson, S. / Smallbone, D. (1998): Business environment for running SMEs in Poland and EU countries, Polish Foundation for SME Promotion and Development, Warsaw, Poland.

Piasecka E. / Rainnie, A. (2000): Small firms and local economic development in Poland: limits and possibilities, in: Journal of Southern Europe and the Balkans, Volume 2, pp. 25-37.

Polish Foundation for SME Promotion and Development (2000): Contribution of small and medium enterprises to the development of the Polish economy, Polish Foundation for Small and Medium Enterprise Promotion and Development, Warsaw, Poland.

Porter, M. (1979): How competitive forces shape strategy, in: Harvard Business Review, Volume 1, March 1979.

Smallbone, D. / Piasecki, B. / Rogut, A. / Venesaa,r, U. / Rumpi, E. / Budreikate, D. (1996): The survival, growth and support needs of manufacturing SMEs in Poland and the Baltic states, Centre for Enterprise and Economic Development Research, Middlesex University, London, UK.

Smallbone D. / Piasecki, B. / Rogut, A. (2001): The implications of EU accession for Polish SMEs, in: Environment and Planning C: Government and Policy, Volume 19, pp. 317-333.

Szreder, M. (2001): Development of small enterprises in Poland: results of a sample survey conducted in the province of Gdansk, in: Statistics in Transition: Journal of the Polish Statistical Association, Volume 5, pp. 56-77.

Appendix

Table 1: Difference Between Proportions Test

Description of variable	Reported %	Z_statistic	Z critical values	Result	Conclusion
Legal form					
Limited Company	Lubelskie 19%	1.74	[-1.96, 1.96]	Cannot reject HO	No real difference between proportions
	Pomorskie 27%				
Network arrangements					
Co-ownership of other firms	Lubelskie 3%	2.21	[-1.96, 1.96]	Reject HO	Real difference between proportions
	Pomorskie 9%				
Participation with foreign firms	Lubelskie 0%	1.85	[-1.96, 1.96]	Cannot reject HO	No real difference between proportions
	Pomorskie 2.5%				
Franchising	Lubelskie 7%	-1.81	[-1.96, 1.96]	Cannot reject HO	No real difference between proportions
	Pomorskie 3%				
Subcontracting	Lubelskie 38%	6.95	[-1.96, 1.96]	Reject HO	Real difference between proportions
	Pomorskie 5%				
Formal Collaboration					
Suppliers	Lubelskie 35%	8.05	[-1.96, 1.96]	Reject HO	Real difference between proportions
	Pomorskie 77%				
Research Institutes	Lubelskie 7%	1.79	[-1.96, 1.96]	Cannot reject HO	No real difference between proportions
	Pomorskie 13%				
Variables indicating Change in Small Firms					
Change in fixed assets:1998-1999	Lubelskie 31%	3.20	[-1.96, 1.96]	Reject HO	Real difference between proportions
	Pomorskie 60%				
R&D	**Lubelskie 0%**	2.91	[-1.96, 1.96]	Reject HO	Real difference between proportions
	Pomorskie 6%				

Table 1: Difference Between Proportions Test *(cont.)*

Description of variable	Reported %	Z_statistic	Z critical values	Result	Conclusion
Innovation giving new products or services	Lubelskie 30%	3.58	[-1.96, 1.96]	Reject HO	Real difference between proportions
	Pomorskie 49%				
Restructuring	**Lubelskie 1.5%**	2.34	[-1.96, 1.96]	Reject HO	Real difference between proportions
	Pomorskie 7%				
Improved or new technologies	Lubelskie 30%	3.59	[-1.96, 1.96]	Reject HO	Real difference between proportions
	Pomorskie 45%				
Sources of Financing					
Profits	Lubelskie 22%	4.97	[-1.96, 1.96]	Reject HO	Real difference between proportions
	Pomorskie 48%				
Owner's capital	Lubelskie 16%	2.82	[-1.96, 1.96]	Reject HO	Real difference between proportions
	Pomorskie 29%				
Bank Loans	Lubelskie 16%	0.24	[-1.96, 1.96]	Cannot reject HO	No real difference between proportions
	Pomorskie 17%				
Leasing	**Lubelskie 0%**	4.57	[-1.96, 1.96]	Reject HO	Real difference between proportions
	Pomorskie 14%				
Grants	**Lubelskie 1%**	2.73	[-1.96, 1.96]	Reject HO	Real difference between proportions
	Pomorskie 7.5%				
% firms Intending to Increase Output in 2000-2001					
by greater than 5%	Lubelskie 40%	4.49	[-1.96, 1.96]	Reject HO	Real difference between proportions
	Pomorskie 64%				

Table 1: Difference Between Proportions Test *(cont.)*

Description of variable	Reported %	Z_statistic	Z critical values	Result	Conclusion
Comparative Educational Level of the Workforce					
Those with higher and/or post secondary qualifications	Lubelskie 19%	2.90	[-1.96, 1.96]	Reject HO	Real difference between proportions
	Pomorskie 33%				

Note to Table 1: the *Difference in Proportions Test for Two Proportions* Calculator allows to test for a statistically significant difference between two proportions drawn from independent samples. This procedure can be validly employed only if both samples satisfy the standard binomial requirement that $n*p$ and $n(1-p)$ must both be equal to or greater than 5, where n=samples size and p=percentage. Eight variables were excluded from entering our test on this criterion.

Selected Issues Relating to Real and Nominal Convergence of New EU Member States[1]

Václav Žďárek[2] and Jaromír Šindel[3]
University of Economics and Management, Czech Republic

1 Introduction

The new EU member states[4] are currently in a situation where plans for introducing the euro are in place and preliminary dates for joining the Eurozone have been set. Decisions on whether or not to adopt the euro will have to be made in a few years time. These countries will be assessed by the EU as to whether they meet the criteria for entering the third stage of the economic and monetary union (EMU). An analysis of the progress regarding the nominal and real convergence of these economies, including comparisons with other new member states, is therefore both relevant and necessary. The experience of selected EU-15 countries before and after introducing the euro are also be taken into account.

Significant changes in the economies of the new member states, can, however, not be expected within a few years. Their standard of living is likely to grow at a slower pace over the next few years, as the new member states are reducing the gap with the average standard of living in the European Union. On the other hand, the growth in price levels, wages, and labour productivity will have to accelerate to ensure a smooth progress of integration into the Eurozone. These changes should arise from an adjustment process that leads to a strong increase in prices and wages, resulting from a corresponding growth of labour productivity. A price and wage spiral, however, could ultimately undermine im-

---

[1] The paper was compiled within the Research Centre Programme of the Ministry of Education, Youth and Sports, project No. 1M0524. The authors wish to express their thanks to Vojtěch Spěváček and Růžena Vintrová from CES VŠEM Prague and Andrea Ingianni from Kingston University for valuable suggestions and comments. All remaining errors and omissions are ours.

[2] Václav Žďárek, Centre for Economic Studies, University of Economics and Management, I. P.Pavlova 3, CZ – 120 00 Prague 2. Tel. +42 (0) 224 941 056. Email: vaclav.zdarek@vsem.cz

[3] Jaroslav Šindel, Centre for Economic Studies, University of Economics and Management, I. P.Pavlova 3, CZ – 120 00 Prague 2. Tel. +42 (0) 224 941 056. Email: jara.sindel@centrum.cz

[4] The new EU member states (EU-10) do not include Bulgaria and Romania. This study, however, focuses on the EU-10 countries with formerly centrally planned economies, excluding Malta and Cyprus. Deviating from its conventional use we refer to these countries as the EU-10. EU-5 countries are EU-4 countries (the Visegrad group of countries which consists of the Czech Republic, Hungary, Poland, and Slovakia) and Slovenia.

provements in the standard of living and would disrupt the convergence process. For this reason the new member states may need decades to reach the European average. After all, some of the less developed countries that joined the EU in the 80s have not yet succeeded in reaching the standard of living or price level of other EU-15 countries.[5]

The paper focuses on selected issues relating to real and nominal convergence of the economies of the new member states. Section 2 addresses selected theoretical and methodological issues associated with the comparison and convergence of economies over time. An empirical verification of the convergence of the new EU member states and selected EU-15 countries is provided in Section 3. The countries that aim to join the Eurozone face problems that relate to the real exchange rate and to the Balassa-Samuelson effect, which are discussed in Section 4. The fifth and final section provides a brief summary of potential issues and problems.

2 Convergence

Convergence is a process defined as "approaching a certain level" or "decreasing a difference between two values" with the difference between the variables reducing towards zero over time. For a rigorous theoretical definition see e.g. Greene (2003). The meaning of the terms nominal and real convergence as used by individual authors is not without ambiguity. Real convergence is defined as the standard of living of one country approaching that of another country or a group of countries. It is usually measured by GDP per capita in purchasing power parity (PPP)[6], which excludes the impact of different price levels and measures the value of goods and services available in the relevant economy.[7]

[5] The experience of united Germany illustrates the consequences of fast convergence (see Rother / Süppel 2003).

[6] GDP per capita in PPP reflects the country's standard of living in international comparisons. When geographic comparisons are carried out, volume indexes are expressed in purchasing power parity to exclude price level differences. GDP expresses the real value of goods and services available to the relevant economy for consumption, investment and the balance of foreign trade. It is necessary to distinguish between the purchasing power standard unit (PPS) and purchasing power parity (PPP) of the currency. PPP is calculated on the basis of US prices, average prices for the 30 OECD Countries or in case of the International Comparison Project (ICP) are used prices of large group of countries. The results are published by OECD or World Bank (ICP). The PPS is an artificial unit created by EUROSTAT based on the average price level in the EU states. Its value varies even within individual EU countries. The PPS is calculated from the average price levels in the EU member states (previously EU-15, currently EU-25) and, thus, acts as a double converter, converting both prices and exchange rates.

[7] Alternatively, real convergence can be understood to include convergence of structural features of the economies and of the technologies used. See e.g. Slavík (2005).

The so-called Copenhagen criteria for countries striving for membership in the EU or for inclusion in the Eurozone are often referred to in this context. These criteria, however, have a broader scope.[8]

The theoretical foundation for real convergence lies in the neoclassical growth theory, which predicts convergence towards a steady state which is identical for all economies. This steady state is influenced by a variety of characteristics and parameters, including savings, population growth, and the rate of depreciation of the capital goods. This theoretical framework, however, fails to provide a satisfactory explanation for the tendencies observed in reality, in particular for the failure of many less developed countries to catch up with their developed counterparts. Empirical studies have produced a range of different and sometimes contradictory results. Some less developed countries remain at their lower standards of living, widening the gap with developed countries, whereas other countries show rapid convergence. This range of results contradicts the neoclassical growth theory and fuelled a persisting search for alternative concepts and explanations.

A number of alternative approaches explaining the above mentioned phenomena have been presented over the last two decades. Modern concepts of the endogenous growth theory were developed. They reflect a range of up to then neglected factors, such as the accumulation and spread of skills and experience, infrastructure, and institutional quality. A common steady state for otherwise identical economies may fail to exist due to these dissimilarities. Endogenous growth models can provide a theoretical explanation for the empirical observation that some countries grow faster than others in spite of their higher standard of living, while others may continue to lag behind. This is described by models of conditional convergence, for instance β–convergence and σ–convergence, as discussed in Barro / Sala-i-Martin (2004).

Nominal convergence in the broader sense is defined as the convergence of absolute values and growth rates of nominal variables – interest rates, inflation rate, exchange rate, fiscal deficit, and public debt – e.g. in connection with the Maastricht criteria.[9] In the narrow sense nominal convergence is defined as convergence of the price levels of individual economies, as in Frait / Komárek (2004).

The relationship between real and nominal convergence, i.e. the relationship between the standard of living and the price level, goes both ways each influencing the other (see for example Dobrinsky 2006). Countries with a lower standard of living typically have lower price and wage levels. As the standard of living increases, the price level tends to rise, due to an increasing inflation differential between tradable and non-tradable goods as well as an appreciating ex-

[8] The main issue being the existence of a functioning market economy and the ability to cope with competitive pressures in the EU (see Čech / Komárek 2002a).

[9] Compare for example Vávra (1999).

change rate. This process gradually leads to the elimination of the cost-based competitive advantage of local companies. If the economy is to retain its dynamics, progress towards forms of non-price competitiveness is necessary (i.e. based on the quality of produced goods and services).

2.1 Price Level and Standard of Living

If the relatively strict assumptions of the PPP-theory (see for example Rogoff 1996) were valid, prices of tradable goods in individual countries, once converted into a common currency, should by identical. International arbitrage would lead to the harmonisation of prices in the long run. Differences in price levels would then be due to differences in the prices of non-tradable goods and their significance in the economy. These, in turn, would depend on the standard of living as indicated by, e.g. income per capita and wage levels. The relationship between the price level and the standard of living would show a positive correlation as is often observed in practice (see for example Vintrová et al. 2002).

This relationship, however, is at times disrupted, which may be caused by a number of factors. The existence of a clear distinction between tradable and non-tradable goods is open to debate and differences between individual countries exist even for tradable goods. Still, empirical observations of the relationship between the price level and the standard of living often find an interdependence of the two. Thus, they confirm the above mentioned theory, which explains differences in national price levels by different levels of labour productivity in the tradable goods sector (see Balassa 1964 and Samuelson 1964). For a more detailed discussions of this issue see, for example Čihák / Holub (2001).

In reality, the harmonisation of the prices of goods and services in different countries is obstructed by a variety of factors. These obstacles are, amongst others, associated with free trade and the existence of transport cost and transaction costs.[10]

The differentiation between tradable and non-tradable goods is not as clear as it may seem. Both the price differential of a particular good between countries and the cost of arbitrage are important factors in distinguishing between them. A good is considered to be tradable only when the difference between its price in individual countries exceeds a certain level. This difference, however, this is itself affected by the arbitrage process. The differentiation between tradable and non-tradable goods is therefore somewhat arbitrary and using terms such as "more or less tradable good" and "more or less non-tradable good" would seem more appropriate (see Skořepa 2001, compare Obstfeld / Rogoff 1998). This differentia-

[10] For an overview of potential obstacles to arbitrage see for example Skořepa (2001) or EC (2002).

tion of goods is applied remainder of this paper while using the abbreviated reference to "tradable goods" and "non-tradable goods".

There are also different views regarding the criteria for real and nominal convergence (see Dědek 2002, 2006). An issue frequently highlighted in the case of transition economies with different economic structures is that excessive efforts to promptly meet the required criteria for nominal convergence may negatively affect economic growth. This is known as the Balassa-Samuelson effect.[11] When a country is about to join a monetary union, as it is in the case of the new EU member states, this is highly relevant.

The price structures of transition economies are not only influenced by the former regimes and their pricing policies, but also by structural changes. Thus, the adjustment of relative prices depends on the flexibility of individual prices. If prices are inflexible downwards – i.e. if prices are "sticky" as is typical for most developed and transitional economies – this process requires an increase in the overall price level to implement changes in relative prices.

Economic growth generates pressure on the current account and causes inflation associated with the adjustment of relative prices and the elimination of regulatory measures. These coincide with the effects of stabilising policies that support smooth progress or aim to eliminate disrupting influences. Benchmark values for the relevant criteria should therefore be applied with caution and the potential risks associated with their use should be highlighted when assessing the convergence process.[12]

In this context it should be noted that an excessively low inflation rate, due to problems with the measurement of inflation, may lead to a reduction in economic growth. On the other hand, exceeding inflation expectations, which often include a significant adaptive element, represents a serious problem for monetary authorities' credibility. When determining their monetary policy stance, monetary authorities should therefore take explicit account of the estimated productivity growth, the expected distortions in the inflation rate, and the relevant convergence criterion. Combining these three aspects should lead to a balanced policy which will neither affect the rate of real convergence, nor the rate of nominal convergence.[13]

---

[11] For an overview of literature on this topic and a more in-depth analysis of Balassa-Samuelson effect, see, for example Čihák / Holub (2001), Holub / Čihák (2003) and Égert (2003, 2006).

[12] See e.g. Sorsa (2006).

[13] In the case of the Czech Republic, the inflation corridor determined in the past was relatively narrow. The current ČNB target (3 %) is closer to the lower border line. The interval for price increases of 0–2 % per year is considered price stability and additional 2 % account for the impact of the Balassa-Samuelson effect. Combined with exchange rate appreciation by 0.5 % this meets the potential ECB target of 2 % plus 1.5 %. Therefore, in combination with the exchange rate changes, the inflation target appears consistent. Problems may occur in the

2.2 Measurement Problems and Issues with International Comparisons

When making international comparisons, additional problems arise from differences in national procedures for constructing identically named indicators. This may occur even within unified methodological standards, such as the national account system ESA 1995. National statistical authorities within the EU apply rules developed by EUROSTAT which allow international comparisons.[14]

Productivity is internationally comparable only if it is defined identically and reported in the same units. In practice this requires converting national prices and currencies to international prices and currencies. Comparisons are normally based on a reference country or a group of countries. The EU uses the Purchasing Power Standard (PPS)[15] for the purposes of comparing standards of living.

For the comparisons made in this paper, the Comparative Price Level (CPL) is another important indicator. It is based on the Price Level Index (PLI), a non-dimensional indicator representing the price level of a particular good in one country compared to another country or a group of countries. CPL is calculated as a fraction of the price of the good in PPP (or PPS) and the nominal exchange rate of the compared countries.

The EU-10 states are undergoing significant structural changes in their economies. This causes a rapid outdating of the prices used in conversions to fixed price indices. More frequent updating would therefore be required for ob-

---

evaluation phase if three Eurozone economies report zero (or even negative) inflation rates. In this case, the criterion would demand an inflation rate of 1.5 % or less. However, according to official EU documents this is not possible (see EC 2005, p. 20). Similar conditions apply to the minimum period required for remaining in the ERM-II, where exchange rate appreciation is allowed. For an alternative opinion see Janáček / Janáčková (2004).

[14] The change in calculation of the GDP indicator in EU countries is associated with the so-called relocation of FISIM. The new method results in changes in the absolute value of GDP and the subsequent impact of the growth rate that may be significant (see EUROSTAT 2005a). Economies that have implemented both of these changes can be used as an example (see World Bank 2006, p. 8). While the change in the growth rate for Hungary is in tenths of percentage points, it may be in the range of whole percentage points for other countries (e.g. Estonia).

[15] Besides the so-called current parity, OECD also constructs fixed parity, which differs from the current parity in having a fixed structure of the relevant aggregate (GDP) during a certain year and for the following period. During the following years the indicator is extrapolated with deflators or real growth rates. Fixed parities are used for monitoring the relative growth performance of a particular economy, while current parities are used for example for quantifying the current position of the economy in international comparisons. Again, deviations of both indicators may be a few percentage points, which is the main reason why countries are classified in groups with certain levels of income (see Spěváček 2003 and Schreyer / Koechlin 2002).

taining a "truthful" reflection. If an index holds the prices of goods that are subject to frequent innovation fixed over an excessively long period of time, this is another source of distortions.[16] This can readily be solved by applying chaining methods in which annual updates of prices are used for the calculation of indicators such as GDP in fixed prices. For this purpose, average prices for the previous period are used.[17] Within the EU-10, statistical authorities in Poland, the Czech Republic and Lithuania have changed to this method. The other EU-10 states, excluding Bulgaria and Rumania, have agreed do so before the end of 2007.[18]

3 Results and Discussion

The empirical part of this paper focuses on the actual development of real and nominal convergence during the period 1995–2005, for which the relevant data is usually available in two individual sections, 1995–2000 and 2000–2005. The choice of these intervals is more of less arbitrary and was made in order to distinguish between different stages of the actual development. Dividing the relevant period into sections 1995–1999 and 1999–2005, arising from the introduction of the Euro, may be an alternative.

3.1 Real Convergence

With a growth in GDP per capita in PPS of only 4.6% during the entire period, the growth rate achieved by the Czech economy is only half of that achieved by Poland, although the higher growth rate of Poland is achieved from a lower basis (see Table 1). It is only one third of Slovenia's growth rate. Looking at the two individual sub-periods we find that is caused by the development of the Czech Republic during the period 1995–2000, in particular by the recession during 1997–1999.

---

[16] See for example Janáček / Janáčková (2004) and Janáčková (1999).

[17] These calculations present a relatively complex task and a variety of procedures for the chaining method provide quite varied figures on the growth rate of the relevant aggregate with identical input details exist (see Landefeld et al. 2003).

[18] It should be noted that modern internationally integrated economies report domestic productivity indicators (such as GDP) that fail to take into account primary income of production flowing to and from abroad. The amount of dividends paid out abroad by affiliated companies is a typical example of this. According to the new national accounts, in 2004 for the Czech Republic this flow accounted for almost 5 % of GDP (4.87 %), while the same percentage for Ireland was more than 15 % (15.4 %), authors' calculation from (OECD 2006a).

A turnaround occurred in the period from 2000 to 2005, when the Czech Republic showed strong real convergence dynamics, ahead of Hungary and Poland.[19] Poland displayed low growth at the beginning of the new century due to macroeconomic problems. The high increase of GDP in Slovakia over the last few years fails to be reflected in real convergence for a number of reasons, which included the effect of fixed prices used in the calculation of GDP. For more details on the issue of reported and actual convergence rates see the section on convergence in Spěváček et al. (2005).

Table 1: GDP in PPS per Capita in the Selected EU Countries, 1995–2005 (EU-25 Average = 100)

	1995[1]	2000	2005	Change (p.p.)[2] 1995–2005	1995–2000	2000–2005
Czech Republic	69.0	64.7	73.6	4.6	-4.4	8.9
Hungary[3]	49.0	53.7	62.6	13.5	4.7	8.8
Poland	40.6	46.8	49.8	9.1	6.1	3.0
Slovakia	44.5	47.3	57.0	12.5	2.8	9.8
Slovenia	68.4	72.6	81.7	13.3	4.3	9.1
Estonia	33.5	42.3	59.6	26.0	8.7	17.3
Lithuania	34.2	37.8	51.9	17.7	3.6	14.1
Latvia	29.7	35.3	48.1	18.4	5.7	12.8
Cyprus	81.9	82.1	88.9	7.0	0.2	6.9
Malta	..	78.1	70.2	..	..	-7.9
Portugal	75.5	80.1	71.1	-4.4	4.6	-9.0
Greece	71.0	72.6	83.8	12.9	1.6	11.2

Note: [1] EUROSTAT estimate. [2] Changes are based on unrounded numbers, so a simple addition of them for a country, might not be equal to the total change of GDP in PPS. [3] Hungary changed the methodology for measuring of GDP since 2002 (allocation of FISIM to user sectors), thus its figures are not compatible with other states of the EU-25 (see EUROSTAT 2005b).
Source: EUROSTAT, Structural Indicators (20/02/07), own calculation.

Figure 1 and Figure 2 show the standard of living of individual EU-10 countries during the period 2000–2005. Figure 1 presents an overview of changes in the levels of the standard of living of individual countries, while Figure 2 illustrates the same development in relation to the EU-25. The EU-15 and the Eurozone are also included for comparison.

Figure 3 illustrates the frequently used relationship between the standard of living and price level for all EU countries. The correlation between the standard of living as expressed by GDP per capita in PPS and the price level in the

[19] See OECD (2006b) for comparison of the presented analysis and discussion.

EU-25 countries is high. The slope of the regression line equals 0.85 and is relatively close to one.

Figure 1: GDP p.c. in PPS in the EU-10, EU-15 and Eurozone (EU-25 = 100)

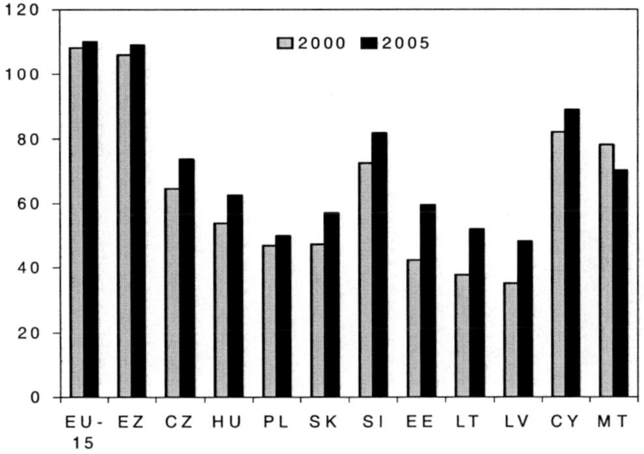

Source: EUROSTAT. Structural Indicators, National Accounts (20/02/2007), own calculation.

As shown by Čihák / Holub (2001, p. 335), the value of this slope is influenced by the proportion of non-tradable goods in GDP and by the share of the capital used for producing non-tradable goods. The explanatory capacity of this simple regression is relatively high (91%).

Figure 3 shows that the price level of the Czech economy is below the price level of the EU-25, even more so than the difference in the standard of living would suggest. The Czech and Slovenian economies differ in this regard from those of other new member states, for whom the difference with the EU-25 price level reflects their standard of living. In Figure 3, these other countries are located close to the regression line. The Northern European countries, France, and Germany stand out from the group of the most developed EU countries. Their price levels show and upward divergence, while the price levels in Belgium, Ireland, the Netherlands and Austria depart downwards from the overall EU level.

Figure 2: Changes in GDP p.c. in PPS in the EU-10, EU-15 and Eurozone in comparison with the EU-25, 2000–2005

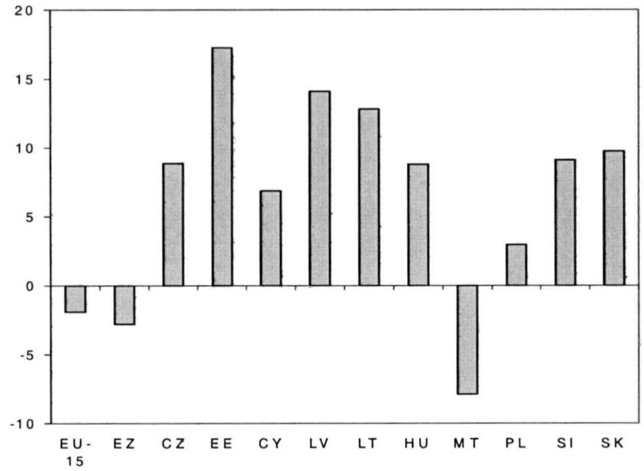

Source: EUROSTAT. Source: EUROSTAT, Structural Indicators, National Accounts (20/02/2007), own calculation.

Figure 3: Relationship Between Price and GDP p.c., EU-25 (EU-25 = 100, 2005)

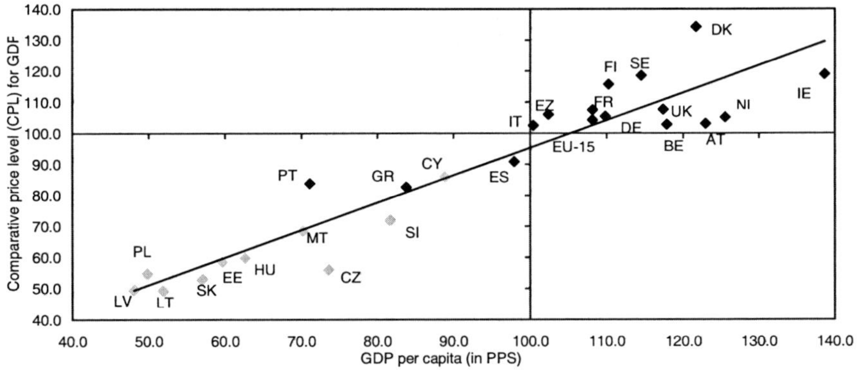

Luxemburg is omitted from the analysis. Linear regression: *CPL = 7.1796 + 0.8768·GDP*, S.E. (6.3921), (0.0673). $R^2 = 0.89$, *F*-test = *170*.

Source: EUROSTAT, Structural Indicators, National Accounts (20/02/2007), own calculation.

The change in the standard of living and the price level in the EU-10 countries as in Figure 4 is also interesting. The first quadrant of the figure shows a group of countries with growth in their standards of living and price levels. Applying an imaginary 45° line to this quadrant reveals a differentiated development between Baltic countries, where real convergence is faster than nominal convergence, and the Czech Republic, Hungary and Slovakia, where real convergence is outpaced by nominal convergence. Only Malta, which combines price increases with and real divergence, and Slovenia, which shows stagnation of the price level and real convergence, display qualitatively different developments.

Figure 4: Changes in GDP in PPS per Capita and Comparative Price Level (CPL), EU-10, 2000–2005 (EU-25 = 100)

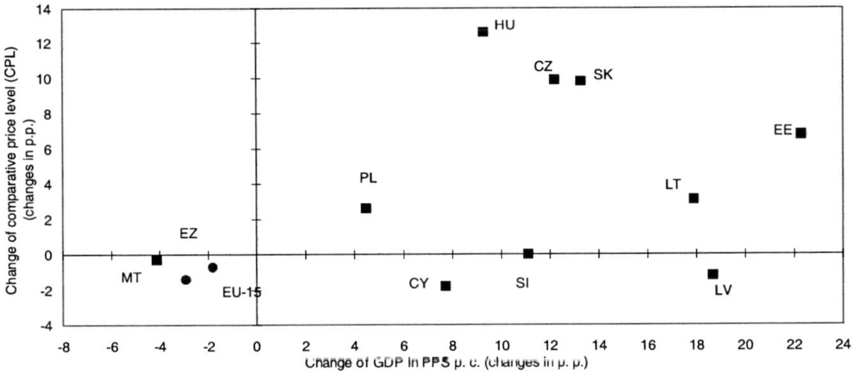

Source: EUROSTAT, Structural Indicators, National Accounts (20/02/07), own calculation.

Table 2 summarises a different perspective on the changes in the price levels in both new member states and selected "old" member states. During the period 1995–2005 only Slovenia showed a decrease in its price level, by 1.7 percentage points (p.p.). The Czech Republic recorded a price level growth by 17.8 p.p., which is nearly equal that observed in Hungary, which equalled 16.4 p.p. While inflation in the Czech Republic was relatively stable over time, in Hungary it was largely concentrated in the period from 2000 to 2005.

The comparison of the price level in the Czech Republic with that of the other EU-5 countries generates interesting results. The standard of living in the Czech Republic is somewhat higher than that of Poland and Slovakia. The price level in the Czech Republic is less than that in Hungary even though its standard of living is higher. The fast growth in the price level in Hungary would be worth analysing in detail in order to find causes that led to this development.[20] The growth in Poland up to 2000 was followed by a significant fall in the price level (according to the available preliminary data the price level for 2005 is back above the 50 % benchmark), which is also remarkable. Portugal and Greece are included for comparison. The implications for nominal convergence are as follows. While real convergence in the selected EU-10 countries between 1999 and 2005 has developed significantly better than in the previous period, nominal convergence falls behind.

Table 2: Comparative Price Level (CPL) for GDP in Selected EU Countries

	EU-25 = 100			Change in CPL (p.p.) [2]			Czech Republic = 100
	1995	2000	2005	1995–2005	1995–2000	2000–2005	2005
Czech republic	38.3	46.2	56.1	17.8	7.8	9.9	100.0
Hungary [2]	43.4	47.2	59.9	16.4	3.8	12.6	106.8
Poland	44.4	52.1	54.7	10.3	7.7	2.6	97.6
Slovakia	40.6	43.2	53.0	12.4	2.6	9.8	94.5
Slovenia	73.6	71.9	71.9	-1.7	-1.7	-0.0	128.2
Estonia	38.5	51.8	58.6	20.1	13.3	6.8	104.5
Lithuania	26.4	46.1	49.2	22.8	19.6	3.1	87.7
Latvia	32.6	50.7	49.6	17.0	18.1	-1.2	88.4
Cyprus	85.8	87.9	86.1	0.3	2.1	-1.8	153.6
Malta	..	68.8	68.5	..	..	-0.3	122.1
Portugal	74.4	74.5	83.8	9.5	0.2	9.3	149.5
Greece	77.3	78.8	82.7	5.5	1.5	4.0	147.6

Note: [1] Changes are based on unrounded numbers, so a simple addition of them for a country, might not be equal to the total change of CPL for GDP. [2] Hungary changed the methodology for measuring of GDP since 2002 (allocation of FISIM to user sectors), thus its figure are not compatible with the other EU-25 states.
Source: EUROSTAT, National Accounts (20/02/0707), own calculations.

[20] Over many years Austrian residents have commuted to Hungary in order to benefit from the cheaper local services, which may provide one possible explanation, as it may have brought local prices closer to the EU-25 price level. More detailed data on price level development would be required for confirming these conclusions.

3.2 Selected Instances of Nominal and Real Convergence

Unlike some other new EU members, viz. Hungary, Poland or Slovakia, the Czech Republic has seen a long-term downward deviation of the price level from its theoretically expected value.[21]

In this subsection, we follow the disaggregated approach to analyse the relationship between the real and the disaggregated nominal convergence process, which distinguishes between the price for goods and the price for services.

Figure 5: Comparative Price Level for Total Services in 2000 (left) and 2005 (right)

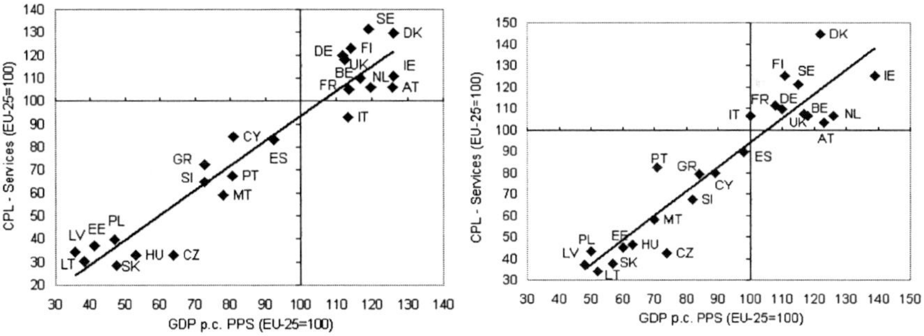

Note: Luxembourg is omitted. Linear regression: $CPL = -14.2 + 1.08 \cdot GDP$, $R^2 = 0.91$ in 2000 and $CPL = -19.8 + 1.14 \cdot GDP$, $R^2 = 0.87$ in 2005.
Source: EUROSTAT, Economy and Finance, Prices (19/02/07), own calculation.

The results from the simple linear regression associated with the disaggregated approach differ from the results in the previous subsection. The slope of CPL-line for services exceeds 1, whereas the slope for goods is between 0.5 and 0.6. This can be roughly explained by the difference in tradability of goods and services, but we can also identify differences among new member states from it.

The CPL for services in the new member states is closely linked to the real convergence process. As the comparative price level for total goods is not connected with the real convergence process (see Figure 6 and Figure 7), we cannot expect a substantial increase in CPL for goods during real convergence process. This is supported for new member states by Figure 7, where the change

[21] For Croatia recorded the opposite holds: the price level was higher than implied by its standard of living, see Nestić (2005). Turkey, Switzerland and Norway or, outside Europe, New Zealand and Mexico are additional examples.

in the real convergence process is correlated with the change of the CPL for services. No such correlation is found for the change of the CPL for goods.

Figure 6: Comparative Price Level for Goods in 2000 (left) and 2005 (right)

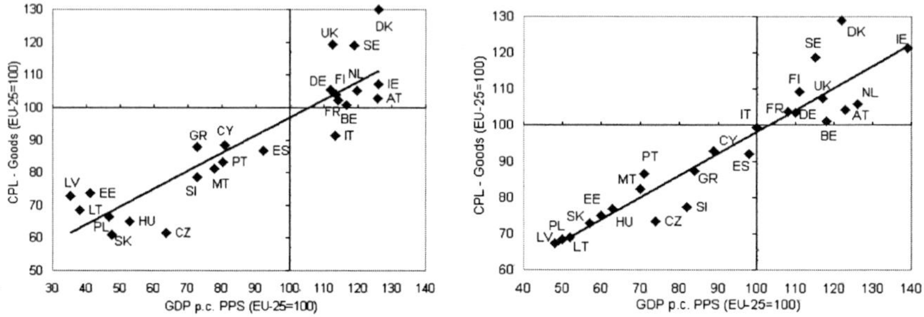

Note: Luxembourg is omitted. Linear regression: $CPL = 42.0 + 0.55 \cdot GDP$, $R^2 = 0.81$ in 2000 and $CPL = 37.3 + 0.61 \cdot GDP$, $R^2 = 0.89$ in 2005.
Source: EUROSTAT, Economy and Finance, Prices (19/02/07), own calculation.

Figure 7: Change of GDP (per capita in PPS) and Comparative Price Level between 2000 and 2005 for Services (left) and Goods (right)

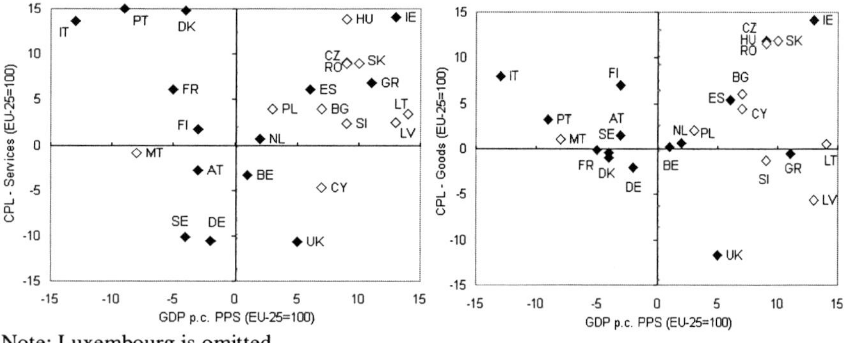

Note: Luxembourg is omitted.
Source: EUROSTAT, Economy and Finance, Prices (19/02/07), own calculation.

By analysing the nominal convergence process we do not just want to focus on the disaggregate price levels for individual new member states. We also want to make disaggregated comparisons with different group of countries. The ongoing real and nominal convergence process among the EU-25 Member States is illustrated by Table 3. The standard deviation of the CPL index[22] for GDP declined from 27.5 in 2000 to 25.4 in 2005 for the EU-25 and is much higher than for the Eurozone (11.1). The differences in CPL result from non-tradables in the service sector and from the role of the government due to regulated prices and non-tradability in government sector.

Table 3: Progress in the Convergence Process

	EU-25		Eurozone		EU-10		EU-4	
	2000	**2005**	**2000**	**2005**	**2000**	**2005**	**2000**	**2005**
GDP p.c. in PPS	31.4	27.3	17.5	*18.4*	16.3	13.2	7.4	*8.8*
Comparative Price Level – GDP	27.5	25.4	12.8	11.1	13.9	11.0	3.2	2.6
Actual Individual Consumption	29.3	27.2	13.6	12.0	15.8	12.7	3.8	2.5
Actual Collective Consumption	36.1	33.4	17.6	14.6	18.9	14.9	4.2	*4.4*
Gross Fixed Capital Formation	19.7	19.6	12.3	*12.9*	6.2	4.4	2.7	*4.7*
Final consumption expenditure	30.2	28.0	14.0	12.2	16.3	13.0	3.9	2.7
Household final consumption expenditure	26.7	24.4	13.6	11.5	14.2	10.8	4.5	2.3
Government final consumption expenditure	38.1	35.2	18.3	14.7	20.7	17.3	2.8	*4.1*
Total goods	19.2	17.7	8.4	*9.6*	8.5	7.2	2.3	*3.0*
Consumer goods	19.8	17.2	7.9	*8.2*	11.9	10.6	3.1	2.1
Non-durable goods	23.4	20.8	10.4	*11.7*	11.8	11.6	3.3	1.5
Semi-durable goods	15.0	10.4	7.8	6.3	10.1	6.9	4.3	*5.8*
Durable goods	13.9	13.9	7.4	6.7	14.3	11.0	2.7	1.1
Capital goods	19.7	19.6	12.3	*12.9*	6.2	4.4	2.7	*4.7*
Total services	35.4	33.2	17.6	14.4	17.7	14.1	4.0	3.3
Consumer services	33.8	31.6	19.3	15.6	16.1	11.5	5.5	3.7
Government services	38.1	35.2	18.3	14.7	20.7	17.3	2.8	*4.1*
Collective services	36.1	33.4	17.6	14.6	18.9	14.9	4.2	*4.4*
Individual services	39.6	36.7	19.3	15.5	22.6	19.5	1.8	*4.3*

Note: The standard deviation of levels (EU-25=100%). EU-10 = New Member States. EU-4 = the Czech Republic, Hungary, Poland and Slovakia. The number in 2005 is in italics, if the standard deviation is higher than in 2000. Capital goods correspond with Gross fixed capital formation and Government services with the Government final consumption expenditure.
Source: EUROSTAT, Economy and Finance, Prices (19/02/07), own calculation.

Looking at the standard deviations at disaggregated levels, we observe an increase in the Eurozone for the gross fixed capital formation (capital goods) and for durable goods. Their CPL, however, have the lowest standard deviation among the EU-25 (19.6 and 13.9 respectively). For the EU-4 countries the increase in the standard deviation, which is visible in many spheres of CPL, is also interesting, as it contrasts to the reduction in standard deviation for the EU-10. The largest differences between standard deviations for both groups of countries

[22] Eurostat publishes the price convergence indicator, which is the coefficient of variation of the comparative price level index for final household consumption in %.

are in CPL for gross fixed capital formation (capital goods) and total goods both in 2000 and in 2005. The CPL decreased in Poland but increased in the Czech Republic, Hungary and Slovakia. Such a different development confirms the modest increase of CPL for Poland from the Table 2. The standard deviation of CPL is higher among EU-25 than among the Eurozone countries, but we can also observe two stable groups from Table 3 – the Eurozone and the EU-10 with similar levels of standard deviation.

One source of the heterogeneity in the nominal convergence process is confirmed by Table 4, where the comparative price level for the government's final consumption expenditure differs among the selected new member states. We now focus on the role of government expenditure in the nominal convergence process. We also seek to identify the driving force behind the progress in the convergence of the household final expenditure comparative price level.

Table 4: Average Annual Contributions to the Change of the Relative GDP Comparative Price Level in 2000-2005

Comparative Price Level	CZ	SK	HU	PL	SI
- Gross Domestic Product	4.1	4.5	4.8	2.5	-0.3
- Gross fixed capital formation	0.8	0.4	0.6	0.2	-0.4
- Final consumption expenditure	3.3	4.2	4.3	2.4	0.1
- Household final consumption expenditure	2.1	3.3	2.6	1.8	0.0
- Government final consumption expenditure	1.2	1.0	1.7	0.7	0.1

Source: EUROSTAT, Economy and Finance, Prices (19/02/07), own calculation.

Figure 8 offers an insight into the role of government services in the CPL analysis. The relative CPL of government services to consumer services is the highest in the Czech Republic, Hungary and Slovakia in 2000 and 2005. These three countries have also the lowest CPL for GDP and for actual individual consumption in comparison with GDP per capita in PPS. Here the government expenditures price level is not the main factor that causes the price level to deviate from its theoretically expected value. An explanation of this apparent paradox is beyond the scope of this paper, but in the next section we offer a possible explanation that relates to regulated prices.

The ratio of government services comparative price level to that for consumer services has increased only for the Czech Republic and for Hungary. The Slovak ratio has substantially decreased since 2000. The regulated prices show a different development. The water supply price index and the electricity, gas and other fuels price index (as included in the HICP), our approximation for regulated prices, were tripled in Slovakia and doubled in the Czech Republic during this period.

Figure 8: Relative CPL of Government and Consumer Services compared with Total Services CPL in 2000 (left) and 2005 (right)

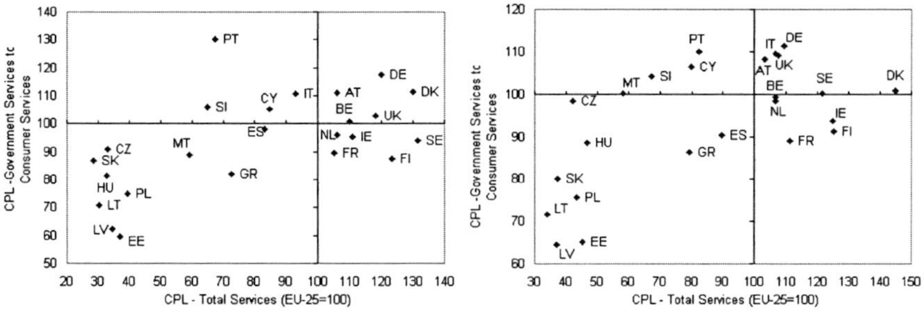

Note: Luxembourg is omitted.
Source: EUROSTAT, Economy and Finance, Prices (19/02/07), own calculation.

Figure 9 only partially reflects the increase of the Slovak comparative price level of regulated items. This is due to the relatively lower appreciation of its nominal exchange rate (9 % from 2000 to 2005) in comparison with the Czech crown (16 %).

Figure 9: The Comparative Price Level for GDP and Housing, Water, Gas and Other Fuels in 2000 (left) and between 2000 and 2005 (right)

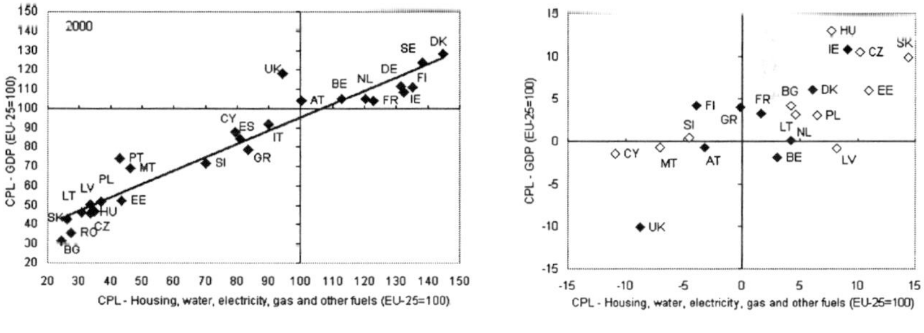

Note: Luxembourg is omitted.
Source: EUROSTAT, Economy and Finance, Prices (19/02/07), own calculation.

3.3 Why are the Differences for the Czech Republic so Significant?

Price adjustment in the Czech Republic is determined to a significant extent by exogenous factors whose impact reflects the share of administered prices in the relevant economy. The development of the price level therefore needs to be considered in the context of price differences between tradable and non-tradable goods and in the context of regulated items.

Prices of tradable goods are determined on international markets and the influence of domestic conditions is relatively small. The prices for some specific commodities may be close to this international level, while other prices may be higher or lower.[23] Their development may be influenced mainly by other factors and may not change much even when other prices converge. It is important to note that differences in price convergence may reflect different developments for tradable and non-tradable goods and for inputs and outputs, because only then the competitiveness of domestic producers can be sustained in the long-term.

Non-tradable goods have a low price level arising from past conditions, which grows slowly as the standard of living and the wage level increase. This growth should not be disconnected from the development in labour productivity, as this could lead to similar consequences as those currently experienced in the former GDR. The adjustment process can be expected to take a long time and it is impossible to predict if the Czech Republic will eventually reach a standard of living similar to that of the EU-15. After all, even some EU-15 countries show a significant difference in this respect many years after their accession.

Different shares of regulated prices in EU-10 countries may also be partially responsible for the observed situation. The Czech Republic and Slovakia are currently the two countries with the highest share of regulated prices in the consumer basket for inflation calculation (see Table 5). Although the weights in this basket differ from those in the national accounts, they are a fair approximation of the actual values.

The shares of administered items in the CPI calculation differ significantly among the new member states – from a few percent in Poland to tens of percents in Estonia, as can be seen in Table 6.

---

[23] In the Czech Republic this is the case for the prices of clothes in 2003 (CPL index = 105), 8th place above the EU-25 level shared with Cyprus; while other EU-10 countries are below the EU-25 level (see EUROSTAT 2005a). On the other hand, the local prices of passenger cars for 2004 were below the EU-25 level (CPL index = 90), Hungary recorded a somewhat higher level (97); while lower levels were observed in Slovakia (88) and Poland (82) (see EUROSTAT 2006).

Table 5: Composition of the Consumer Basket (HICP)

Total index = 1000	CZ	EE	HU	LT	LV	PL	SI	SK
Regulated prices	250.5	178.0	200.6	171.3	205.9	206.0	166.9	258.2
Other prices	749.5	822.0	799.4	828.7	794.1	794.0	833.1	741.8

Note: the total HICP basket = 1000.
Source: World Bank (2006), p. 12, own adaptation.

Other reasons for the significant divergence of the price level in the Czech Republic have suggested (see Skořepa 2001, Čihák / Holub 2001 and Égert 2006):

- Statistical deception (associated with international comparisons where identical items may fail to exist in the compared countries. Clothing is a good example of this),
- Tax burden (indirect taxes affect the potential for arbitrage),
- Arbitrage rate (not a temporary price difference),
- Arbitrage cost (relates to obstacles to arbitrage between countries),
- Monopolist competition on markets with tradable goods (sophisticated products with emphasis on their quality rather than price),
- Productivity (this value for the Czech Republic is higher than in other new member states and most of the old EU members),[24]
- Prices of food have not been influenced by the EU agricultural policy (minimum prices, volume regulation, etc.) but instead were influenced by strong pressures from retail chains over the last few years.

Table 6: The Share of Administered Prices in the CPI (in %)

	CZ	EE	HU	LT	LV	PL	SI	SK
1998	13.3	25.6	17.0	16.9	20.4	10.6	17.0	17.8
1999	13.3	25.6	18.2	22.0	16.2	9.0	14.3	17.8
2000	13.3	25.6	18.3	22.3	18.1	2.6	13.7	17.8
2001	12.4	28.9	18.5	22.0	20.4	1.2	13.2	17.8
2002	12.4	28.5	18.9	20.7	21.5	1.0	14.0	21.1
2003	10.9	24.9	19.4	16.3	23.5	1.0	15.4	20.7
2004	10.9	26.9	17.9	16.0	19.8	1.0	16.1	19.9
2005	10.9	26.7	17.0	14.3	*na*	1.2	16.7	*na*

Note: EE – the high share is due to including of gasoline into basket.
Source: EBRD (2004, 2005).

[24] Productivity is reflected in GDP per worker rather than GDP per capita. The relative productivity of the non-tradable sector represents the second distorting factor. Higher relative productivity decreases unit costs in the tradable sector and the overall price level.

Some related issues should also be mentioned. The price level increase in the Czech Republic will clearly need to accelerate as the current substantial (be it declining, see Čihák / Holub 2001) downward differential is not sustainable in the long-term under normal circumstances. Since inflation in the tradable sector is lower than that in the non-tradable sector (the Balassa-Samuelson effect), the overall inflation rate will be particularly influenced by the following factors (see Janáčková 1999):

- Growth in labour productivity for tradable and non-tradable goods (the so-called dynamic Balassa-Samuelson effect, see Skořepa 2001);
- The difference between the growth rates of productivity in both sectors of the Czech economy;
- Opportunities for and the size of wage increases in both sectors.
- Growth of the output level leading to changes in the consumer demand structure towards a higher share of non-tradable goods.[25] The price elasticity of these goods tends to be higher and this ultimately leads to a faster growth in prices.

Another possible explanation for the divergence of the Czech price level is linked to the specific situation within the EU (see Canzoneri at al. 1996), where the process of creating a single market resulted in increased competition in the tradable goods sector. In many cases labour was re-allocated to the non-tradable sector – especially the state sector and services – which provides greater protection and barriers against competitive pressures. The growth of this part of the economy has led to higher wage increases and inflation in countries with higher output levels.[26]

The nominal convergence in the Czech Republic is interpreted as a long-term process similarly to real convergence. However, if the rate remains stable, the non-tradable sector will create a positive inflation differential, the extent of which will depend greatly on development in the prices of tradable goods. Moving from the macroeconomic level to a more detailed structure of good groups or individual items and assessing the structure of their relative prices and their changes over time would be necessary for a more in-depth analysis. This was the case in the results of the international comparison for the period from 1996 to

[25] This fact arises from the microeconomic theory of the Engel curve.

[26] The planned change in the conditions for conducting business in the services sector within the EU (the so-called Bolkenstein's directive) should ensure a higher level of competition in this sector. However, the proposed changes have significantly weakened the original intentions and no significant increase in competition in the services sector can therefore be expected.

1999 (see for example Čihák / Holub 2001); no study has so far published similar results thusfar.

3.4 Open Issues

Within the EU there are groups of countries with inflation differentials that exceed the Eurozone average, e.g. the Mediterranean countries, Ireland and the Netherlands, as well as countries with inflation rates below this level. Countries with higher inflation rates also tend to have higher growth rates. Low price levels are therefore associated with the risk of increased inflation. This was the case in Mediterranean countries, which, in the context of fixed exchange rates, compensated price differentials arising from different growth rates of productivity in this manner. If this development continues on a long-term basis, ECB or ECOFIN can be expected to require that the limit laid out by the Maastricht criteria be observed. The experience of some countries suggests that applying anti-inflation stabilising policies carries the risk of reducing economic growth.[27]

EU countries that face lower output levels or significant structural changes are listed in Table 7. Except for Greece, which did not join the Eurozone in 1999 with the other 11 countries but attempted to meet the Maastricht criteria, all other countries have higher inflation rates from 1999 to 2001 than during the previous stage from 1996 to 1998, which are associated with decreased GDP growth rates, except for Greece and Spain.[28] The higher inflation rates persisted even in the following period from 2002 to 2004, although the lower growth dynamics during this period may have been caused by a number of adverse external factors.

The experience of countries that became EU members during the 1980s and 1990s may prove useful in this case. This applies especially to the Mediterranean countries (Portugal, Greece and Spain), which upon their accession to the EU had standards of living and price levels comparable to that of the Czech Republic. These countries experienced a dynamic development before and after their accession. Ireland could also be considered as a country at a similar level when it entered the Community. This country, however, is excluded from the comparison due to its specific characteristics regarding language, location, etc. Countries involved in the previous wave of enlargement in 1995 will also be excluded.

[27] The disinflation process is connected with loss of output (although the growth rates may be positive) relative to potential output. It is therefore possible to conclude a static and dynamic sacrifice ratio of this disinflation process for the relevant economy.

[28] This phenomenon is described in Szypáry (2000) and has the nickname "boxer effect", see Brook (2005).

Table 7: Differences in HICP and GDP Before and After Entry into the Eurozone (Annual Percentage Changes)

	Before entering the Eurozone		Eurozone					
	1996–1998		1999–2001		2002–2004		2005	
	HICP	GDP	HICP	GDP	HICP	GDP	HICP	GDP
Ireland	1.8	9.5	3.9	8.6	3.7	4.9	2.2	5.5
Netherlands	1.7	3.7	3.1	3.5	2.5	0.8	1.5	1.5
Portugal	2.3	4.2	3.1	3.3	3.2	0.3	2.1	0.4
Greece	5.9	3.1	2.9	4.3	3.4	4.4	3.5	3.7
Spain	2.4	3.6	2.8	4.4	3.3	3.0	3.4	3.5

Note. Figures for Greece are for comparison since Greece entered the Euro area in 2001.
Source: Structural Indicators, EUROSTAT (2007a), own calculations.

But even the Mediterranean countries differ from the EU-10 countries in important aspects. Portugal differs due to its history as an industrially and agriculturally backward country. Greece both in being influenced by the prolonged unrest in the country and for its large share of agriculture in its national product.[29] Spain joined the EU after a prolonged period of under an authoritarian regime.[30] However, the level and structure Spain's output is significantly closer to the EU-10 and therefore Spain is the most relevant country for our purposes.

The overall price level of GDP in Portugal at the time of its accession to the EC was around 55% (1986) of the average level at the time and had risen to approximately 70% in 1996, amongst others due to the price level of individual consumption increasing from 60% to 74%. During the same period, Spain recorded a lower rate of price increase from 76.9% to 85% of the EU-average level, while Greece practically stagnated from 83.3 % (1981) to 80%.[31] The nominal convergence of these countries developed gradually and has on a long-term basis been at a level equal to output growth. However, a more detailed analysis of the structure of price relations and the adjustment process is not expected to be completed for quite some time.[32]

---

[29] However it is true that very similar economic structure shows Poland.

[30] The central planned economy "experiment" and the type of government regime *sui generis* (one party government regime) in the post-communist countries is very difficult to compare with the dictatorship regimes in Portugal or Spain due to the fact of long durability of the regimes in the CEE countries.

[31] Numbers vary depending on the method of constructing the average for all countries during the relevant period. This is why these values must be considered only approximate price level indicators. See for example Janáčková (1999, 2000), EC (2003) and Nestić (2005).

[32] In order to examine this issue in greater detail, development of individual items in the main consumption groups would need to be monitored and tested.

Real Exchange Rate

A low level of inflation accompanied by a significant exchange rate appreciation currently characterizes the development in the Czech Republic and Poland. The clearest illustration of the impact of the inflation and exchange rate differential on the competitiveness of the relevant economy is provided by the so-called real effective exchange rate (REER).[33] This issue is addressed in more detail in, for example, Frait / Komárek (2004). While inflation affects most of the economy, exchange rate appreciation has a significant impact on exporters and importers. Its impact is positive for importers as it allows them to compete with local companies. Exchange rate appreciation, however, presents a major problem for exporting companies. In this context Čech / Komárek (2005) refers to exchange-rate hysteresis, which means that significant currency appreciation can result in the closure of companies which are not re-opened when the currency returns to its original value.

In the case of accession to a monetary union or of adherence to a fixed exchange rate – e.g. the so-called central parity within ERM II – only appreciations remain possible, but depreciations are effectively ruled out.[34] An incorrectly or unsuitably set conversion ratio of the domestic currency to Euro could lead to problems. Such problems can, for example, be observed in Germany which faced an overvalued exchange rate and experienced the resulting negative shock. In other countries the undervaluation of the exchange rate caused a positive cyclical fluctuation. Neither alternative is desirable[35] and this is why the issue of determining parity is perhaps the most important problem to be solved.

Balassa-Samuelson Effect

The impact of Balassa-Samuelson effect needs to be considered for a more detailed explanation of the difference in price levels of individual countries. The aggregate price and output levels need to be decomposed into sectors in order to

[33] According to database of the EUROSTAT, the real effective exchange rate for the Czech Republic for 2005 (index 1999 = 100) is 137.3 (year-on-year change of + 7.9 %), which is the second highest value after Hungary (144.9, change of + 0.5) and before Slovakia with a value of 134.6 (change of + 6.6, see EUROSTAT, 2007b).

[34] Interpretation of the exchange rate criterion is complex and it is not clear as yet which rules apply – whether the original range ± 2.25 % or + 15 % / – 2.25 %, or the broadest version applied by many countries after the black autumn in ERM in September 1992, i.e. ± 15 %, which was used by Dědek (2002). Currently the concept of a narrow range of ± 2.25 % prevails with the assumption that exchange rate appreciation or exchange rate adjustment in this direction practically is not a problem. Short-term depreciation below the 2.25 % level is also discussed, but its assessment is not clear (see Čech / Komárek 2002a and Čech / Komárek 2002b), see Dobrinsky (2006).

[35] The first scenario may slow down the catching-up process, while the second one may result in rising inflation (and wages) pressures influencing competitiveness of the country (REER appreciation).

allow for an assessment of the Balassa-Samuelson effect. As Balassa (1964) and Samuelson (1964) show, different levels of labour productivity between sectors in individual countries are reflected in the price levels. A higher productivity in the tradable sector compared to the non-tradable sector results in a higher price level for the economy as a whole. If the law of one price holds for tradable sector, the formal expression for this relationship leads to the following equation:[36]

$$(1) \qquad CPL = \left(\frac{A_T}{A_{NT}}\right)^{1-\delta} \Bigg/ \left(\frac{A_T^*}{A_{NT}^*}\right)^{1-\delta^*},$$

where CPL is the comparative price level, A_T (A_{NT}) is the productivity in the tradable (non-tradable) sector, the asterisk denotes the foreign country and the parameter δ is the estimated share of tradable goods in consumption.
After rearranging Equation (1) into growth rates and taking into account that the change in CPL is the inverse of the change in the real exchange rate, one obtains the following equation in logarithmic form

$$(2) \qquad \Delta cpl = \Delta p - \Delta p^* - \Delta e = (1-\delta)(\Delta a_T - \Delta a_{NT}) - (1-\delta)^*(\Delta a_T^* - \Delta a_{NT}^*) - \Delta e,$$

where Δ denotes first differences and e is the nominal exchange rate. The Balassa-Samuelson effect on the CPL development is expressed in Equation (2). The higher the difference of labour productivity in the tradable sector corrected for the difference in the non-tradable sector are in the new member states, the higher inflation differential in these countries will be.

The assumed level of the Balassa-Samuelson effect for the new EU countries is estimated at 2% (see Kovács 2002), for more recent estimates see Égert (2003, 2006). Mihaljek / Klau (2003) estimate the impact of the Balassa-Samuelson effect at 0.1 to 2.0% per year for the EU-10 countries. Growth in productivity is a minor factor for price differentials of the EU-10 countries compared to its impact in the Eurozone.

The Balassa-Samuelson effect is a tool for explaining the differences in price levels, but its predictive capacity is low compared to that of real income. Real income, however, is influenced by a range of factors that also influence the price level. Finally, the Balassa-Samuelson effect can be reduced by changes in employment and in the mark-ups at the sector level, which themselves can be obscured by the structural changes in the new member states.

[36] This relationship is frequently tested for inflation rates and the productivity differentials, a higher differential leading to a higher inflation rate. See for example ECB (1999).

Path to the Eurozone

The next few years will be characterized by the efforts to gradually meet the Maastricht convergence criteria. Even though this will be demanding for the stabilisation policies, both real and nominal convergence should be continued. An acceptable solution regarding nominal convergence needs to be found that will not jeopardize competitiveness of the corporate sector, while at the same time supporting real convergence.

A number of options are available regarding the development of the exchange rate and the price level. The influence of the exchange rate channel will weaken in the phase where the exchange rate is fixed as part of ERM II. The impact of meeting the Maastricht criteria for inflation will differ for countries with a fixed exchange rate – for whom this de facto means free movement of inflation within the target zone – compared to countries with a flexible exchange rate – for whom the exchange rate will have to be contained within the bound of ERM II.[37]

In the cases of the Czech, Polish, and Slovak economies the exchange rate channel appears to be important. The exchange rate in the short and medium-term, however, is influenced by a range of factors, including the inflow of foreign investment and expectations. In a liberalised environment, capital flows are to some extent detached from the underlying real economic processes.

A reduction in interest rates has positive effects on the corporate and public sectors of countries with inflation levels that exceed that of the Eurozone, e.g. Slovakia and the Baltic states. On the other hand, countries with a low and stable inflation rate, such as the Czech Republic, will gain little advantage from this.

The EU-10 are likely to face great challenges in the fiscal area. Relatively strict criteria for fiscal deficits and the levels of public debt are in place, whereas the convergence process forces these countries to make significant investments which, even though heavily subsidized by the EU, require co-financing from public resources.

4 Conclusion

After the fall in output at the beginning of the 1990s, the economies of the EU-10 countries gained significant momentum, which allowed them to renew the real convergence process. Some of the countries did not manage to avoid a deceleration in the mid 1990s or at the turn of the century.

[37] One of the options is modifying the convergence criteria for countries with a fixed exchange rate regime (a higher inflation rate limit) and for countries with a flexible exchange rate regime, as suggested by Dobrinsky (2006). In the case of the inflation criterion differentiation between benign inflation arising from growth of productivity and malign inflation caused by policies should be introduced.

Securing a relatively smooth convergence process requires harmonised progress of both real and nominal values. However, a number of issues regarding nominal convergence remain unresolved (e.g. the Balassa-Samuelson effect) and these will sooner or later need to be addressed. Their significance is likely to increase when the date of accession to the Eurozone draws nearer.

The significant difference between the actual price level in the Czech Republic and that predicted by its standard of living represents a major potential problem. A number of ways to address this problem have been mentioned, as the frequently proposed method of price regulation is not sufficient. The excessively low price level not only has serious implications for the present, but even more so for the future development of the Czech economy. Its price level will continue to increase over the next few years, not only due to the inflation differential and the exchange rate, but also as a result of spontaneous processes. Inflation will result from growing labour productivity and real income, as well as from the convergence in consumer habits.

The disaggregated approach to comparative price level indices indicates important consequences. The most often used regression in the real and nominal convergence process shows that the slope of comparative price level to GDP per capita in PPS is between 0.8 and 0.9. If we follow the disaggregated approach, however, we obtain qualitatively different results. The expected real convergence process will affect the increase in the comparative price level through the price increase in services, where the slope to GDP per capita is higher than in the comparative overall price level. The driving factors of differences in comparative price levels in the new member states are price (de-)regulation and the growth of the share of services within individual consumption, as well as the price development in government services.

If the nominal convergence process continues to occur through changes in the exchange rate rather than changes in the price level, significant changes in the exchange rate caused by improved competitiveness of some domestic companies and industries, can be expected to pose threat to the exports of others. This could lead to problems with the current account of the payment balance and the subsequent overshooting of the exchange rate could potentially lead to the opposite effect: price level divergence.

References

Balassa, B. (1964): The purchasing-power parity doctrine: a reappraisal, in: Journal of Political Economy, Volume 72, pp. 584–596.

Barro, R. / Sala-i-Martin, X. (2004): Economic Growth, 2nd edition, MIT Press, Cambridge, MA, USA.

Brook, A. (2005): The challenges of EMU accession faced by catching-up countries: a Slovak Republic case study, OECD Economic Department Working Paper No. 444, Organisation for Economic for Co-operation and Development, Paris, France.

Canzoneri, M. / Diba, B. / Eudey, G. (1996): Trends in European productivity and real exchange rates: implications for the Maastricht convergence criteria and for inflation targets after EMU, CEPR Discussion Paper No. 1417, Centre for Economic Policy Research, London, United Kingdom.

Čech, Z. / Komárek, L. (2002a): Konvergence a vstup do eurozóny I: Existuje pro kandidátské země možnost volby? in: Finance a úvěr, pp. 322–337. In Czech: Exchange rate convergence and entry to the Eurozone I: is there any choice for the candidate countries?

Čech, Z. / Komárek, L. (2002b): Kurzová konvergence a vstup do eurozóny II: Komparace zkušeností členských zemí EU, in: Finance a úvěr, pp. 522–538. In Czech: Exchange rate convergence and entry to the Eurozone (II): a comparison of experiences from member states of the European Union.

Čech, Z. / Komárek, L. (2005): Kurzová konvergence a vstup do eurozóny III: Vybrané problémy nových členských zemí EU, in: Finance a úvěr, pp. 483–505. In Czech: Exchange rate convergence and entry to the Eurozone (III): selected issues of the new member states of the European Union.

Čihák, M. / Holub, T. (2001): Cenová konvergence k EU – pár nezodpovězených otázek, in: Finance a úvěr, pp. 331–349. In Czech: Price convergence toward the EU: a few open issues.

Dědek, O. (2002): Česká ekonomika a euro, in: Politická ekonomie, pp. 361–375. In Czech: The Czech economy and the Euro.

Dědek, O. (2006): Rizika výzvy měnové strategie k převzetí eura, in: Politická ekonomie, pp. 1–21. In Czech: risks and challenges of the monetary strategy for Euro adoption.

Dobrinsky, R. (2006): Nominal versus real convergence: the balancing act for new EU entrants, Mimeo, Spring Seminar Wider Europe: Opportunities and Future Challenges, Vienna Institute for International Economic Studies, Vienna, Austria.

EBRD (2004): Transition Report 2004: Infrastructure, European Bank for Reconstruction and Development, London, United Kingdom.

EBRD (2005): Transition Report 2005: Business in transition, European Bank for Reconstruction and Development, London, United Kingdom.

European Central Bank (1999): Monthly Bulletin October 1999, European Central Bank, Frankfurt am Main, Germany.

European Commission (2002): Technical barriers and functioning of the internal market, in: Internal Market Scoreboard, No. 10, pp. 17-34, European Commission, Luxemburg.

European Commission (2003): New member states have substantially lower prices, in: Internal Market Scoreboard, No. 12, pp. 26-30, European Commission, Luxemburg.

European Commission (2005): Convergence report 2004, *European Economy Special Report No 2,* European Commission, Luxemburg.

Égert, B. (2003): Nominal and real convergence in Estonia: the Balassa-Samuelson (dis)connection, oil shale, tradable goods, regulated prices and other culprits, Working Paper, No. 556, William Davidson Institute, University of Michigan, Ann Arbor, MA, USA. [www.bus.umich.edu/-KresgeLibrary/Collections/Workingpapers/wdi/wp556.pdf]

Égert, B. (2006): Real convergence, price level convergence and inflation, Mimeo, presented at conference ICEG EC: Growth and Jobs: Challenges to the Lisbon Strategy and European Competitiveness, Budapest, Hungary.

EUROSTAT (2005a): Clothing and footwear – comparative price levels in EU, EFTA and candidate countries for 2003, Statistic in Focus, No. 13, Eurostat, Luxemburg.

EUROSTAT (2005b): Changes to national accounts in 2005, Eurostat, Luxemburg. See europa.eu.int/estatref/info/sdds/en/na/na_changes2005.pdf (15th February 2006).

EUROSTAT (2006): Relative price levels for new passenger cars in Europe for 2004, Statistic in Focus, No. 3, Eurostat, Luxemburg.

EUROSTAT (2007): Economy and finance: prices, wages and labour costs, Eurostat, Luxemburg. See epp.eurostat.ec.europa.eu/portal/page?_pagid=1996,45323734&_dad=portal&_schema=PORTAL&screen=welcomeref&open=/&product=Yearlies_new_economy&depth=2 (19th February, 2007).

EUROSTAT (2007a): Structural indicators: national accounts, Eurostat, Luxemburg. [epp.eurostat.cec.eu.int/portal/page?_pageid=1996,45323734&_dad=portal&_schema=PORTAL&screen=welcomeref&open=/&product=EU_MASTER_national_accounts&depth=2] (20th February, 2007).

EUROSTAT (2007b): Sustainable development indicators: economic development: competitiveness: international price competitiveness (real effective exchange rate), Eurostat, Luxemburg. http://epp.eurostat.ec.europa.eu/-portal/page?_pageid=1996,39140985&_dad=portal&_schema=PORTAL&screen=detailref&language=en&product=SDI_MAIN&root=SDI_MAIN/sdi/sdi_ed/sdi_ed_com/sdi_ed1300. (20th February, 2007).

Frait, J. / Komárek, L. (2004): Exchange rate and monetary developments in accession countries, in: Reforming the Financial Sector in Central European Countries, edited by S. Polouček, pp. 169–210, Palgrave Macmillan, Houndmills, Basingstoke, United Kingdom.

Greene, W. (2003): Econometric Analysis, 5th edition, Prentice Hall, Upper Saddle River, NJ, USA.

Holub, T. / Čihák, M. (2003): Price convergence: what can Balassa-Samuelson model tell us? Working Paper No. 8, Czech National Bank, Prague, Czech Repbulic.

Janáček, K. / Janáčková, S. (2004): Evropská měnová unie a rizika pro reálnou konvergenci, in Politická ekonomie, pp. 435–449. In Czech: European Monetary Union and Risks for Real Convergence.

Janáčková, S. (1999): Příprava české ekonomiky na vstup do Evropské unie, in: Politická ekonomie, pp. 435–448. In Czech: Convergence of the Czech price level toward European Union must be based on productivity.

Janáčková, S. (2000): Price convergence and the readiness of the Czech economy for accession to the European Union, in: Eastern European Economics, Vol. 38, pp. 73-91.

Kovács, A. (Ed.) (2002): On the estimated size of the Balassa-Samuelson effect in five Central and Eastern European countries, NBH Working Paper No. 5, Nation Bank of Hungary, Budapest, Hungary.

Landefeld, J. / Moulton, B. / Vojtech, C. (2003): Chained-dollar indexes: issues, tips on their use, and upcoming changes, in: Survey of Current Business, Volume 83, pp. 8–16.

Mihaljek, D. / Klau, M. (2003): The Balassa-Samuelson effect in Central Europe: a disaggregated analysis, BIS Working Paper No. 143, Bank for International Settlement, Basle, Switzerland.

Nestić, D. (2005): Price level convergence: Croatia, transition countries and the EU, CNB Working Papers W. 13, Croatian National Bank, Zagreb, Croatia.

Obstfeld, M. / Rogoff, K. (1998): Foundation of International Macroeconomics, MIT Press, Cambridge, MA, USA.

OECD (2006a): National accounts of OECD countries: main aggregates. Volume I: 1993–2004, Organisation of Economic Co-operation and Development, Paris, France.

OECD (2006b): Economic policy reforms: going for growth, Organisation of Economics Co-operation and Development, Paris, France.

Rogoff, K. (1996): The purchasing power parity puzzle, in: Journal of Economic Literature, Volume 34, pp. 647–668.

Rother, P. / Süppel, R. (2003): East Germany, Central Europe, and risk of real convergence overshooting, in: Finance a úvěr, pp. 374–393.

Samuelson, P. (1964): Theoretical notes on trade problems, in: Review of Economics and Statistics, Volume 23 , pp. 145–154.

Schreyer, P. / Koechlin, F. (2002): Purchasing power parities – measurement and uses, OECD Statistical Brief, No. 3, Organisation of Economic Co-operation and Development, Paris, France.
Skořepa, M. (2001): K rozdílům v cenových hladinách mezi ČR a Německem. in: Finance a úvěr, pp. 350–363. In Czech: On the differences in price levels between the Czech Republic and Germany.
Slavík, C. (2005): Reálná konvergence České republiky k EU v porovnání s ostatními novými členskými zeměmi. Praha, CESES UK, (Pracovní sešit 3). In Czech: Real convergence of the Czech Republic to the EU in comparison with the other new member countries.
Spěváček, V. (2003): Parita kupní síly – nástroj mezinárodního srovnávání, in: Politická ekonomie, pp. 59–78. In Czech: Purchasing power parities – a tool of international comparisons.
Spěváček, V. (2005): Economic growth of the Czech Republic in the light of real income indicators, Working Paper No. 2, Centre for Economic Studies VŠEM, Prague, Czech Republic. www.vsem.cz/data/docs/gf_WPNoII.pdf
Spěváček, V. / Vintrová, R. / Hájek, M. / Žďárek, V. (2005): Růst, stabilita a konvergence české ekonomiky v letech 1996–2005, Working Paper No. 12, Centre for Eeconomic Studies VŠEM, Prague, Czech Republic. In Czech: Growth, Stability and Convergence of the Czech Economy in the Years 1996–2005.
Sorsa, P. (2006): Macroeconomic challenges with EU accession in South-eastern Europe: an overview, IMF Working paper No. 40, International Monetary Fund, Washington DC, USA.
Szapáry, G. (2000): Maastricht and the choice of exchange rate regime in transition countries during the run-up to EMU, NBH Working Paper No. 7, National Bank of Hungary, Budapest, Hungary.
UNECE (2001): Economic Survey of Europe, United Nations Economic Commission for Europe, United Nations, New York.
Vávra, D. (1999): Nominal versus real convergence in a CEE transition country: do the Maastricht criteria make sense for the Czech Republic? CERGE-EI Discussion Paper No. 16, Center of Economics Research and Graduate Education, Charles University Prague, Czech Republic.
Vintrová, R. (chairman of the group) / Fassman, M. / Klvačová, E. / Pick, M. / Ungerman, J. (2002): Sociální a ekonomické souvislosti integrace České republiky do Evropské unie, Advisory Council of the Czech Government for the Social and Economic Strategy, Prague, Czech Republic. In Czech: Social and economic consequences of the integration of the Czech Republic to the European Union.
Vintrová, R. (2005): What GDP indicators do not tell you: alternative indicators of economic growth and real convergence, in: Finance a úvěr, pp. 579–595.

World Bank (2006): EU8 Quarterly Economic Report, World Bank, Washington DC, USA. http://siteresources.worldbank.org/INTECA/Resources/EU8-QER-Feb06-Main-Report.pdf

List of Contributors

Anıl Akçağlayan, Department of Economics, Ankara University, Ankara, Turkey.

Elif Bascavusoglu-Moreau, Business School, Imperial College London, United Kingdom.

Victoria Dobrynskaya, State University – Higher School of Economics, Moscow Russian Federation, and London School of Economics, London, United Kingdom.

Ayşe Ertuğrul, Sorbonne Economic Centre, Université Panthéon-Sorbonne (Paris I), France.

Alan Mulhern, School of Economics, Kingston University, London, United Kingdom.

Laura Ruud, Bank of Estonia, Talinn, Estonia and Faculty of Economics and Business Administration, University of Tartu, Tartu, Estonia.

Jaromír Šindel, Centre for Economic Studies, University of Economics, Prague, Czech Republic.

Willem Spanjers, School of Economics, Kingston University, London, United Kingdom.

Václav Žd'árek, Centre for Economic Studies, University of Economics, Prague, Czech Republik.

New Developments in Economic Research
edited by Christian Richter, Edward Shinnick and Jan Van Hove

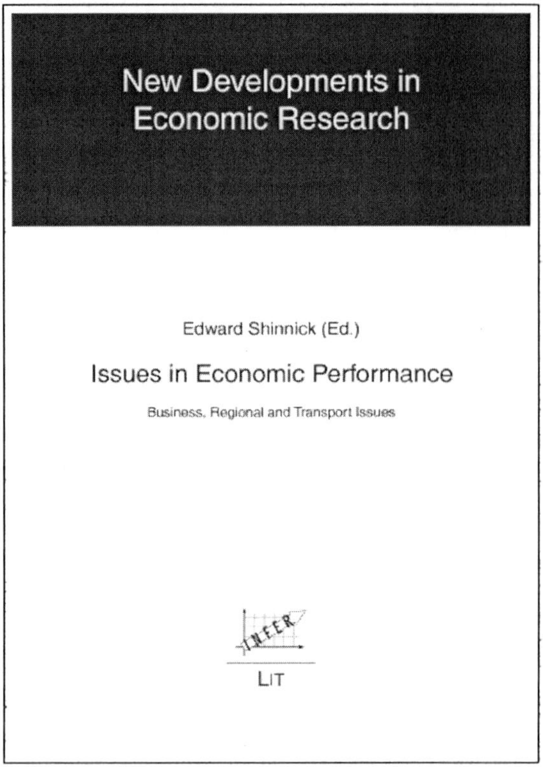

Edward Shinnick (Ed.)
Issues in Economic Performance
Business, Regional and Transport Issues
This volume analyses three themes of economic performance. The first theme looks at how business culture influences firm behavior, how the human resource function, and corporate governance aids firm performance. The Second theme focuses on how integration policy increases competitiveness and how social, economic and institutional factors contribute to economic development. The final theme analyses the impact of air transport regulations on growth, and economic policy in railways. This collection will appeal to those in academia, business and policy institutions. .
Bd. 1, 2009, 152 S., 39,90 €, br., ISBN 978-3-8258-1963-7

LIT Verlag Berlin – Münster – Wien – Zürich – London
Auslieferung Deutschland / Österreich / Schweiz: siehe Impressumsseite